Introduction

If you spend a year or more of your life writing a screenplay, don't you want it to have lasting value if it is made into a film? Of course. Is it possible to assure that this will happen if you use a particular screenplay-writing formula? The answer is no. But you can certainly increase the odds that your hard work and vision will stand the test of time by working from the inside out—the technique of the character-driven screenplay.

Look at any "Best 100 Movies" list created by critics, filmmakers, film schools, or magazines, and ninety percent of the selections are character-driven films, such as *M*, *Citizen Kane*, *The Godfather*, *8 1/2*, *Chinatown*, *The Searchers*, *Some Like It Hot*, *It's a Wonderful Life*, *Mean Streets*, *Rio Bravo*, *The 400 Blows*, *The Lady Eve*, *Dr. Strangelove*, *Badlands*, *Unforgiven*, and *Who's Afraid of Virginia Woolf.* These films have survived the test of time because they combine content, craft, a fresh perspective, and possess a single guiding intelligence. Their screenwriters pushed the rules to the edge or broke them. They are, quite simply, one of a kind.

The power of the character-driven film is undeniable. It seeps into the bones and souls of viewers and haunts them for a lifetime. These films have lasting meaning because they have the power to awaken an audience to what they did not know they knew or felt before. Watching *M* we are awakened to how we judge and condemn others too quickly. In *The Godfather*, we recognize the craving for a family that protects and gives us security and the price that must be paid; in *Mean Streets* we see how our guilt can blind us. The great character-driven movies are reference points marking the first time viewers experience some new aspect of themselves—their suffering, joy, love lives, evil natures, sense of terror, or use of power.

There is no magic formula for creating the character-driven screenplay. But there is clearly a process that can be learned for writing a screenplay that will have content, craft, and staying power. This book is an attempt to communicate a way to work from the unconscious imagination to discover complex characters and resonant stories. Parts one and two of the book examine the principles and standards that screenwriters should use to guide themselves during the process, and part three provides a step-by-step guide to the process of creating a character-driven screenplay.

It took me a long time to learn the process of writing the character-driven screenplay. In fact, when I began as a screenwriter I did not even know that I wrote character-driven screenplays. I found out in 1990 when I sold my screenplay, *Arab Bride*, to Hollywood Pictures, a division of the Walt Disney Company. The proposed film was a romantic comedy about a suburban housewife, who meets a rich Egyptian at the Sign of the Dove, an upscale restaurant on the isle of Manhattan, and marries him within a night. I flew to LA with my executive producer, John Patrick Shanley, the author of

Moonstruck, to meet with the head of the studio. Shanley had one request—let him do all the talking at the meeting. I agreed: he had been through this many times before, while I was a New York playwright who had never been an official writer-for-hire. The purpose of our meeting at Hollywood Pictures was to discuss revisions to my script. As a playwright, I am a habitual revisionist, so the idea of it posed no real threat. I sat through the meeting a perfect solider, silent. Ricardo Mestres, the President of Hollywood Pictures, a boyishly handsome Harvard grad, certainly not the stereotypical cigar-smoking movie mogul, kept saying, "Jim, jump in, any time." Finally, after politely enduring thirty minutes of my studied silence, which was putting a damper on the whole room, he said, "Jim, you know what your script reminds me of?" "No," I mumbled. "*A Clockwork Orange*," Mestres said. I was stunned. Stanley Kubrick's work is magnificent, but I was certain I had written a romantic comedy and didn't quite get the connection. I looked at Shanley who reacted with his aggressive Bronx charm, "It is not! It is *The Prime of Miss Jean Brodie!*" he said, pounding his fist on the table. More confused than ever, I returned to silence. Mestres took a noticeable pause, grinned and nodded, as if some fear, unnecessary to mention because it was so clearly self-evident, had been put to rest. I grinned, faking comprehension.

"Did you see what they tried to do to you in there?" Shanley asked after our meeting. "No. What?" I replied. "When he said *A Clockwork Orange* he was testing you, to see if you wanted to write art house films." *A Clockwork Orange* is intellectual, cool, edgy, at times harsh and scary; it is perceived by the industry to be an example of a commercial "art house" film. *The Prime of Miss Jean Brodie* with its charming, sexually repressed main character, is entertaining, sentimental, and more accepting of the status quo, than *A Clockwork Orange;* it is an example of a commercial "commercial" character-driven film. There is a significant difference between the commercial "art house" film and the commercial "commercial" film: the box office for the latter is much bigger. While *A Clockwork Orange* may be perceived as a stellar, breakthrough movie that has influenced and inspired many filmmakers, its net profit is far less than *The Prime of Miss Jean Brodie*—and that does not warm the hearts of movie executives. The movie business is, after all, a business. Let's not forget that. And we live in a time when the studios must not only make a profit, they must make a big profit to stay solvent and competitive.

"Oh, so that's why you said that thing about Miss Jean Brodie?" "Yeah," he replied. "*The Prime of Miss Jean Brodie*? I mean seriously, John." "It was the best I could do," he said with a shrug. "What exactly do they mean by an art house film?" I asked. "You know, personal, quirky, character-driven," John responded. "Well, isn't that what I do?" "Of course, but don't ever say that to anyone. You want a career, don't you?"

Shanley knew what he was talking about; he had an Academy Award to prove it. Mainstream Hollywood is about action flicks that sell overseas because they are marvelous cartoons. These films have a lot of physical action, very little dialogue, and archetypes—the hero, the mentor, the trickster, and so on—rather than complex characters. They are "high concept" movies: an entire film could be summarized in one or two

Screenwriting
from the Heart

The Technique of the
Character-Driven Screenplay

JAMES RYAN

BILLBOARD BOOKS
An imprint of Watson-Guptill Publications
New York

Acknowledgment is made to the following for permission to reproduce the material indicated:

Welcome to the Dollhouse, copyright © 1996 Suburban Pictures, Inc.; *Secrets and Lies,* copyright © Mike Leigh, 1997; *The Apostle,* copyright © 1997 Butchers Run Films, Inc.

Senior Editor: Bob Nirkind
Editor: Margaret Sobel
Book Design: Cheryl Viker
Production Manager: Ellen Greene

First published in 2000 by Billboard Books, an imprint of Watson-Guptill Publications, a division of BPI Communications, Inc. 770 Broadway, New York, NY 10003

Library of Congress Cataloging-in-Publication Data

Ryan, James, (James Edward)
  Screenwriting from the heart : the technique of the character-driven screenplay / by
James Ryan.
     p. cm.
  Includes bibliographical references and index.
  ISBN 0-8230-8419-1
  1. Motion picture authorship. 2. Characters and characteristics in literature. I. Title.

PN1996 .R93 2000
808.2'3--dc21

99-087771

Printed in the U.S.A.
First Printing 2000

2 3 4 5 6 7 8 9/05 04 03 02 01

Acknowledgments

I am indebted to Steven Valentino, a former student, for being the catalyst for this book. Steven accidentally ran into Jerry Rudes and Fifi Oscard, both literary agents, while dining at an outdoor café, one Manhattan evening. A former Wall Street executive turned professional screenwriter, Steven talked so highly of his experiences with The Brass Tacks Screenwriting Workshop, a writing class I began seven years ago in New York, that he inspired Jerry to approached me about writing a book on screenwriting. I am also grateful to Jerry, who served as agent for this book, for his pluck, editorial contributions, and unswerving loyalty.

I must thank Bob Nirkind, Senior Editor at Billboard Books, for gracefully extending my deadline—several times. I cannot imagine this book without Margaret Sobel, my editor. Like a patient drill sergeant, she whipped the manuscript into fighting shape. Her commitment and insistence on clarity helped me to become a better communicator, writer, and teacher of screenwriting.

I am thankful to my colleague at the Actors Studio MFA Program, Laura Maria Censabella, for reading various parts of the first draft and giving invaluable criticism.

I had many great teachers, over the years, who have helped me to understand my craft. Uta Hagen showed me that dramatic writing is about giving the actor something to do; Curt Dempster, as artistic director and producer, gave me the support I needed to experiment and grow as a dramatist; Ralph Toporoff taught me about filmmaking; and Richard and Beverly Mehrlich, my friends and executive producers, with their "hire 'em and let 'em loose" management style, taught me that working from the inside out always makes for a better movie.

I am grateful to my mother and father who taught me how to be funny and tell a good story. To William and Tina Flaherty, who supported me as a playwright, screenwriter, and film director for many, many years. And to my daughter, Liana, who with her directness and idealism, helps to keep me honest.

Finally, I must thank the hundreds of students I have taught over the last decade, who with their queries and hunger to express themselves, have challenged me to refine and deepen my knowledge of dramatic writing. Collectively, they gave me enough to fill a book.

Contents

Contents *(continued)*

lines, or with an image on a poster. The lack of complexity means most foreign audiences would understand and enjoy them, so they are highly marketable around the world. Romantic comedy, however, despite its reliance on character and language, is still something an executive could take a risk on; there is box office to prove it— *Moonstruck, When Harry Met Sally, Sleepless in Seattle*. What I didn't fully understand at the time is the enormous pressure studio executives are under. I know this sounds, well, unforgivable, but it is true; I had always heard about this pressure, but now I had experienced it, felt it. As a friend said to me once, "you're just not gonna understand this place till you come here. Then you'll get it." My friend was right. One movie can make or break a career. Romantic comedy, Shanley explained to me, works for executives as long as it doesn't break too many rules. That is, isn't too personal, too quirky, too specific, or too original. I reminded him that *Moonstruck* broke some basic rules and was a big hit. "Luck counts, you know," he replied.

Several months after I signed the deal for *Arab Bride*, the Persian Gulf War began. Saddam Hussein was portrayed as a "madman" on CNN and Arab-Americans complained that Arabs were being portrayed negatively in Hollywood films such as *Operation Condor*, which portrayed Arabs as cruel and cowardly terrorists, replacing Indians as the "bad guys." The American-Arab Anti-Discrimination Committee claimed that *Condor* glorified killing Arabs, and therefore promoted a fear and hatred of them as an ethnic group. Disney put my project in "turnaround" (i.e., on the shelf). "We've decided we just don't want to make it anymore," Mestres explained to me over the phone. I knew what he was afraid of: The American-Arab Anti-Discrimination Committee. But I am sure it was far more complicated than that. There could have been budget constraints, my film may have lost out to priority projects, or there may have been some political infighting at the studio. Disney is a huge multinational corporation and no doubt has its share of Byzantine intrigue. Whatever the case, Mestres' decision to cut bait was most likely predicated on the convergence of a number of factors entirely out of my control and perhaps, even out of his control. Nonetheless, I tried to keep the project alive. I explained to Mestres that my stepfather, the inspiration for the screenplay, was an immigrant from Egypt who had succeeded at the American dream. I told him I hoped he didn't think I wrote a clichéd, bigoted portrayal of an Arab. "Not at all," Mestres said cheerily, moving us expeditiously to the next subject, "and don't worry, I'm gonna get you a lot more work here."

An executive from the studio called me several days later to pitch an idea he had for a film. During our conversation, the executive told me that one of the reasons he was considering me for the project was because he had heard that I could "do character really well." I thought, "shouldn't every writer be able to do character very well? Isn't that the essence of a good screenplay, novel, or play?"

For many months after my first sale I was in and out of Disney talking to executives about scripts they wanted me to "give some character to." Nothing ever worked out; none of the projects offered to me had a voice or vision. I knew my efforts would simply be a matter of script-doctoring, keeping the patient heavily sedated until death inevitably arrives, when the script would be put on the shelf and never looked at again. Like empty eggshells, these scripts followed the formula: a central protagonist, most likely a thirty-five to forty-year-old male (i.e., a bankable star, who in "real life" is probably forty-five to seventy years of age), is dutifully set up and assigned a major plot point by page thirty, which then spins the action in a different direction and begins the second "act of confrontation," which of course leads to a happy ending. And if the ending is not happy, it is certain to deliver one thing: order is restored, society is once again stable, the status quo survives. Unless I could wire these contrived and dead scripts like *Frankenstein*, they were beyond resuscitation.

What became clear to me was that the language used by most executives, directors, actors, producers, and agents to diagnose and discuss scripts inevitably dictated a particular result: the three-act linear screenplay with a happy ending. "Why should I 'care' about this character?" or "How does this character's 'arc intersect' with our hero's?" or "I don't get it: what's the 'inciting incident?'" Rarely did anyone paraphrase the deceptively simple, yet more fluid and complex set of questions formulated by Goethe: "What's the writer trying to do, how well is he doing it, and is it worth doing?" Their analysis seemed inorganic and imposed upon the work. Instead of helping writers to shape their impulses, they were binding them, stunting possibility.

I believe people come to the movies for the same reason they read a novel or attend a play: to have their emotions aroused, mind engaged, and spirit exalted. The only way to deliver such an intensified experience is to write about something about which you are passionate, something you obsessively need to say. "Write something from your heart so that you know it's solid all the way through. When you write something from your heart, it's going to be your best work," said Billy Bob Thornton, author of *Sling Blade*.

In 1997, seven years after I sold my first screenplay to Disney, this note appeared in the *New York Times*:

> With the exception of *Jerry Maguire*, which was made by Tri-Star, a division of Sony, the 69th Academy Award nominations, announced Tuesday, were overwhelmingly dominated by independent films like *The English Patient*, with 12 nominations, followed by *Shine* and *Fargo*, with 7 each. In fact, some of Hollywood's biggest studios, like Warner Brothers and Universal, were virtually shut out of top nominations, underscoring the contrast between the often edgier, provocative movies released by independents and the increasingly by-the-numbers action film and comedies from these big companies.
>
> Harvey Weinstein, co-chairman of Miramax, the New York-based and Disney-owned company, which dominated the field with 20 nominations, said over the phone: "All these movies that were honored Tuesday have one thing in common: they were writer-driven with good sound stories."

The Academy Awards in 1997 proved the tide had indeed turned and the old rules were no longer working. Small independent distributors like Miramax mushroomed during the nineties, and then Disney bought Miramax so they could be competitive in a niche they had lost a foothold in: the character-driven film. Audiences clearly now had a thirst for films that are more personal, quirky, edgy, and original. The American films of the 1930s and 1940s, such as *Bringing up Baby, Fury, His Gal Friday, Citizen Kane,* and *Sullivan's Travels,* filled this niche, but over the decades the studios moved more and more toward spectacle films and lost sight of this market. By the 1990s, independent distributors saw their opportunity and outflanked the major distributors by seizing and cultivating this niche. Also, as high culture and content-based media (books, plays, and works of fine art) diminish globally, and the world is bombarded by visual media (movies, television, and the internet), audiences are looking for more content in their films to replace the content lost by the shrinking power of the printed word. The character-driven film satisfies this hunger for content, which makes it all the more popular.

Today, forces have converged to make it a fertile time for the character-driven film. Character-driven films like *Shakespeare in Love, Pulp Fiction, The Crying Game, Sling Blade,* and *Life Is Beautiful* have all been highly profitable. To survive and prosper today, the screenwriter must learn a new way of scripting a movie, because it is obvious that the spectacle and follow-the-genre films that follow the traditional three-act structure are fast becoming dinosaurs. Screenwriters today cannot not do it by the numbers and hope to have success; they must learn screenwriting techniques that value originality and specificity and understand how to work from the inside out. In other words, they must learn how to create true and original characters. This book is an attempt to put forth a technique and process to do precisely that.

In a mad rush to create the spectacle film, Hollywood has developed standards that produce dead projects. This seems odd because a dead movie does not attract an audience or make a profit. But upon closer examination, it is not just standards, but the burden of a process that produces lifeless films. The "three-act structure" is a template that is laid on top of all stories; it acts like a compactor in a junkyard, compressing everything into a cube that can be stacked, assembly-line fashion, for the smelting pot. If it doesn't fit, it must be made to fit, even if it means eviscerating precisely what is compelling about the narrative. This process makes for bad art, certainly, but given the recent change in taste at the box office, it also can make for bad business.

I consider myself a working writer who teaches. I feel there is nothing very abstract or academic about writing; it is an art form, yes, but first and foremost it is a craft. "The stage is life, music, beautiful girls, legs, breasts, not talk or intellectualism or dried-up academics," said Harold Clurman, the stage director and critic. I feel the same is true about movies.

Writing for film, theater, or the novel is about expressing oneself by shaping a story. The story is the outcome of a writer trying to give clarity and meaning to intense feelings and experiences. I have found writing to be an extremely chaotic, unpredictable task, so any technique used to accomplish this mammoth challenge should not be "by the numbers." It should instead be open-ended, organic, and allow for the assembly of very complicated and often contradictory choices. Sometimes the dramatic question you want to explore is best structured in one, two, or four acts instead of three. Sometimes your real interest as a writer is just to reveal the many complex layers of character and world rather than force a fast-tempo unfolding of plot.

Creating a screenplay is too complex and fluid a matter to be enclosed in any single form. The most powerful and effective writing is the result of constant discovery, governed by a single guiding intelligence. A useful technique must be flexible, yet disciplined and conscious. "Sean O'Casey had a sign over his desk that simply said, 'Write the damn play,'" said playwright/screenwriter and two time Academy-Award nominee, Robert Anderson, *(I Never Sang for My Father, Tea and Sympathy, The Sand Pebbles* and *The Nun's Story)* in a recent interview. "The important thing for me is the enthusiasm of 'Now, what are they going to say?' It's the surprises. I write to discover what I didn't know I felt or didn't know I knew."

A decade ago, when I first began teaching screenwriting in my private workshop in New York City, The Brass Tacks Screenwriting Workshop, I was amazed at how many students, many of them graduates of the best film schools in the country, hadn't the slightest idea of how to create complex and specific characters. Yet they could recite the three-act formula like the Baltimore Catechism. It seemed as if they learned everything from the "outside," from the point of view of the producer or agent or development executive. Very few had experienced letting the story rise from their unconscious imagination and soul, rather than recycling the stereotypes, familiar symbols, and contrived images of our time.

I discovered the most common reason for this lack of dramatic skill was that none of these students had ever studied acting. "It is true that playwrights [and I believe the same holds true for screenwriters] must learn the art of the theatre, and above all its central art: that of acting," wrote Eric Bentley, critic and playwright, in his essay, "Letter to a Would-Be Playwright." Many of our great playwrights—from Shakespeare, Molière to the more contemporary Sam Shepard, David Mamet, August Wilson, and Maria Irene Fornes—all studied acting. To act is to become. To become is to inhabit, from head to toe, a character and a world. Acting technique recommends that the actor explore the behavior, previous circumstances, needs, desires, actions, and emotional life of the character he or she wants to become. It begins with Konstantin Stanislavsky's dictum, "'What If?—Here, Now, Today," a technique that values and supports surprise and being in the moment, which will be examined in greater depth throughout this book.

Having worked early in my career as a professional actor on stage, film, and television, I tried an experiment: I got my writing students on their feet doing improvisations. It helped enormously, even if they were lousy actors. They began to understand that good dramatic writing is acting on the page and there must be truthful moment-to-moment behavior for their characters. I devised "simple-stupid" exercises to get all their "learning" out of the way, so that they could access their deeply felt imagination and find that place in themselves that would give them a sense of prowess—a feeling of being alive and true. I asked other screenwriters for help and learned how they did their work. What I have tried to put together is a very practical process, a technique, that allows one to discover substance first, and then the form it will need to support its full expression.

The book is divided into three parts. The first part, "The Character-Driven Approach," is concerned with the theory and tenets of the character-driven screenplay—although practical exercises and examples are provided. Parts two and three "Finding Your Structure" and "Crafting Your Script: Step by Step" focus more on the actual "doing." To the screenwriter who is impatient and itches to "get on with it," the first section may, at times, seem unnecessary. However, I don't know how many times I have given students a bit of practical advice on what or what not to do, and they invariably ask what they should ask: Why? They want to know the aesthetic values that lie underneath this practical advice. The first part of this book considers the why behind the actual practice of writing a character-driven screenplay. It is important to understand and examine the underlying assumptions that support a writing technique; without this awareness a screenwriter becomes exactly what caused the problem with many films today—a by-the-numbers guy or gal. If a driver learns to stop at a red light only because all drivers are required by law to stop at the red light, all he or she knows is a rule. If the driver learns that he or she is required to stop at the red light for his or her safety, the safety of the pedestrian, and to participate in a very effective way to control the flow of traffic, then the driver will have a fuller understanding of this practice, as well as a greater awareness of the risk that is taken if the rule is ignored. Or, more interestingly, because the driver understands why one must stop, he or she may discover an even more effective and original way to control traffic—and with this discovery, revolutionize driving as we know it. If the objective of the character-driven screenwriter is not only to create something effective but to discover new ways to do things—to be original—then it is necessary to become aware of the theory behind any particular choice of technique or process, despite the natural eagerness to "just do it."

Finally, this book is an attempt to change a pervasive problem in movies today. As the actor Sean Penn said, "we have become a cinema of impression rather than a cinema of expression." Meaning and transcendence is thought to be best expressed in metaphor, by giving an audience a snapshot, a sound byte, or MTV montage, rather than digging deeply into character. In light of recent box office results and Academy-Award nominations, the rise of the immature film—from cartoonish spectacle action movies to overly ironic adolescent "all-authority-figures-are-hypocrites" films—has peaked. A new period is beginning: a renaissance for the mature film—one that is specific, complex, and original. This book is an attempt to help screenwriters to become adult screenwriters, that is, to know who they are, what they want, and to commit to a purpose.

PART 1

THE CHARACTER-DRIVEN APPROACH

Defining the Character-Driven Screenplay

The character-driven story is not a new concept. It is axiomatic that all stories, to some degree, are character-driven. Many people refer to a film as "character-driven" if it doesn't have much plot, or if it's a "slice-of-life story," a "small" or "independent" film, or "independent in spirit"—meaning that even if it is made by a major studio, it somehow breaks the rules. The term is vague. It has been co-opted by so many to say too much, and consequently it now says very little.

Very simply, the character-driven screenwriter is someone who understands that the permanent value of any film is in the complexity of the characterization, not in the suspense and thrills—although these elements should certainly not be overlooked. Renowned film director, Martin Scorcese has said that he starts first with the characters, and from that base he constructs a movie. This process of developing the character and then building the story is unique to the character-driven screenplay.

To create complex characters, paradoxically, the writer needs to avoid complicated plot because it decreases the opportunities to show the audience deep and meaningful revelations about character. A string of mounting plot points pushes the character, setting him or her on the run, and the audience does not have a chance to observe a character. It is those seemingly less "thrilling" moments, when a character is centered and present and free to open up about deeply held thoughts, feelings, secrets, and longings, that will give an audience some deep understanding of a character. To captivate an audience, the character-driven screenplay employs similar strategies to that of the modern narrative.

The Modern Narrative

The modern narrative is a way of telling a tale that has been a part of Western culture, at the very least, since Cervantes published the first part of his novel, *Don Quixote,* in 1605. I do not presume to be a scholar of literature, but I draw this watershed mark with Cervantes because it goes back far enough in time to make the point that the modern narrative is not so modern.

The modern narrative is not plot-driven. Cervantes entitled his chapters: "The Character of the Knight," "His First Expedition," "He Attains Knighthood," "An Adventure on Leaving the Inn," and so on. Leaving an inn or just simply noting the character of the knight are not, ostensibly, earthshaking events or topics. There is an understatement and a certain irony to these chapter titles, implying that the author did not think "big events" were all that important. His tale is about Don Quixote having a meal, sleeping on rocky ground, or just hanging out. Cervantes was interested in creating a slice of life to reveal his character and his world so that the sum of this approach would accumulate to create impact. He digressed frequently, providing many insights into death, love, learning, and charity, among other things, and his digressions were great counterpoint; they filled out the irony of Quixote's attempts at adventure.

Character-driven screenwriters are much like Cervantes. They are not interested in huge events and the unfolding of plot. They are interested in showing the contradictions and idiosyncrasies of character and revealing a specific world and the people in it, allowing for digressions to bring insight and counterpoint. Cervantes' standards were low. He originally intended Don Quixote to be a mere riff on the traditional popular ballads. Initially he wrote only part of what we now know to be the complete book, but because it was so successful, he wrote the second part to continue to give readers the pleasure of living in the world of Don Quixote with the quirky main character and the idiosyncrasies of many of the other characters—Sancho Panza, and Dulcinea. With very little ego and a sense of fun, Cervantes created a major hit, certainly the most famous book in Spanish literature. Screenwriters can learn a lot from him.

The modern narrative has been in the theater for over a century. In 1888, with the production of his first serious play, *Ivanov,* Anton Chekhov began his exploration of the modern narrative. He wanted to deflect emphasis from the plot and traditional melodramatic devices (still used today in most traditional three-act screenplays) of suicides, attempted murders, shootouts, duels, love triangles, interrupted love scenes, hero/villain characters, or the great reversals when virtue triumphs over vice. He wanted to excise the unnatural and the untruthful. Chekhov was compassionate towards his characters and strove to depict their full humanity at all times, dramatizing the internal and external forces on individuals, their motives, and the complexity of every choice. "Let things that happen onstage be just as complex and yet as simple as they are in real life," he said, "for instance, people are having a meal, just having a meal, but at the same time their happiness is being created, or their lives are being smashed up."

The character-driven writer is not, as author Milan Kundera said in *The Art of the Novel,* "an author on a horse cracking a whip at his characters as they run down a narrow alley." A character-driven screenplay, of course, has plot, but it comes second in priority to character. In the character-driven screenplay the story is the relationship between the characters. The plot is what changes these relationships. Seymour Chatman, a specialist in the study of narrative structure and Professor of Rhetoric at the University of California, Berkeley, writes in *Story and Discourse* that in the modern narrative:

> The plot is not an intricate puzzle. In the traditional narrative of resolution there is a sense of problem solving, in things being worked out some way. "What will happen" is the basic question. In the modern plot of revelation, however, the emphasis is elsewhere. It is not that a state of affairs is resolved (happily or tragically), but rather that a state of affairs is revealed. Revelatory plots tend to be

strongly character-oriented, concerned with the infinite detailing of existents (the characters and the world), and events are reduced to a relatively minor, illustrative role. Whether Elizabeth Bennet (*Pride and Prejudice*) marries is a crucial matter, but not whether Clarissa Dalloway (*Mrs. Dalloway*) spends her time shopping or writing letters or daydreaming, since any one of these or other actions would correctly reveal her character or plight.

Specificity is one very modern aspect of the modern narrative. Ancient writing, Biblical or mythological, never valued details that much. When the oracle told Oedipus that he would kill his father, he did not say it would be at 4:30 in the afternoon just before rush hour. Charles Pierce Baker, the legendary Harvard professor who taught Eugene O'Neill and Thomas Wolfe, and created the first practical course in playwriting ever presented in an American college, wrote in *Dramatic Technique,* "in drama, individualization is always the sign of developing art. In any country, the history of modern drama is a passing, under the influence of the audience, from abstractions and personifications, through type, to individualized character."

Characters can be general and stereotypical like the "village idiot," but specificity gives characters more layers and compelling contradictions. Without a character's very specific worldview, likes, dislikes, sensitivities, life experience, habits, patterns of speech, and idiosyncrasies, there can be no layers to a character, which is the source of complexity. When a story has less complexity, it doesn't resonate in the minds and hearts of the viewers. And with less resonance, a story will never be lasting and meaningful.

Character: The Single Most Powerful Element of Any Story

I have read screenwriting books that promote the idea of using archetypes—the hero, mentor, trickster, and so on—as the basis for creating "real" characters. This strategy concerns me because a real character and an archetype are two very different entities. Archetypes are generalized, simplified characters. They can be helpful to a storyteller who is exploring the mythic, but the writer of the character-driven screenplay is looking to detail a character, to find the many layers of competing characteristics, not simplify. It is true, if you do choose to use archetypes, you will have a wider audience; the eight-year-old boy in Japan who does not speak English will certainly understand an action film hero created in Hollywood: the action film hero is good, there are bad guys who are in his way. Physical actions rather than mental actions are the vocabulary of such a film. However, nearly any moviegoer, no matter what level of education or what culture they belong to, knows on some level that there is a falseness to "type" characterization. When the lights come up after a farce, melodrama, or musical comedy, an audience will certainly admit that they did not believe in the truth of the characters, but they will qualify it by saying that "that is not where the pleasure lies." In farce the pleasure lies in the verbal wit and examination of a central idea; in melodrama it is in the thrills, the suspense, and making the improbable probable; and in musical comedy it is in the tunes that we can sing after the show.

Think about your favorite movies. If they are films like *Citizen Kane, Godfather II, Jules and Jim, Contempt, Casablanca, The Silence of the Lambs, Steel Helmet,* or *Secrets and Lies,* what do you remember first? The plot or the characters? Charles Foster Kane, Michael Corleone, Catherine, and Hannibal Lecter are complex characters who come to mind first, rather than the contrivances of plot or the chance events that unfold to twist the action in another direction. Charles Foster Kane is remembered for his monumental egotism, and his obvious self-loathing; Hannibal Lecter for his mysterious sexiness; and Catherine for how she could seduce, transport, and at the same time, destroy her lovers.

Most executives who run Hollywood, in my experience, are incredibly bright and often very well educated. But Hollywood is in constant flux; people go in and out of favor with alacrity. It is a town that constantly forgets and rediscovers just about everything, including this dictum: the true value of any story lies first and foremost in character. "In drama, undoubtedly the strongest immediate appeal to the general public is action. The permanent value of a play, however, rests on its characterization," wrote Charles Pierce Baker. The writer of the character-driven screenplay is concerned with plot, but she or he gets to it by first focusing on unique characters in a unique world.

2

How to Write from the Inside Out

Let's examine the very different writing process required by the character-driven versus the plot-driven screenplay. The screenwriter of the plot-driven movie most often works from the outside in rather than the inside out, using a cerebral and rational process that does not tap the unconscious imagination. The plot-driven screenwriter first looks for a concept that can be pitched in one line: "a train is taken hostage by a madman with a ticking bomb" or "people are trapped in a skyscraper that is burning from the bottom up." Clear and simple concepts are perfect because he or she can immediately concoct a plot from a strong, clear concept that can be played out for two hours on film with lots of physical action and twists and turns in the plot.

With the concept established, the plot-driven screenwriter then begins to think about "peopling" it—whipping up characters that will service the plot. "Okay, we have a burning building and so the first thing we need is a character that will lead the fight to put out the fire," thinks the plot-driven screenwriter. He or she will think about it for a while and then come up with a character that we most probably have seen before—the same old cliché, recycled over and over again. Perhaps it is the demanding, controlling, fiery, and no-nonsense fire chief, who has worked his way up over the years and comes from a long line of firemen who died putting out fires. The screenwriter is smart enough to know this character is a cliché and quickly tries to come up with one or two distinguishing characteristics that will make this character different—perhaps the fire chief has lost a hand and has a drinking problem. "Yeah, that's special," thinks the plot-driven screenwriter, "a General Patton sort of guy who has a bottle stashed in his boot and dives in at the last minute to save the day, despite the fact that he has a prosthesis for a hand."

The writing process of the plot-driven screenwriter forces creation from a conscious place; traits are imposed on an "idea" for a character. This is a recipe for disaster. Why? Because there is no real discovery in this process. The writer has not gone deep enough and discovered something unknown. Without factoring in discovery into the writing process, the results will lack vitality, specificity, surprise, truth, and originality—all things that make a movie lasting and meaningful. At first glance, it appears that the plot-driven screenwriter is having lots of "ah-hah" experiences in the process briefly described above. But the plot-driven screenwriter is writing from the head, not from the heart; the mind is leading the process, not the soul. Our brains are simply not as powerful, wise, or effective as our mysterious unconscious for creating original stories and characters.

The character-driven screenwriter creates stories that are personal, edgy, quirky, surprising, specific, and original. Only the unconscious, not the conscious, can deliver these results. Thus, in order to meet the goals of the character-driven screenplay the writer must learn how to access his or her unconscious.

Flow: Creating Story from the Unconscious Imagination

How does the character-driven screenwriter work from the inside out rather than the outside in? By becoming aware of and understanding flow—the unconscious imagination—and developing tricks to trigger and free it. The essence of the writing process is to free up the unconscious and allow it to take over and lead you to both character and story; to discover what you did not know you knew or did not know you felt. It is a process that requires you to "to take the trip," to become fully immersed, and discover concept, rather than impose one.

For the writing process of the character-driven screenplay to work, you must have faith that the story will define itself—eventually. Story and character are discovered by opening up to your unconscious flow and being surprised by your own feelings and thoughts. Consequently the audience will also be surprised, and you will have created a powerful and resonant screenplay.

We experience the unconscious imagination when we daydream, or when we shut our eyes and sit in a quiet room and watch the movie that begins flowing before our mind's eye. This movie or daydream just seems to flow with no beginning, middle, and end, and it appears to always be there, brewing ceaselessly whether we are aware of it or not. "Flow" is all the thoughts, feelings, sounds, images, character, story, and so on, that flows into the conscious mind when the unconscious imagination is set free. The writing process proposed in this book is essentially a process of triggering flow—opening the door to it while the writer is in a conscious state—and deciding what to use or discard in order to build a story.

The discovery process is a "backwards and forwards" procedure. The writer must first dive into the realm of the unconscious imagination for material, and then, move out of it to a conscious state to craft a screenplay. The process continues, back and forth, literally hundreds if not thousands of times before the writer can complete a screenplay.

Flow occurs every day of your life. You pick up an old pair of boxing gloves in an antique shop while your wife (or husband) impatiently waits for you to look at a candelabra. You feel the cracked leather of the gloves, get a whiff of its odor: sweat and rawhide. You pound one fist into the mitt and you suddenly feel yourself on your toes, recalling newsreel footage of Muhammad Ali doing his rope-a-dope. You hear the *Rocky* theme song, and Robert DeNiro's bruised and swollen face in *Raging Bull* flashes before your eyes.

You get past all of these references to popular culture—flow that really doesn't belong to you but to the world, the images and romances that have influenced and inspired you—and you recall a tall, distinguished man you met once at work. He is going to be seventy next year, and even though he is a great success as a father, husband, businessman, and member of his community, there is only one thing he was really ever good at—boxing. He tells you about a time just before World War II when, on his way up, he would box at Gleason's Gym in New York. He was raised as a foster child, his mother was institutionalized soon after he was born; his father, a good man, was an artist and could not make a living, and unfortunately succumbed to the bottle. He discovered boxing while at an orphanage, and with it, found himself. But at the same time, another opportunity came his way. He was awarded and took a full scholarship at Columbia University, following the advice of his boxing coach, who advised him to get out of the racket because it was corrupt and a dead end. But he regrets it today because he believes boxing was his one and true talent.

Suddenly you begin to see what he was like as a child. You imagine his father and mother and his boxing coach. Characters and a unique world come to mind. Images spring up: a worn pair of red high-top sneakers; rain sluicing into a New York City sewer; creamy chipped beef on white toast; a leather strap; several stalks of corn sprouting out of a tenement roof garden in Brooklyn. You are experiencing a flow that belongs to you, your unconscious, not the old man that inspired it or to popular culture. You are entering the realm of the unknown, the deeper imagination—inspiration. You feel very alert, lose track of time, and are completely engaged; you are having a breakthrough.

Amidst all this enthusiasm you ask yourself why you are interested in this man's story—here, now, today. Obviously you are haunted by the elements of this story: an old man looking back on his life and recalling when he had prowess and regretting selling out and not sticking to the one thing he did best—boxing. But what does that have to do with you and your life today?

A sinking feeling quickly replaces your enthusiasm, you are entering threatening territory. You have turned the focus away from the story and onto your motive for being so drawn to it, requiring you to face what you are projecting onto the story. You must dig deep into your soul and extract the truth.

You consider what you like about the elements of your flow: an old man defying old age, an old man who has the courage to still pursue his dream, the honesty the old man must possess, and so on. You consider what you don't like about your flow: it's corny and grandiose. This critical reflection guides you; you are warning yourself to avoid the traps you feel are inherent in the story, and at the same time, you are developing a greater awareness of what you want to emphasize and explore in the story. But you still have not answered that most difficult question: "What has this story got to do with you and your life—here, now, today?"

To answer this question, you must assess your own life. You decide that you don't like the way your life is proceeding today—its present course. You realize you are in a rut, something is missing. What could it be? What do you need? "The reward is in the struggle," a little voice whispers in your head. "The reward is in the struggle." You are at the halfway point in your life; you have wasted time, detouring to keep others happy. "The reward is in the struggle," is heard in your head again.

Suddenly, the lightbulb goes on. That's it! It is so clear, yet simple. This story, for me—here, now, today—is about how this old man, so late in life, comes to understand that the reward is in the struggle. He left boxing because he misunderstood its reward. He thought it had to do with money, status, and being number one, but it didn't. It was about just doing it—meeting the challenge, and it was the one challenge in all of his life experience for which he was the most suited. He missed a golden opportunity: he could have been great at something. Your "purpose" for writing this story is to examine the idea that true engagement and satisfaction in life comes from new challenges and we must strive to create these adventures for ourselves. This purpose puts a new spin on your story, giving it focus and direction. You decide your story is about a man who, having this insight, acts upon it and tries to make up for lost time. At age seventy, he will go back in the ring.

Suddenly you hear your wife calling your name. You come out of your dream world, you are all charged up. Curious, she wonders why you are so happy, and you realize you have just experienced the rush of a breakthrough and discovered your purpose—the spine that supports your unconscious flow.

You will notice several things about this process. It begins with an object (a boxing glove), that, when experienced through the senses, opened the door to the conscious imagination. Second, you personalized the experience by recalling, intuitively, a specific man from your past. Third, you felt the power of a breakthrough when you entered into the realm of the unconscious imagination—the point at which you began to discover unknowns—the boxer as a young child, his parents, his coach, a string of apparently unrelated images, and so on. Fourth, you asked yourself why you are interested in this story and discovered your purpose. You just worked from the inside out, not from the outside in, which is what formulaic and plot-driven screenplays demand.

The Breakthrough: The Building Block of the Unconscious Writing Process

It is important to note that you arrived at a more inspired and unknown place only after you experienced a breakthrough; the breakthrough is a sign you are in the land of the unconscious. In a sense, it was the breakthrough you were searching for all along as you followed your flow; it opened the gates to inspiration. All of which begs the question: what exactly is a breakthrough and how do you know you are having one?

Borrowing from Mihaly Csikszentmihalyi, professor of psychology and education at the University of Chicago, and author of *Finding Flow: The Psychology of Engagement with Everyday Life* (1998), an illuminating study on the psychology of engagement, a breakthrough can be defined as a level of consciousness when you feel there is no room for anything else because you are so completely immersed in the activity at hand. Athletes talk about this experience as being "in the zone," musicians refer to it as being "in the groove," mystics call it ecstasy. Csikszentmihalyi notes that when a breakthrough occurs "there is no space in consciousness for distracting thoughts, irrelevant feelings. Self-consciousness disappears, yet one feels stronger than usual."

Most people just simply know, a priori, they are having a breakthrough; they can feel it. A breakthrough is that moment when writers have the feeling that what they are discovering is something never seen before. When a breakthrough occurs, an imagined character takes off in a completely surprising way and acts independently of a writer's desire or ego demands; story just appears. Montages or images spring up and flow of their own accord and the writer feels a loss of control—in a wonderful way.

EXERCISE

SHAPING STORY FROM UNCONSCIOUS DISCOVERIES

Sit in a chair in a quiet room. When you are totally relaxed open your eyes and look about the room until you find something you have never noticed before. What does this object evoke or suggest to you? What feelings, thoughts, and images? For instance, you may notice for the first time that the room has a dead moth trapped in a light cover. Perhaps this trapped moth brings up the thought of the death of someone you loved, and/or makes you feel afraid and unclean, and/or reminds you of a young boy you knew who happily spent hours by himself cataloging butterflies.

Once you have chosen a thought, feeling, or image write whatever comes into your mind about it. Let one sentence lead you to the other without fear of what it all means. Do not take your pen off the paper until you are experiencing a breakthrough, which could easily take thirty minutes or more.

Once you have a breakthrough about one thought, feeling, or image, make another choice. For instance, using the example above, after you have written about the boy collecting butterflies, start to write about someone you loved who just died. Continue this until you have made five different choices about the same thing you never noticed in the room before.

I have observed that when people start to work on their second, third, and fourth choices, they either laugh, grin, giggle, squirm, mutter, or do something else to indicate they are uncomfortable. This is because they have moved beyond the obvious first choice, which is usually safe, and are now coming up with something that does not make sense, that is out of their control. This uncomfortable feeling is a good sign that you are getting somewhere surprising, yet truthful. Don't submit to this natural defense. Go toward what scares you, but, again, be utterly honest.

Put these notes aside for a day. When you come back to them, what patterns do you see? Are there similarities in terms of moods and feelings expressed, themes, stories, characters, worlds, images, styles, etc.? Can you create a story with a beginning, middle, and end from any of these threads?

Purpose: What the Writer Is Trying to Do

As discussed, the character-driven screenwriter places a high value not only on character, but also on content. The only way to truly give a work content is to have something that passionately needs to be said or examined—a "purpose." This may seem like a contradiction at first. If the writing process of the character-driven screenplay is all about freeing up the unconscious and allowing it to lead the way, isn't having a conscious purpose the opposite of this? The answer is no. Having a conscious purpose is just another way to free up the unconscious. Without a clear, conscious purpose, the writer will not be able to work as deeply and freely with the unconscious. A screenwriter's purpose may, and most likely will, change and evolve as she or he continues to work on the story. But a purpose must be in place from the start of the journey if the screenwriter is ever to arrive at a completed screenplay with some genuine content.

What is a purpose? A purpose, very simply, is the deepest and most personal reason a writer is writing a story. It is what the writer needs to say. Which means, if you have nothing to say, then you have no purpose, and without a purpose, you will not have a deep foundation for your screenplay.

A purpose can be many things. For example, I need to create a story to give expression to the sense of loneliness and having no one to love that I have been writing about in my diary for the last year; I want to write about what it is like to commit murder; I want to explore the real consequences of sin in today's world; I want to capture and express the feel, excitement, and complex world of car racing; I want to express what I think and feel about life in the suburbs; I would like to know what it is like to be sexually addicted; I want to explore what it was like to be the pilot who pushed the button that dropped the bomb on Hiroshima; I want to show people what it is really like to survive an Ivy League law school; I want to show the destruction a parent can have on a child; I want people to see what it is really like to be a genius at playing the piano; I want to express what it is like to be gay in America today; I want to tell the story of my grandmother; I want to express the utterly misunderstood and overlooked complexities of farm life. A purpose can be connected to a subject you know very well or something you want to get to know more about. To formulate a purpose, you must start with "I want to..." Your purpose is the focus point for exploring a topic or issue. It should be something you can state clearly in a line or two and it should come from your heart, simply and truthfully.

To find the purpose, a writer examines some notion, proposition, idea, or feeling for a test of truth, just as I discovered my purpose, "the reward is in the struggle" for the boxing story. Knowing this purpose will not only free me up and give me direction, but it will also lead me to real content. I will write the story to see what the statement—the reward is in the struggle—truthfully means for me. Perhaps I will discover or learn that this statement is utterly false—that the reward is not in the struggle, it is in winning. Or perhaps this statement may lead me to discover that the real truth of the story—and therefore my real purpose—is that dreams die hard. In either case, I would still have a personal statement that tells me what this story is all about, a purpose, that evolved organically, like all the other elements of a story.

A purpose represents what the writer cares about at the moment he or she is writing the story. If you don't have anything to say or express, then don't write until you do. Without a purpose, a writer is a boat without a rudder—there is no way to navigate or take control; it is all journey and no destination. Unfortunately, discovering purpose is the one step that many beginning writers overlook. It is the most difficult step to learn. But if this step is not taken, your screenplay, play, or novel, will never reach the level of specificity, originality, and complexity it could achieve.

Grounding Purpose in a Central Emotion

Discovering purpose requires the writer to interpret why he or she wants to write the story and to simultaneously translate that interpretation into dramatic action. When doing a self-examination, most beginning writers, will abstract matters instead of distilling the "why" (why the story must be written) into simple truths. They often complicate the reasons they are writing a story, concocting abstract, fuzzy, and generalized theories that are just not useful when it comes to writing a screenplay. Writers must learn to "get out of their heads," and discover a purpose that is not metaphysical, but one that is grounded in a basic human emotion. They must learn to make their assessments about their story from a calm, centered place, inside themselves, rather than a frenetic, defensive, and untruthful place, in their heads. When searching for the truth about the essence of their stories, beginning writers should keep this maxim in mind: "Keep It Simple, Stupid."

In the boxing story about the old man, the purpose hovers around "the reward is in the struggle"; it becomes the spine of the story. I use the phrase "hovers around this statement" because a purpose, if it is a true one, can be stated in many different ways, yet essentially be about the same thing. "The reward is in the struggle" can also be stated as not wasting your life, not following your bliss, or the shame we feel about our lack of courage, and so on. Each of these statements has a different nuance, but they are essentially about the same thing. What do each of these statements have in common? A central emotion.

In the case of the boxing story, the central emotion is remorse. Remorse about wasting a talent, not pursuing a dream, letting other people lead our life for us, not taking responsibility for our lives, and so on. Of course there are other emotions being expressed in the story about the older boxer, but a purpose is the emotion the writer chooses to place the central focus on.

Purpose Gives Focus to the Story

Having discovered my purpose, I use it to put together the elements of my flow—to make them be *about* something. I give focus to my story by extrapolating from my purpose and postulating a "what if?"

With my boxing story, I begin to meditate on my purpose by elaborating on why I chose it. I chose it because it summarizes for me what I think my central character is going through: a crisis in his life. He has come to learn, at the age of seventy, that the most important thing in life is to find new challenges, to have new dreams, and to go for them. And the reward in all of this is simply the "doing" of it. I then put myself in the shoes of my central character. I ask myself a "what if?" What if he came to this understanding today, what would he do? He would follow his dreams, I immediately realize. Which directly leads me to another "what if?" I wonder what if this old man decided, for his seventieth birthday, to have one more go in the ring? Perhaps there is some opponent that he wants another chance at beating. Or perhaps he wants to prove he could go three rounds with the latest amateur champ, even at his age.

I now have a strong direction. There are many questions that still need to be addressed, much work to be done, but because I have this strong sense of purpose, my unconscious imagination is now free to lead me to discover what I did not know I knew or what I did not know I felt.

Different Grades of Flow

Breakthroughs give your screenplay brilliance, scope, size, and luminosity. But sooner or later you will be faced with the task of arranging and proportioning your breakthroughs. Often, you will need to discard some of your most brilliant, unconscious excavations. It is difficult to do, but you should not cling to something that does not add to the whole experience of the screenplay.

In the course of this book, I occasionally stop and suggest something that can be an excellent trigger for flow. Physical or mental actions, sound, picture, dialogue, reexamining your purpose, finding different layers of conflict, or simply changing the setting, can all help unblock you, create flow, and trigger your unconscious imagination. Crafting the character-driven screenplay is essentially about the management of flow—from developing and applying dependable triggers to set off flow to devising practical ways to select, apportion, and arrange flow to shape a fully considered screenplay.

Flow is a source of material that can sometimes be contaminated by triggering it in the wrong way. For instance, if you conjure your flow in order to satisfy your ego, to prove to the world how funny or clever you are, you will receive stuff from your flow that will not be you. It will belong to your peers, parents, ideology, or your screenwriting teacher. It is very hard to use that type of flow to make anything lasting, original, or surprising. If you are naturally funny, your flow will be funny. But you can't make it funny. If you are smart, so will be your flow, but its IQ can't be pushed up by your control. If you are thinking through every detail as you are trying to access your flow, your flow will be labored and self-conscious.

You are your flow, which, for most of us, is a frightening proposition. If you hate your flow, you hate yourself, and nothing good can come of that, can it? Trust your flow and it will lead you to the answer. Its power lies in the fact that it is flowing. If it stalls or is encumbered, consider it a warning sign that something is wrong. Immediately lower your standards; you are becoming too ambitious in the worst sense, as you are not honoring your skills and self-knowledge at this point in your life or the limits of the form you are working in. Stop, let go, you have a monkey on your back and it is causing writer's block. Reflect, study, reconsider, play tennis, go for a walk in the woods, give up entirely, and just when you do, the flow will begin again, with the answers that you need. But this time the flow will not be forced, it will be organic and true.

EXERCISE

DISCOVERING YOUR PROFILE AS A WRITER

Make a list of ten likes and ten dislikes (preferences and prejudices) about films, plays, novels, or television shows you have watched in your lifetime. For instance, if under the category of likes, you include *The Honeymooners*, discuss in one or two lines, in utterly simple stupid terms, why you like *The Honeymooners*, i.e., fat people interest me; things are always blowing up in Ralph's face and I like that; I like characters who are over the top and Ralph is over the top. Or suppose you choose *Terminator 2: Judgment Day*, you could write: I like science fiction, as a writer it lets you be really imaginative; I like the way someone destroys himself in every way possible, in order to save someone else in every way possible; I like films in which young boys find a father figure; I love action films.

When making your list of likes and dislikes, try to draw out what scares you and reveal likes and dislikes you have never revealed to others or yourself. For instance, you might write: I like *Jules and Jim* because I want to sleep with my girlfriend's best friend, or, I dislike such and such a film because it has too many bird's eye shots in it and I hate heights and I have never told anyone. Share your secrets, puzzling thoughts, ideas, fears, desires, dreams, recurring images, and so on—things that you do not have clarity on, but that haunt you just the same.

After you have completed your list, analyze and assess it. What does this list suggest to you about your preferences or prejudices? What do these likes and dislikes tell you about yourself as a writer, as an artist? What is it that haunts you, holds your interest, inexplicably, obsessively? What haunts you in terms of subject matter, theme, form, and style?

Finally, how can you put this self-knowledge to practical use in creating a screenplay? For instance, if you discover your intense fear of heights perhaps you could write a screenplay that deals that that issue. How can this information give you confidence and direction as a writer?

3

Contingent Causation: Accumulation Creates Impact

Flow is the unleashing of the unconscious imagination. It is messy, non-linear, inexplicable and unpredictable, with no order and coherence. When experiencing flow, you may imagine a boy dancing by the seashore, next you see him diving in the water, and finally he is in his bathing suit driving on the freeway at breakneck speeds. You wonder how one thing causes the other in this chain of imagined events. What does the dancing have to do with the diving and the driving? To make sense of these three events, to make them into a story, you must provide some causation, some linkage, that explains why these three events belong together.

To borrow from E. M. Forster, imagine telling a group of people to gather around the campfire because you want to tell them a great story. Everyone leans forward to give you their attention. You then stand up and say, "The king died and then the queen died." The group would not feel like you have told them a story, because you have given them a mere chronicle of events. No link or cause-and-effect relationship between the two events—the king and the queen's death—was provided. If you were to tell them that "the king died and then the queen died because of grief," they would be far more satisfied. This addition of causation that links the two events is what creates a narrative.

In order to give shape and coherence to flow and make it into a story, the screenwriter must provide causation—a way to join things together so they make sense. In the character-driven screenplay, the causation is usually contingent rather than linear.

With linear causation A directly causes B and B directly causes C, and so on. With contingent causation A does not directly cause B and B does not directly cause C, but it all adds up to D. In other words, D is not directly caused by any one reason that proceeded it, but rather, it is caused by the accumulation of reasons that proceeded it.

For instance, if the first thing we see in a movie is a man walking down a street who randomly punches a complete stranger in the nose, we wonder why he did that. If the screenwriter then shows us that this man has lost his home, suffered the death of a child, has no job or future prospects, cannot break his drug addiction, and is hungry and lonely, then we begin to understand that many complex reasons have accumulated and indirectly caused his action. This contingent causation is a hallmark of the character-driven screenplay. Contingent causation is more complex than linear and therefore has more resonance.

In the plot-driven screenplay, the causation is linear and more direct. With linear causation, the man punches the stranger because the stranger insulted his wife in the previous scene. There is a direct, one-to-one, action/reaction mechanistic explanation for the event in the scene. The linear causation suggests that things do not happen for an accumulation of reasons, which may take a long time to weave together and explain. Instead, one concrete thing happens and then causes something else to happen.

The character-driven screenplay progresses by the sheer accumulation of compelling scenes and moments, made cohesive by a common theme. Because the scenes are glued together by theme rather than by mounting plot points that provide a direct bridge to the climax of a story, the linkages are indirect rather than direct.

Indirect Linkages Are More Truthful

The Russian novelist Leo Tolstoy explored similar notions of contingency in his story-telling. Isaiah Berlin, Oxford educator and scholar, observed that Tolstoy believed that war and history, as expressed in his novel *War and Peace,* was "only a succession of 'accidents' whose origins and consequences are, by and large, untraceable and unpredictable." For Tolstoy, battles and the course of history represented loosely strung groups of events in an ever-varying pattern, with no discernible order. The "great illusion" that Tolstoy seeks to expose in *War and Peace,* noted Berlin, is "that individuals can, by the use of their own resources, understand and control the course of events." And that anything told to us otherwise is "elaborate machinery for concealing the spectacle of human impotence and irrelevance and blindness." Tolstoy's underlying vision was that an accumulation of complex forces creates our reality. The character-driven screenwriter embraces this complexity, and uses contingent causation to express it.

The writer of the character-driven screenplay is trying to express the complexity and relativity of the world we live in; that moral and social certitudes and absolute standards of any kind, are difficult to find in postmodern times. With the more traditional plot-driven approach to screenwriting, the writer is communicating something very different: all effects have causes; all can be explained and predicted; what goes up comes down; and truth can be found through empirical evidence.

The Fugitive clearly has a linear, every-action-has-a-reaction causality. Dr. Richard Kimble comes home and discovers his wife has been murdered. This directly causes him to look for the murderer, which directly leads to a scuffle with the murderer, a one-armed man in Kimble's home. The one-armed man escapes, which directly leads the police to perceive Kimble, with blood on his shirt and no real alibi, as their prime suspect. Home alone with his dead wife, Kimble looks very guilty indeed. A gross misreading of the evidence on the part of the police and district attorney directly causes Kimble to be convicted of the murder of his wife and directly sent to jail. On the way to jail, a scuffle between an escaping prisoner and a guard directly causes the bus, transporting Kimble to jail, to crash. The crash directly leads to an opportunity for Kimble to escape, and so on.

The causality of *The Fugitive* is a line of dominos, one directly taking the other down. Each time something happens, it clearly and simply, without the slightest ambiguity, leads directly to the next event. This strategy communicates to the audience that there is order in the world, that all will be restored since the mechanism of change is so apparent and predictable.

The TV series of *The Fugitive* has more contingent factors than the movie: the wife was an alcoholic, the couple had a troubled marriage and was debating whether or not to have a child. None of these factors are directly linked to Dr. Richard Kimble's need to prove his innocence, but they are indirectly linked. In the television series, Kimble had the persona of guilt, which resulted in a far more complex characterization than the movie. He had guilt about his wife because of their history together but he did not commit the murder; so he was guilty but not guilty. The appearance of guilt in Kimble was caused by an accumulation of factors that added layers to the characterization and story—all giving further resonance to the TV series.

I am not proposing using contingency just for the sake of being obscure, profound, or indulgent. The trick is to create as much contingent causation as possible in your work without losing clarity. With too much contingent causation, a story will soon mimic a person with a multiple-personality disorder. The use of contingency should always be in the service of illuminating complex connections, rather than befuddling an audience. Clarity is key.

EXERCISE | **COMPLICATING A STORY**

Take *The Fugitive*, or any other traditionally structured film, and in less than three pages of outline, come up with ways to complicate it, focusing on changes in character and back story. How do these changes make your version of the film unique? How do they make the story more character-driven?

Examples of Contingent Plotlines

With contingent causation, to borrow from Milan Kundera in *The Art of the Novel,* subplots are "polyphonic" in structure: they are simultaneous voices of equal weight that run parallel to one another, or form tangential connections rather than direct intersections. In a character-driven screenplay, a story frequently has more than one plotline, which are not directly related. In fact, the characters of one plotline may have no relationship whatsoever with the characters of another plotline. The plotlines may never intersect and push each other forward; they may simply run parallel to each other. However, in order to make them cohesive, they must be tied together by theme. This contingent approach to plot adds complexity to the story—one of the main goals of the character-driven screenplay.

In *Pulp Fiction* there are four essentially separate plotlines: the travails of two mid-level hit men, Vincent Vega (John Travolta) and Jules Winnfield (Samuel Jackson); the boxer, Butch (Bruce Willis), who refuses to throw the fight; the overripe couple, Honey Bunny (Amanda Plummer) and Pumpkin (Tim Roth) who hold up a diner; and the mob boss, Marsellus Wallace (Ving Rhames) and his girlfriend, Mia (Uma Thurman), who likes to date the boss's employees. Finally, there is the subplot of Mr. Wolf (Harvey Keitel) who must help Vega and Winnfield dispose of a dead man. Their stories go as follows:

Butch is pressured by the mob boss to throw the fight, but he cannot. After the fight, while trying to get out of town, he realizes that he has lost the watch that belonged to his dad, an irreplaceable heirloom. He must find the watch, despite the danger of being caught by the mob boss, whom he has betrayed. Butch must pay the price for his betrayal—he will be whacked, shot to death. Meanwhile, Honey Bunny and Pumpkin hold up a diner and narrowly escape death.

The plotline of Honey Bunny and Pumpkin does not connect or intersect with the plot of Butch at any point in the film; they are entirely separate. Butch's plotline is tangential to the plotline of the bumbling hit men, Jules and Vincent; they briefly meet, but their stories certainly do not directly intersect. And the subplot of Mr. Wolf (Harvey Keitel) is entirely separate except for an intersection with the plotline of Jules and Vincent.

So what ties *Pulp Fiction*'s plotlines together if they do not intersect? Theme is the cement that makes them cohesive. All of these plotlines have a common line of investigation, they represent a "meditation about tough guys with too much or too little time on their hands," wrote Richard Corliss, film critic for *Time* Magazine. All of these plotlines, which form a polyphonic structure, are shaped into a unified whole around the question: how does a "man of the pulp" keep his status and self-respect in this hierarchical, boys-will-have-big-guns world, when he has been humiliated or has made a serious error of judgment? The strategy of using contingent causation works to create a fresh perspective, more complexity, and resonance for *Pulp Fiction*. If the screenwriters, Roger Avary and Quentin Tarantino had used a linear strategy the film would have been the same old cliché gangster tale. What elevated it and spun it ironically was the complexity created by shaping the material in a contingent way.

In a drama of much greater complexity and specificity of character, *Before the Rain*, which was written and directed by Milcho Manchevski and awarded the 1996 Independent Spirit Award, there is a similar polyphonic structure. The plotlines run parallel to each other and are enclosed in a circular tale. However, unlike *Pulp Fiction*, the film's effect is not distancing or overly ironic. Instead, this strategy deepens and illuminates the theme of the film: how the effect of the impending war in Macedonia spreads throughout the world in circular and contingent ways, like a virus.

Before the Rain elicits a very strong emotional response from the audience by using three separate plotlines. The first takes place in Macedonia and concerns a young monk, Kiril, who falls in love with a runaway girl. Escaping the wrath of a vigilante, the runaway girl seeks refuge in the monastery where Kiril is a novitiate. Once Kiril declares his love for this young woman, he must leave the monastery forever since he has broken his vows. The second plotline concerns Anne who, having left her marriage to pursue an affair, meets her estranged husband in a London restaurant and he pleads for her to return. During all of this, a stranger enters the London restaurant, argues in a foreign language with a waiter and returns with a gun. He shoots the waiter and sprays the dining room with bullets, venting an unknown rage. Anne's husband is shot in the head and dies in her arms. The third plotline concerns Aleksander, a war photographer who is having an affair with Anne. He breaks off the affair and returns to his native Macedonia only to be faced with the ethnic and religious conflict that has overrun his homeland. The brewing violence and impending war in Macedonia forces Aleksander to take sides on the matter—something he has steadfastly avoided. The plotline of Anne and her husband barely even touch the plotline of Aleksander and his troubled homeland; they are tangential in relationship. The plotline of the young monk and his girlfriend are entirely separate, running parallel to the plotline of Anne and her husband. The plotline of the monk and the girl do eventually flow into the plotline of Aleksander, however, it serves as a bookend rather than a direct intersection. Like *Pulp Fiction,* the unifying factor of the contingent structure of *Before the Rain* does not rely on intersecting plotlines to push the main plotline forward, but rather a common theme or line of investigation that gels all of the actions of the separate, parallel plotlines into a coherent whole.

Manchevski has a minor character, a doctor, boldly state the major theme of the movie: "war is a virus." Like a virus, war spreads randomly, can be carried by good as well as by bad people, and will infect anyone and cause meaningless death. By using the strategy of contingent causation, Manchevski succeeds in giving fuller expression to this metaphor; the audience can feel and experience the viral madness of war more powerfully. The strategy also effectively communicates the ideas associated with the virus metaphor—randomness, inexplicable terror, unfairness, sad irony, and chaos.

How to Create Contingent Plotlines

The writing process examined in this book places a high priority on the unconscious imagination; it is from this well that the writer of the character-driven screenplay draws most frequently. A plotline is an element of a screenplay that is also drawn from the unconscious imagination. The best way to excavate a plotline from the unconscious is to choose an emotion—envy, joy, anger—and an idea correlative to that emotion— entitlement, kindness, abuse. Using both the emotion and idea as a theme, begin to explore your unconscious by asking, "What does this combination evoke or suggest to me?" "What image, person, place, thing, or sound springs to mind in my wildest imagination and feels truthful and excites me?" A plotline will eventually emerge from this kind of meditation. It may be evoked or suggested by elements excavated from the unconscious, or it may appear in clear-cut form.

If a writer finds one plotline in this manner, and then continues, using the same combination of emotion and idea, yet another plotline will soon present or suggest itself. Ideally, if a writer continues this process until five plotlines emerge, it is likely that these five plotlines will be contingent—unexpectedly related to one another—since they were unconscious meditations on the same theme.

Let us examine an example of this process of discovering and shaping a contingent plotline. Taking the screenwriter Paul Schrader's *(Affliction, Taxi Driver, Mishima)* advice, I attempt to create a screenplay by beginning with my most personal, pressing problem today, which is spending too many hours on-line trading stocks. This trading is an obsession, like gambling, that has affected my peace of mind and robbed priceless hours of psychic energy that I should be expending on more important matters, such as meeting the deadline for completing this book. I wonder what is driving this behavior. What is at the bottom of it all?

I go for a walk in Central Park and as I meditate on these questions, answers come to me in little epiphanies. I painfully realize that I am greedy. Certainly this on-line trading reflects my compulsive nature, but that doesn't interest me as much as the emotion of greed. Writers should always pursue what haunts them—and greed haunts me. I wonder: what is greed? Why does it have such power? I ask myself what idea immediately springs to mind when I think of greed. The answer is self-worth. Now I have both an emotion and an idea to guide my unconscious exploration.

The next step in the process is to find a way to personalize this combination of greed and self-worth. I immediately recall a man I once knew. At this point, I have no idea why I am recalling this particular man from my past, I just do. Trusting this unconscious association, I allow it to lead me. I recall that, in an effort to break the chain of poverty in his family, this man worked nights and attended college during the day. He became a high school teacher, admired by both his students and fellow teachers, and was eventually elected to represent the Teacher's Union in his district. I feel I understand his profession since I once worked as a conflict resolution specialist with gang members at several high schools in the South Bronx. I am familiar with the realities, the real ups and downs of being an educator. This past experience gives me the confidence to tackle this challenge that my unconscious presented because it is best to write what you know.

The next step in this writing process is to ask a "what if?" question: what if this man, a respected teacher and elected representative, became obsessed with on-line stock trading? How would his obsession break the stasis of his world? What new forces would be unleashed? How would he deal with these forces?

Asking the "what if?" questions lead me deeper into the unconscious imagination. At this point I sense a breakthrough. I imagine that his obsession with on-line trading, breaks the stasis of his world by robbing his students and girlfriend of his time and focus. The force unleashed by the break in this stasis of his world and character is rapacious greed. He deals with this unleashed force by finding a way to use pension funds for his own investments, working with other corrupt union officials. At first, he is fabulously successful. He moves into a much better apartment, buys a new car, clothes, and so on. Inevitably, he makes the wrong move, and an investment goes sour. His greed turns into panic and he convinces his cohorts that he can cover his losses with more misappropriated funds. But this plan does not pan out, as another investment goes sour. He is exposed and forced to face his shortcomings.

As I reflect on this story, I find it unsatisfying. It feels derivative of the Bud Fox story in *Wall Street*. My story has a traditional structure with a central protagonist and a linear, cause-and-effect plot, and the hero of my story is similar to Bud Fox because both characters must learn a lesson. Both stories are tales of caution or morality narratives. I am not satisfied because the purpose of my story is not to teach lessons. I want the audience to watch a movie to discover where their own values lie.

I begin again the next day. I am depressed. The story had seemed so exciting when it first came to me the day before. In fact, for a brief while, I thought it was brilliant. It is a difficult time because all I have to follow are my instincts. I throw away the whole idea. I decide the best way to begin again is to just recall all the people, at any point in my life, who I thought were greedy and were connected in some way to the idea of self-worth. Evidently, the last person I used, the schoolteacher, led me down the wrong path, so I choose another person from my past to personalize this exploration.

I quickly flip through the Rolodex in my head. I try not to pressure myself and keep my standards low; it is just a simple, fun game. I recall a very greedy little girl (again, I have no idea why—it is strictly an unconscious choice), an only child who was bullied in subtle ways by her parents, both high-powered New York surgeons. She was my daughter's playmate and they attended the same nursery school. This child was remarkably greedy. If another child brought in a new toy to school, this greedy little girl invariably wanted it. She would do anything in her power to get her way, and all the teachers at the nursery school joked about her tenacity.

This greedy child felt much better than the previous choice, the greedy teacher. I felt I had not seen a character like her before, so perhaps she will lead me to a world and other characters that are just as unique. To delve further into the unconscious imagination, I decide to name this greedy child by recalling people from my past who remind me of this character—someone named Betsy, another named Marcia. I try their names on for size and they do not feel right. I have found from past experience that I cannot create a character until I have a name that fits. I suddenly think of my neighbor's cat: Chloe. My neighbors and I joke about this cat, and project upon it a kind of childish, silly greed and selfishness. "That's it," I think—Chloe is perfect (again, there is no conscious reason for this choice, it is just a feeling). Like every choice made in creating a screenplay, it may change later on in the writing process.

I continue by proposing another "what if?" What if Chloe stole something and got away with it at school? How would she do that? To address this question the first thing I do is a meditation through the senses. I want to anchor my imagination in a specific place to help free it up. Using my experience with my daughter's nursery school, I imagine what Chloe's classroom is like: I recall the smell of the clay the children used; I hear the buzz of the overhead fluorescent lights; I can feel the sticky hands of a child after snack time. This sensory recall further frees up the unconscious and creates a new flow.

I discover that Chloe desires a Barbie doll that belongs to another young girl, Grace. Chloe is warned by her teachers that she cannot have the doll. Finally, Chloe constructs an elaborate manipulation, one that is oddly far beyond her years of maturity. Chloe fakes a fainting spell and while her teachers are in a panic looking for Chloe's pills in her lunchbox, she steals the child's Barbie. She executes her manipulation with great success and suffers no negative consequences. I am delighted with this discovery, especially the discovery that the manipulation was far beyond her years. I sense this detail is very telltale, and note it.

As I reflect at this point in my process, I discover that my line of investigation, greed, as connected to the idea of self-worth, has changed. I now feel that I am really interested in writing about the emotion of envy and how it connects to the idea of evil. The theme of the exploration, as any other important element of a screenplay, will often change as the writing process proceeds.

Starting with this new exploration, I see in my mind's eye a lonely, wealthy man, who is dying. He needs a new kidney and is on an organ donor's list, but no matter how much he tries to use his influence to get an organ sooner than the others on the list, he cannot. The list is completely democratic and protected by vigilant and honest administrators. This older gentleman's chances of survival would be greatly increased if he could quickly find a donor. This man is considered a great philanthropist, honored by the community for his generosity. At a charity benefit, he asks his lawyer if there is any way to speed up the process of organ donation. The lawyer will consider the matter.

Several days later, the lawyer makes a proposal: he will arrange for the robbery of a kidney from a healthy young man. The lawyer rationalizes the idea by saying that it will not kill the healthy young man, since we all can live with one kidney. The wealthy man, whose name now occurs to me, Fredrick, is appalled at the suggestion. The lawyer says he has contacts who can execute this crime, but it will cost $10 million. It seems the lawyer, who is in the middle of a very messy divorce and wants to secure the hand of a much younger woman needs money and he will do anything, however destructive or compulsive, to accomplish his goal.

After days of deliberation, Fredrick reluctantly agrees, but wants to know every detail about the personal history of the healthy young man who will be plundered for a kidney. Fredrick's final demand is that he wants to meet this young man before the crime is committed. The lawyer is concerned about Fredrick's request to meet the donor, but since he desperately wants the money, he agrees to the terms.

At this point in the writing process I become aware of three very distinct plotlines: Fredrick, the lawyer, and the healthy young man being set up to have his kidney stolen; the lawyer and his bride-to-be; and Chloe and her manipulations at school. I can follow traditional advice and make one of these plotlines the central plotline, and then conceive of ways the others could intersect with that main plotline. As I quickly consider the outcomes of using this strategy, my truth meter goes off. All of the outcomes seem forced, and therefore untruthful. How could Chloe's plotline truthfully intersect with Fredrick's? Could Chloe be Fredrick's granddaughter or his neighbor? Is Fredrick a pedophile? All of these choices feel contrived and they should because the ego, rather than the unconscious imagination is now shaping the story. I am following formula and prescription, not the unconscious, and the results are deadly. Ultimately, it is your individual truth meter and purpose that should guide you about what strategy to pursue. If I could find a truthful way to have these plotlines intersect, I would certainly give further consideration to those possibilities. But since I can find no truthful way to do this, I accept the way the plotlines run parallel or are tangent to one another.

The three plotlines that evolved in my writing process are already tied together by theme and therefore do not have to be forced into an unnatural marriage in which all plotlines should intersect. Each of my plotlines examines a central idea: why are people evil? Why do people do whatever they can to get what they want, regardless of other's needs? Why are people willing to destroy someone else emotionally, spiritually, or physically in order to preserve a sick sense of themselves? Because these plotlines are tied together by theme, the screenplay will have clarity.

I discovered these three contingent plotlines by entering the unconscious imagination and asking "what if?" guided by an emotion—greed—and its correlative idea, self-worth. My unconscious imagination presented three characters: Chloe, Fredrick, and the lawyer. I had absolutely no rational, conscious idea at the time of the excavation why these three characters were linked. I trusted my instincts and organically excavated from my unconscious the story of each of these characters until I had an awareness of their potentialities in separate plotlines, which I did not try to force together. I examined the possibilities of having the plotlines intersect or marry, but these possibilities felt false and contrived and led me dangerously away from the unconscious imagination and into the realm of the ego, which often blocks writers from their most specific, original, and complex creations. The emotion/idea of greed/self-worth changed into a new comination—envy and evil. This change is a surprising, yet wonderful, discovery and I do not resist it because it has brought me a story that is more fresh and original than my first choice.

Using contingent plotlines is an excellent strategy to add layers and complexity to the story. They also help the screenwriter to express the complexity, relativity, and ambiguity of the world we live in today. This approach supports a view that reality is an ever-varying pattern that follows no discernible order.

4

Character or Story: Which Comes First?

The most effective way to fulfill the requirements of the character-driven screenplay—originality, specificity, and complexity—is to build your plot from character rather than your character from plot. This strategy will help you discover more organic plot (what happens to change the relationship of the characters) for your story. Since the plot is not imposed on the characters it will be less contrived. And when a plot is less contrived it will feel more truthful to an audience because the dramatic logic of a character has been respected. A cheap man will not suddenly become generous so the plot can work out, or a virtuous woman will not suddenly lose her integrity so the author can fill the holes in a contrived plot. When a plot is imposed on a character the writer will often violate the true nature of a character. So in order to keep a screenplay truthful, it is important to build story from character.

The writer who first creates magnetic characters and tries hard to not get in their way during the writing process greatly increases the odds of creating a story that is specific, complex, and original. It is important to let the characters react honestly in any situation, regardless of how the writer wants the plot to unfold. And since the characters will not be hammered into a linear way of behaving in order to service the logic of a demanding, extraneous plot, they will be like real people filled with complexity. There will also be greater surprise and originality to the screenplay because the idiosyncrasies of the characters—their quirky, unpredictable, surprising ways of behaving—have been respected. The most resonant aspects of a story come from the surprises characters create, so if the writer celebrates their idiosyncrasies and creates a plot that illuminates these quirks rather than smothering them, the story will stay surprising and fresh.

Would *Hamlet* Still Be *Hamlet?*

Lajos Egri, author of *The Art of Dramatic Writing* argues that the story of *Hamlet* is what it is because of Hamlet's character. He suggests that Shakespeare, in his writing process, first created Hamlet, and out of that creation, a story unfolded. Based on this theory, if Macbeth were in the same situation as Hamlet, the play would be over in ten minutes. Seeing the ghost of his father, Macbeth would simply take out his sword and kill the king without a torturous examination of conscience. Egri concludes that "every great literary work grew from character, even if the author planned the action first. As soon as the author's characters were created they took precedence, and the action had to be reshaped to suit them."

So, back to the question: character or story, which comes first? Don't embarrass yourself by trying to take a position one way or another. To ask which came first is to indicate that you have most likely never had the actual experience of writing a story, being up against the demands of craft. If you have truly been up against the demands of craft then you know the question is mute. Just as it is difficult to pinpoint whether wind or temperature causes a hurricane because they are too synergistically linked, separating character and story as two independent processes indicates a lack of understanding of their true nature. Even if you begin with character first, which is the technique I promote in this book, you will discover that once you get into the story you will inevitably make adjustments to your character. Because of the pressures around them, certain characters may be forced to change or take tactics that you could not have predicated.

Yes, if Macbeth was Hamlet in *Hamlet,* it would be over sooner. But wouldn't Macbeth still have to deal with the realities of the court and its politics and his responsibility as an educated prince? And wouldn't that suggest that Macbeth would somehow not be exactly the same person, once he is put in these newly imagined circumstances, as he is in the play *Macbeth?* He is as much acted upon by others and the external forces of his world as he acts upon them. This implies that there will inevitably be similarities in the story of Hamlet, even if Macbeth became Hamlet.

Things are never so black and white in writing to be able to isolate any one, pure cause. If this were possible, there would be no such thing as character as we know character: a dynamic unto itself, a complex stew that is always brewing. There are only probabilities in writing, and again, all attempts to make it a science have failed. Results are hard to predict and that is why all hinges on the "what if?" question. The writing process is in many ways an endless round of asking yourself "what if?" and assessing the results to see if they add to your purpose for writing a particular screenplay.

UNDERSTANDING THE RELATIONSHIP BETWEEN CHARACTER AND STORY

EXERCISE

Take a character from a classic film such as Hannibal Lecter *(The Silence of the Lambs)* or Michael Corleone *(The Godfather),* and imagine plugging him or her into a major scene of another classic. Make the choice extreme; choose a character that would clearly not fit into the world of the film you choose. For example, place Hannibal Lecter into a major scene from *The Godfather,* replacing Michael Corleone. Write the scene in no more than ten pages.

How has the character changed in this scene? How has the plotline of the scene changed? Which changes most: character or plot? What seems truthful in the scene and what seems false and contrived?

Even though we cannot say definitively which comes first, story or character, we must start somewhere. The best way to create a screenplay with complex characters is to always start with your characters and let them lead you to story rather than the other way around. The screenwriter of the character-driven screenplay tries to "crack" the characters, get in their shoes and really become them, before shaping a plot.

The character-driven screenwriter seeks to fully develop all characters, not just the main characters. Why? If the premanent value of story lies in character, then a story is only as strong as its weakest character. Therefore, in order to maintain the strength of a story, a screenwriter must try to fully develop every character.

Why Characters Do Not Change

As we have seen, one of the major traps in the plot-driven screenplay writing process is that character is thought to be action. This misunderstanding leads to flat, one-note characters. Character is a dynamic—ever-changing, complex, and full of surprises. It is all the traits and qualities of a person. A strong fictional character represents what it is to be human. And all humans have the potential to surprise us and themselves because so much of what they truly are and what they can be lies dormant, unexpressed. The plot-driven author has been trained to force the character to go through some kind of transformation. This wrong-headed approach gives a contrived feeling and falseness to the story and character. Instead of forcing a character to go through a change, the writing process for the character-driven screenplay asks the writer to find a compelling "what if?" by imagining situations with high stakes and personal costs, and discovering, along with the character, what the character will do to get what he or she wants. By keeping the focus on the character rather than the result—the transformation—the author will create specific, complex, highly original, and truthful transformations for the character and thus the story.

Character is not easy to bend to suit your needs, but plot certainly is—a car accident could change a character's life, so could falling in love, or making millions of dollars. But can Don Corleone easily change his sense of what it is to be a man? Could Charles Foster Kane easily change his need to control and conquer the world? Bending character only creates an untruthful story.

What does happen in any good story is not that characters change, but rather, their circumstances have forced them to take a new tack, and parts of their character that were previously dormant, suddenly open up and are revealed. This new side of the character that is exposed and awakened because of a change of circumstances is often wrongly perceived as "the character changing."

How many times have we heard from people who were suddenly subjected to great trauma, such as the loss of a child, a home, a marriage, a job, that there was something positive to the experience because with it they "found the strength and resources they never knew they had?" For example, suppose a woman is suddenly faced with the loss of her husband, and, because she must raise four children alone, she starts a business importing soaps and creams from a monastery outside of Rome. The business grows, giving her confidence, and she discovers that she is a great businessperson. She soon becomes fabulously wealthy. Sought after by many for advice, she runs for a government office and becomes one of our leading congresswomen. She is a wonderful debater and has great skill for consolidating power and bringing opposing forces together.

Now has that woman suddenly changed? On the surface it would seem so; she has changed profoundly, from diffident housewife to one of the country's leaders. The truth is that she was always a great entrepreneur and leader, but that part of herself had remained dormant for the first half of her life. Because of the change in her circumstances, the dormant part of her character expressed itself.

Would the Matthew Modine character, Private Joker, in *Full Metal Jacket,* have become a killer if circumstances had not forced him to kill? *Full Metal Jacket* is about Private Joker's relationship with the Marines. The plot of the story is what happens to change that relationship. It is the pressure of the circumstances—the relentless Sergeant Hartman, making endless demands to live up to Marine standards, and the stress of getting ambushed with his company—that cause the "change" in Private Joker. Would Rick ever have found a way to let go of Ilsa in *Casablanca,* if Ilsa had not appeared and forced him to make a choice? Again, no. He would most likely have pined the days away, drinking too much. Would U.S. Marshall Gerard befriend Dr. Kimble in the third act of *The Fugitive* if there had been no change in circumstances that forced Gerard to alter his tactics towards Kimble? Did Gerard change his attitude toward Kimble because Gerard was suddenly struck with some profound insight into himself and the universe? After Kimble convinced Gerard that he was not the murderer, Gerard changed his attitude toward Kimble and befriended him only because circumstances changed. Kimble's and Gerard's goals were no longer in opposition; something dormant in both of them could now be expressed.

A character is a dynamic entity—the possibilities are nearly endless. There is much about characters an author will not know until the characters are forced by circumstances and external pressures to express parts of themselves that are dormant. A writer can only make new discoveries about a character by finding compelling high stakes circumstances for the characters to uncover their dormant, surprising, and unexpressed sides.

The highest priority of the character-driven screenplay is always character, but there are other important considerations in screenwriting including substance, form, and technique.

5

Substance, Form, and Technique

Narrative film (a movie) is an art form. And like all art, it is judged on substance, form, and technique. There is a clear hierarchy of priorities to follow when creating a movie: substance is the highest priority of the artist, followed by form, and lastly, technique. If a film is weak on substance but strong on technique, an artist has either reversed these priorities or is unaware of the demands of art. When substance is weak, technique often becomes a tool to hide or distract the viewer from a film's lack of content.

First, let's define our terms. "Substance" is the subject matter of a film. It asks the following of the artist: Does the treatment of the subject matter have depth, a fresh perspective, and provide insight? If the film's treatment of its subject matter has no depth or insight, then it lacks substance. There are other components that contribute to the substance of a film: the complexity and truth of character; the strength of the dialogue; and the originality and depth of the cinematic language. Substance can also be defined as what the writer is trying to say—his or her feelings, ideas, thoughts, and purpose. Substance is judged on truth, originality, specificity, and complexity.

Since the character-driven screenplay pivots on character, then it stands to reason that the true value and substance of the character-driven screenplay resides first and foremost in the depth of characterization. No matter how complex and resonant the subject matter and theme, or other elements of substance, if a character-driven screenplay does not have specific, original, and complex characters, it lacks substance.

Art can be described as an artist's interpretation of reality; what he or she believes is the real truth of our existence. "Form" asks the artist what the best way is to illuminate, suggest, evoke, or present his or her perception of the core truth of our existence. Form consists of the "type" and "style" of the film. A screenplay can be one or a combination of the following types: tragedy, comedy, farce, satire, or melodrama. Most movies are never purely one type, but are usually a combination of types. However, the type that predominates the blend often becomes the identifying label of the film. There are also different styles for writing screenplays, such as naturalism, realism, expressionism, symbolism/fantasy, and so on. Style is what makes an artist different, memorable, and original. If Bruce Springsteen, Ray Charles, Frank Sinatra, and Tiny Tim were all to sing "Happy Birthday," each would bring his own style to the interpretation. Despite the fact that the song (substance) is the same, the singing style can be altered and the results will be distinctively different, because the substance is filtered through the style.

THE PRIORITIES OF THE CHARACTER-DRIVEN SCREENPLAY: SUBSTANCE, FORM, AND TECHNIQUE

Highest Priority

SUBSTANCE
- Treatment of the subject matter: does it provide insight, have depth, and offer a fresh perspective?
- Resonance of theme: does it mean something for today and forever?
- Characterization: how specific, complex, and original are the characters of this film?
- Dialogue: how idiosyncratic, well-informed, and resonant is the talk?
- Cinematic language: does it break past the clichés?
- Clarity and depth of purpose: what is the artist trying to do?

FORM
- How can I best illuminate my perception of reality?
- What type of screenplay do I want to write—tragedy, comedy, melodrama, or satire/farce?
- What style best expresses and communicates how I see the truth— naturalism, realism, expressionism, fantasy/symbolism, and so on?
- How should I evoke, suggest, or represent the elements of my screenplay?

TECHNIQUE
- Arrangement and proportioning of material; act structure; contingent or linear plotlines.
- The use of the montage, close-up, and moving picture or unique camera angles.
- Tactics employed to create mood and atmosphere; rhythm and tempo of a film.
- The use of flashbacks and narration; juxtaposing and counterpoint.
- The savvy employed by the artist in blending substance into form and technique to create a unified whole.

Low Priority

"Technique" is the arrangement and proportioning of all of the elements of a film. It is the strategy and tactics employed by the artist to create mood and atmosphere and to structure all elements of a film into a unified whole; it is the rhythm and tempo of a film.

The realm of technique includes many decisions, such as whether to use one, two, three, or more acts and how to present the scenes, i.e., will the first part of the third act be a series of short scenes intercut with a long flashback with no sound, or a short, fast-moving montage with heavy metal rock music playing under it? Rhythm, tempo, and intercutting of scenes can also help to illuminate the subject matter and characters. Specific camera angles, extreme close-ups or wide angles—can be used to create a feeling or mood that helps to illuminate the substance. Transitions between scenes—jump cutting, fading in, or dissolving—are also matters of technique. In general, technique is about orchestration, and much of it is accomplished in the editing room, after a film has been shot. However, as mentioned before, screenwriters should be as specific as possible about the matters of technique and communicate them briskly and clearly in their screenplays. But it is important not to overdo it because a screenplay must be, first and foremost, readable. Too many camera angles make a script less readable. The writer should note a change in camera angle only if it will illuminate a scene or transition. It is the director's job to work out camera angles, and the editor and director make the decisions on how to edit the film. But their decisions are largely influenced by the screenplay itself. In fact, a film editor will consult a copy of the screenplay as a reference and guide for all decisions regarding editing.

In the process of creating a character-driven screenplay, the writer must first give full consideration to substance; once the requirements of substance have been met, the writer moves on to the other considerations: form, and lastly technique. To focus on technique or form before giving a well-considered examination of substance is to put the cart before the horse. Form serves substance, and therefore substance must be discovered and considered first; technique serves both form and substance, and should be the final consideration for the artist.

Film Type and Style

As a screenwriter, you should constantly be challenging yourself to make the screenplay better—to refine it and give it the "feel" you want. This challenge is complex and endless, and the more tools you have to meet these challenges the better. Not only is it important to learn how to layer a character and create contingent plotlines, but you should also have a basic understanding of styles and types of films so you can choose one that will best illuminate your purpose.

For instance, you may have finished your first draft, and after reading it as one complete script, you say to yourself: "I don't know, there's something missing. I just feel it." Upon further reflection you realize, "I want it to feel more tragic. It just doesn't come across that way right now." You have diagnosed your screenplay and you want it to be a tragedy. "So how do I make it more tragic?" you wonder. If you have an understanding of the basic requirements of tragedy, you can proceed to adjust and revise your screenplay according to these guidelines.

Or suppose you are in the middle of working on your screenplay and you say to yourself, "I don't like how the characters are talking to each other. It has been done a million times before and I want to do something different. I want the characters to burst out and say things we never say to each other." Again, you have diagnosed a problem that needs to be fixed. You have a screenplay that has a naturalistic style and you want to shape it in a more expressionistic way.

But how can you fix it if you do not know the basic requirements of at least several different styles? With a basic understanding of styles and types of screenplays, you will have more tools in your kit to create original, specific, and complex movies.

Type

There are four basic types of screenplays: tragedy, comedy, melodrama, and farce/satire. Most movies are never purely one type. They are often a type to a greater or lesser degree, or a combination of types. I define the categories as types rather than genres because I do not want to be too ironclad. There are many genres of film. Daniel Lopez, in his book, *Films by Genre,* lists 775 categories! This plethora of categories is simply not useful for the screenwriter. Also, since the categories are so specifically broken down, following the rules of a genre will produce very predictable scripts. Writing for a specific genre is not a wise strategy for the character-driven screenwriter because it works against originality. Using categories that are not fluid and that fence the writer into distinct defined forms goes against the goals of the character-driven screenplay. With more fluid definitions (types), the writer will be free to produce more varied results, yet still have a tool that can be very useful.

Tragedy

Tragedy is concerned with man's individual responsibility and the belief that people must claim ownership of their actions. A tragedy, as Aristotle postulated, should be absolutely honest and truthful in its depiction of character and story; it should avoid contrivance, chance encounters, or improbable reversals of fortune. The central character of a tragedy is usually a great and powerful figure, such as a distinguished doctor, popular politician, CEO of a multinational corporation, or a successful artist. The central character can also be representative of a class, such as Eddie Carbone, a longshoreman, in Arthur Miller's play, *A View from the Bridge,* or Hans Beckert (Peter Lorre), the child murderer, in Fritz Lang's *M.*

Tragedy requires a catharsis, an emotional purging on the part of its protagonist, and following that release of pent-up emotion, an enlightenment. The protagonist of a tragedy has a flaw: a blind side, an inability to see a weakness in character that eventually causes the protagonist to fall. The audience can see this blind side, but the character cannot, which elicits a complex response from the audience. The tragic character embodies both positive and negative values; warring characteristics that the audience can both identify with and are repelled by. We both pity and fear the main character of a tragedy. Finally, most tragedies are about a central protagonist's life and death struggle. As the playwright Arthur Miller wrote in 1949, "tragic feeling is evoked in us when we are in the presence of a character who is ready to lay down his life, if need be, to secure one thing—his sense of personal dignity."

Citizen Kane and *The Godfather* are predominately tragic stories. In *Citizen Kane,* Charles Foster Kane is a powerful figure who is blind to his tragic flaw—his insecurity, which leads him to control or abuse others. Kane's blindness leads to self-destruction, emotional isolation, and the alienation of friends or family. In the first act of the film, Charles Foster Kane is deeply betrayed by his parents—he is essentially sold to a bank. This betrayal elicits a compassionate response from the audience; we suffer with Kane and feel his pain. However, his egomaniacal and narcissistic ways repel us at the same time. His character evokes a push/pull response from the audience, they both pity and fear him.

In *The Godfather,* Don Corleone is like Shakespeare's King Lear—fighting to keep his kingdom intact. His tragic flaw leads to the destruction of his sons. Don Corleone loves his family: he is loyal, self-sacrificing, and protects his tribe. These traits elicit a compassionate response from the viewer. However, Corleone is blind to his ruthlessness, he is not honest to himself about his thirst for vengeance, his disregard for the rule of law and human life, and his criminal and immoral behavior. Don Corleone's tragic flaw indirectly causes the death of all three sons—two are eventually murdered. The viewer infers that their deaths, however indirectly linked, are the result of Corleone's actions. Michael (Al Pacino), who eventually takes over the throne and becomes the new godfather, is also killed by his father's actions: his soul is destroyed. At the end of the film, Michael is no longer the independent, rebellious, yet honest man the viewer witnessed in the beginning of the film. That part of him has been crushed and destroyed by the circumstances set into action by his father.

The writing process for a tragedy requires writers to hone their "truth meter." There can be no sense of contrivance in either character or plot. The writer must continually ask: "Is this utterly truthful for this character to do? Here, now, today? Would this really happen?" The writer needs a deep understanding of the major characters of the story to create specific, detailed personages. The writer of a tragedy must feel comfortable working with deeply felt emotions in order to experience and express the darkest thoughts and feelings of the main characters. Writing a tragedy takes a psychic, emotional, and spiritual toll on the storyteller. Digging deep is painful. If, after honest self-assessment, you determine that you prefer styles that are less emotional and more cerebral, then your purpose may be best illuminated with satire/farce, or a combination of types that are less tragic.

Melodrama

Melodrama, as Sidney Lumet notes, "is about making the improbable probable." The author of a melodrama asks, again and again: "What is the worst thing that could happen?" And how can I make this choice utterly believable—in the moment?" This tactic leads the author to discover the traditional elements of melodrama: love triangles, hero/villain dichotomies, interrupted love scenes, shoot-outs, murders, sudden reversals when virtue triumphs over vice. This type of screenplay stimulates and excites an audience by shaping a thrill ride. Examples of this type of film are *The Fugitive, Heat,* and *The Verdict.*

The writing process for this type of film requires a focus on plot more than character. The writer is constantly searching for the worst thing that could happen, topping the previous worst thing that happened in the story. Complexity of character is often sacrificed for the sake of complicating the plot, to provide the next thrill for the audience. Developing strong plot-writing skills is important and the writer should always be looking for the new, inventive reversal—the surprising thrill. If the writer feels the thrills when writing, so will the audience; the thrills allow both the author and audience to escape.

Comedy

Comedy can be broken down into several categories: low comedy, comedy of manners, and satire/farce. Low comedy is slapstick: laughs are elicited by having characters slip on bananas, get kicked in the butt, or through obvious plot devices. Examples of this type of film are *Austin Powers* and *The Three Stooges*. Many of Cary Grant's performances were riddled with low comedy; one need only think of *Bringing Up Baby* or *Arsenic and Old Lace*. The resonance of this type of comedy is usually short-lived; the goal is to get the audience to laugh just to laugh; the more laughs the better. However, when low comedy is mixed with other types, tragedy for example, it can have great resonance. When Don Corleone puts the skin of an orange in his mouth and becomes a monster for his grandson, low comedy is woven into the fabric of tragedy and melodrama (Corleone's heart attack and death in front of his grandson is a melodramatic device). The combination is surprising and effective and the scene has great resonance.

A comedy of manners is a situational comedy and the humor is the result of the inconsistencies of character (the apparent humorous contradictions) and clashing values among the characters of the story. Characters that are "opposites" are forced to deal with one another or characters from different cultures or classes are placed in situations where they must get along. With this type, comedy grows out of character and verbal wit. Stories are gently ironic, accepting of the status quo. The insights provoke a sense of tolerance in the audience: tolerance for differences of personality, culture, class, or socioeconomic factors. Examples of this type of comedy are *The Odd Couple* and *Eat, Drink, Man, Woman*.

Satire/farce is the flip side of melodrama, because the strategy the author employs is the same for both types: continually asking "what is the worst thing that could happen?" Satire/farce has sudden reversals, love triangles, and highly improbable and contrived plots. The characters are stereotypes or archetypes, without much specificity. The characters need only appear real in the moment, since the goal of this type of screenplay is escape and laughter. The story usually pivots around an absurdly improbable situation with fast-paced, dramatic progression.

The image that best represents the farce is a character bursting onto the scene through a door, making many entrances and exits during the course of a story. With each pass through the door, the character makes another reversal—a sudden, improbable about-face of action. For satire, the pace tends to be a bit slower. The impulse behind satire/farce, unlike other comedies, is to explore and bring insight to a central idea, such as greed, dishonesty, infidelity, or war. There is a sense of morality about satire/farce.

Often satire/farces are tales of caution, alerting an audience to the immoralities of the world. If you scrape away the veneer of comedy, a satirist is a disappointed moralist.

Examples of this type of film are Mel Brook's *The Producers* and Stanley Kubrick's *Dr. Strangelove. Shakespeare in Love* combines several types: low comedy is blended with satire/farce in the plotline of Philip Henslowe (Geoffrey Rush) and Hugh Fennyman (Tom Wilkinson), melodrama and situational comedy is blended in the storyline of Viola (Gwyneth Paltrow) and Will Shakespeare (Joseph Fiennes). The characters of Will and Viola are more rounded, believable, and have greater resonance than Henslowe and Fennyman who are type characterizations. Melodrama adds romance to Will and Viola's plotline, placing them in the forefront of the story in the viewer's mind.

The writing process for low comedy requires a strong sense of physicality. Low comedy often involves a visual trick—a joke. A comedy of manners requires the writer to create fully developed characters. Satire/farce requires the writer to provide fresh insights about a central idea. Many writers of satire/farce talk about writing the script "in a fever," in order to focus on comedic reversals and the honing of verbal wit rather than labor over developing character. The satirist or writer of farce does not seek to elicit a sense of tolerance from the audience. The audience should feel a comedic sense of outrage, so the choices should be riskier and more extreme.

Mixing Types

Since the character-driven screenplay places a high priority on complexity, the screenwriter should try to combine several types in a screenplay. For instance, in tragic moments the author could uncover low comedy or accompany moments of gentle irony (situational humor) with the danger and edge of melodrama. Mixing types will create more resonance.

Style

Style is born out of the question every screenwriter should ask, consciously or not: "what is the best way to illuminate how I see reality or life?" Style should be chosen based on the writer's purpose, not to imitate or pay homage to another writer. Like form, style communicates a worldview. The screenwriter should study styles to develop a well-informed understanding of how other writers have translated their views of reality into tone, texture, and distinctive characteristics—a signature—which effectively illuminates and communicates their purpose. Understanding the vocabulary of style will aid the writer in developing a personal style. And as with types, no screenplay is ever purely one style or another; usually, it represents one style to a greater or lesser degree, or a combination of styles.

Based on a perception of reality, the screenwriter creates his or her style. For example, if a writer thinks the real truth of existence is that nothing can be believed, everything is false or meaningless, or that we are all in a state of perpetual delusion and denial, then he or she may best illuminate this belief with a style that is hyper-ironic.

The hyper-ironic style, a tactic employed in *Happiness*, creates a distance between the characters in the story and the audience, forcing the audience to question the characters' motives and perception of reality. When the irony is excessive, it underlines the meaninglessness and falseness of existence, rather than evoking a sense of tolerance.

If a writer believes that truth resides "only on the surface" in this world, and motive can never be truthfully delineated, then a heightened naturalistic style may be used to illuminate the substance of the screenplay. A writer using this style observes behavior scientifically, trusting only empirical evidence, and makes no inferences about what cannot be seen below the surface of the material world. Heightened naturalism is a tactic used in Jim Jarmusch's *Stranger Than Paradise;* the camera observes, records, chronicles and documents, playing with the audience's expectations about the internal workings and motives of the main characters.

The styles we will briefly examine are romanticism, naturalism, realism, expressionism, fantasy/symbolism, and excessive irony.

Romanticism

Romanticism is perhaps the most predominant style in film today. It values subjective thought, the imagination, freedom of expression, and the individual above all else. Romanticism was a style that appeared in the theater with Goethe's dramatic poem, *Faust,* in 1808. Romanticism scorns tradition and practical matters of life. It is a style that led to the melodramatic form—which in the theater was best expressed with three acts rather than the more classical structure of five acts. The melodramatic three-act form was later carried over to film and is the basis of the classic Hollywood three-act structure. Romantic styles, like melodrama, evoke excitement and suspense. Characters behave impulsively and spontaneously, doing what we, the audience, would like them to do. They embody our need to break with convention, follow our bliss, and do the impractical thing. And, like melodrama, a romantic character provides escape for the audience. An excellent character-driven example of this style is John Patrick Shanley's *Moonstruck.*

Naturalism

Naturalism appeared in the theater in 1888, with Johan August Strindberg's *Miss Julie.* Naturalism's take on reality is that humankind is controlled by instinct, emotion, and socioeconomic climate and forces; a person's future and lot in life is determined by genetics and class structure far more than free will. This style often has the feel of a documentary. Besides *Stranger Than Paradise,* already mentioned, Sidney Lumet's *Dog Day Afternoon* and Richard Brooks' *In Cold Blood* shot in semi-documentary style, are excellent examples of this style.

Realism

Realism is very similar to naturalism: it depicts life as real. It accounts for time, and portrays a locale or setting as it really is, with all of its ugly and beautiful aspects. However, unlike naturalism, realism does not embrace a deterministic worldview—humankind does have free will. *Twelve Angry Men* is a classic example of this style: the jurors fight their backgrounds, prejudices, socioeconomic differences, and the blindness of their instincts and emotions to freely choose the truth and set an innocent man free. Realism is a style often associated with a "thesis" play or screenplay in which a lesson is taught by the narrative, all elements progress to a climax that proves the truth of a proposition set forth by the author. In this style the psychology of the individual is very important; characters either develop self-awareness or not. Realism is the style most used in mainstream films and television today. Example of this style are *Life Is Beautiful, Secrets and Lies,* and *Rio Bravo.*

Expressionism

Expressionism is a style that seeks to illuminate the unconscious thoughts, feelings, and ideas that control us all. The expressionistic style creates films that are dreamlike and chaotic with a powerful grip on the viewer. Subjective perceptions and knowledge of the world take precedence over notions of dramatic logic. The style is free of the conventions of time, place, and discernable lines of dramatic action. Story is often exposed as our worst nightmare—its subject matter is wildly violent and excessively erotic, perverse, or grotesque. *Blue Velvet, Barton Fink,* and *Five Corners* are recent examples of the use of expressionism. In *Five Corners,* Heinz (John Turturro) is truly an expressionistic creation. He has a thick scar across his face, the result of a beer mug being cracked on his head by Harry (Tim Robbins), who was trying to protect Linda (Jodie Foster) from being raped by Heinz. Heinz beats penguins to a pulp with a baseball bat and tosses his mother, who is also grotesquely out of control, out of her bedroom window.
The effect is nightmarish; it is both claustrophobic and wildly out of control. This strategy helps to illuminate not the psychology of Heinz, but the deep-seated, unconscious primal desire that has a firm and unrelenting grip on him.

Fantasy/Symbolism

Edward A. Wright, actor, director, and teacher, notes in *Understanding Today's Theater,* that "symbolism tells two stories at once in that what we see or hear recalls a parallel situation or emotion. Fantasy is thoroughly imaginative and embodies purely hypothetical or fairy-story situations." Symbolists express content through symbols rather than directly. An example of the symbolic style is Krzystof Kielslowski's *The Double Life of Veronique.* Two women, Veronika, who lives in Poland, and Veronique, who lives in France, have never met, yet they affect each other in mysterious ways: both have heart problems, both are incredible singers, both feel the same feelings, sometimes at the same time. What connects them? This is never answered in the film.

When Veronika dies suddenly in Poland from a heart attack, Veronique, in France, just as suddenly announces to her teacher she is leaving her profession. Veronique can feel something suddenly missing in her life but cannot explain it. At the same time, Veronique begins to get late-night phone calls from a secret admirer, a puppeteer,

Fabbri. Fabbri builds a puppet that looks like Veronique and with the puppet performs a story about how lives are mysteriously interconnected. Fabbri and his puppet are clearly symbols rather than characters. The idea that there can be deep and mysterious connections between ourselves and another person we have never met in our lives is communicated by this use of symbolism.

In *The Wizard of Oz* symbolism abounds: the ruby slippers symbolize adulthood; the Tin Man, Scarecrow, and Cowardly Lion, with their quest for a heart, a brain, and courage, symbolize a child's basic fears. And more recently, in *Terminator 2: Judgment Day*, the "good" Terminator (Arnold Schwarzenegger) and the "bad" Terminator (Robert Patrick) symbolize the positive and negative aspects of our ever powerful modern technology. *Terminator 2* also makes use of fantasy: the world of the story, 1997 after a nuclear holocaust, is a fantasy world.

Excessive Irony

Excessive irony is a style which can be seen on television shows like *Talk Soup*, an American show that summarizes the week's highlights in soap operas and talk shows, and in recent films like *Happiness*. It is a style that seeks to underscore the paradoxes, contradictions, and hypocrisies of people and society, especially the middle-class and suburban worlds. Its humor is dry and often bitterly sarcastic. The screenwriter who uses excessive irony is often called the "disappointed moralist." Since the targets of this style are stupidity and vice, one can infer a very moral point of view on the part of the screenwriter who uses excessive irony.

Irony occurs when a character takes an action or says something and the intended meaning is different than what is apparent to the spectator. If a character proclaims very sincerely, "Oh, I don't know, I guess I'm just a good-natured slob," and we know that this character is the cheapest, meanest, most self-centered human on earth, an irony is created and we laugh at him. There can also be visual irony: a close-up of two men having a sincere, heartfelt debate about the relative beauty of two tree species and the camera pulls back to reveal these two men are pissing on one.

Irony is a marvelous tool for the screenwriter to awaken the viewer to the underlining lies and blindness that every character possesses. When well done, irony presents proof positive to the audience that there is a contradiction, paradox, or hypocrisy in the actions of a character. However, when overused, this style will eviscerate tolerance and compassion; the insights turn distinctively derogatory and bitter and hence have less complexity. The style of excessive irony can become a relentless rant because the screenwriter judges a character too harshly and frequently.

Recently, while moderating a panel discussion with several screenwriters at the Avignon Film Festival in New York, screenwriter/director Paul Schrader said he quit teaching screenwriting at Columbia University when he realized how much his students were invested in the "ironic character." He felt he had nothing to give to them because he fundamentally did not understand their preference for excessive irony. He explained that he likes to use the existential character because it has greater dramatic potential. "The existential character is always asking what is the meaning of everything, my life, my work, my existence. The ironic character responds with: 'why bother?'" said Schrader. "Dramatically, where can you go from there?" he remarked.

Postmodern irony stands back with a bemused smile and shrugs, accepting the status quo. The author basically says, "Hey, that's just the way it is—and we all know it's bullshit." Postmodern irony can never be revolutionary or incite moderate social change since the postmodern ironic writer is not committed to any beliefs and therefore cannot offer direction. And, as Schrader points out, from a purely dramaturgical standpoint, postmodern irony stalls dramatic progression.

The screenwriter who is excessive with irony may in fact honestly believe he or she is giving the work meaning. In truth, the screenwriter evades meaning if irony is overused. Although excessive irony can bring insight to a situation, it is at the cost of complex characterization; it sticks pins in characters and holds them up for observation. Unlike humor, excessive irony does not evoke a sense of tolerance or understanding. Too much of this strategy extinguishes the animating force of a character and flattens the story into one dimension—a cartoon.

I am not suggesting that a writer never use irony. That would be ridiculous. Irony is one of the most powerful tools a writer possesses, a story without it would be insufferable. But there needs to be a balance, a sense of proper proportion for every element of a film. As in cooking, using too much of any one ingredient invariably overwhelms the bouquet of flavors of the entire dish, and eviscerates its complexity and subtlety.

Technique

Today, many cliché notions of film have become pervasive. A movie has been described as a story in pictures, writing with light, or a visual concept, and these ideas have dominated many of the films of today, especially among younger filmmakers, who are mistaking technique for substance. The blanket acceptance of these cliché notions has caused a shift in focus; many filmmakers have become insensitive to content and craft. This constant attempt to innovate technique has led to an affected and mannered cinema.

My espousal of the character-driven screenplay is an attempt to address the problems that have arisen because filmmakers are mistaking technique for substance. Having something true, complex, and original to say is the first requirement for writing a screenplay and making a film. Technique ultimately is the personality of a film, so it is no surprise that in our culture of celebrity we have confused it for substance. No matter how complicated the shot; how brilliant the production design; how wonderful the editing; how innovative the use of sound; how ironic, fast-paced, MTV montage-driven, complex and surprising the structure; if there is nothing below all the stimulating and colorful presentation, there can be no art.

If technique is given priority over substance by the writer, content will suffer. There is often more focus in today's films on how well the camera is used or how well irony is applied rather than on the purpose of the project—what the filmmaker is trying to say. This focus is so pervasive that many critics, filmmakers, and even the public have become insensitive to lack of content. Hence, the character-driven screenplay fills an important hole, offering a solution to this lack of content.

As with irony, it would be equally ridiculous to say the character-driven screenwriter should be anti-technique. Technique, when used with originality illuminates, a subject matter. The playwright and screenwriter, Harold Pinter, took a rather overworked subject, the betrayal of one spouse by another, and gave it a fresh perspective by playing with technique in the film *Betrayal* (1983). Orchestrating the story as a series of flashbacks, he made the tale move backwards chronologically. Traditionally in stories of marital betrayal, the writer sets up the major characters, giving bits and pieces of backstory, letting the audience experience the couple as loving, gradually moving them to being at odds, and finally leading to the climax—the betrayal. Pinter reversed this pattern. By moving us backwards, we view the betrayal story anew; like peeling an onion, we first see the whole and then experience the deconstruction of the whole, until, at the center, there is nothing but a mystery. His innovative use of technique brings us to a more mystical understanding of marital betrayal: one mystery after another, all adding up to an even bigger unknowable paradox. This graceful use of technique underscores the treachery of an affair, the step-by-step lying and mounting deceit, creating a moral resonance. Finally, the ending is both ironic and emotional because of Pinter's use of technique: since we already know what will happen to our loving couple when we see them together at the end of the film, we view them with a sad irony.

EXERCISE

EXPERIMENTING WITH FORM: WRITING YOUR PARENTS' FIRST DATE

Imagine your parents' first date. Where did it take place and what happened? Write a scene about it. Now write the scene again, using a different type and style. For instance, if you wrote the first scene as a comedy in a naturalistic way, now write it as a melodrama in an expressionistic way. Once you have completed the first revision, do another one, altering type and style again. At the end of this exercise you should have three different scenes about your parents' first date.

Analyze and assess the scenes for the following: what were you able to express and communicate with one style and type that you were not able to communicate or express with another style and type? Do you prefer one style and type or a particular combination of style and type? And if so, why? How does your choice help you to illuminate what you think is important about the scene—the inner life of the characters, the unspoken rather than the spoken, and so on? How does it help you to communicate what you think is true about life, reality, or our existence?

6

A Movie: Not Just a Story in Pictures

A prevailing dictum, unfortunately taken as a bible among screenwriters today, which promotes the misguided practice of mistaking technique for substance, is "a movie is a story in pictures." This statement is dangerously reductive and too often interpreted by the screenwriter to mean the power of a movie resides first and foremost in the visual—the selection, manipulation, and orchestration of the moving picture. A movie is made up of many elements—picture, sound, and dramatic action, among other components—with one or more taking emphasis, depending on what needs to be said. The moving picture is clearly the most "vocal" element of a film, but that does not mean it is always a great source of substance. The moving picture is the poetry and beauty of film and because it is so seductive and lush, it can cover up for lack of content. Content resides in the choice of subject matter and its treatment; permanent value is in the depth of characterization. The character-driven screenwriter understands that the moving picture, as with all elements of a film, should be used in the service of these priorities.

There are clearly times when telling the story with the moving picture is the most effective strategy for the character-driven screenwriter. Since the moving picture is the most powerful element of a film, it has the greatest grabbing power for an audience and can most easily draw the viewer into the world of the story, Consequently, a montage is often used to begin a film. Director Orson Welles and screenwriter Whit Masterson created one of the longest (and justifiably famous) continuous shots in Hollywood history in order to begin *Touch of Evil.* The shot allows the audience to sweep through the Mexican town—the multi-layered world of the story—and enter it swiftly and fully. In spectacle films, in which the dramatic progression is predicated on physical rather than mental action, the moving picture is often the best choice for telling the story. In *Titanic,* the progression of the film is due primarily to the assembly of pictures.

In Krzysztof Kieslowski's *A Short Film about Love,* a haunting and complex drama, the beauty of the acting and the reaction shots—the way the actors react to what has just happened to them, give us information without using a word. All is expressed and propelled forward by the moving picture and sound, as the viewer observes a nineteen-year-old boy focus his telescope on the windows of the apartment of a beautiful and much older woman. Like *Titanic,* Kieslowski's film is propelled by the visual, yet rather than observing the unfolding of spectacle—the sinking of an ocean liner—the picture evokes and suggests the layers of conflict between the young man and his infatuation, an older woman, across his apartment courtyard.

Dramatic structure and dialogue both contribute equally to creating progression in *Citizen Kane*. Despite superb cinematography, it is the bricks and mortar construction of the screenplay that leads the audience by grabbing their attention with the central dramatic question: what makes Charles Foster Kane tick? Orson Welles addresses this question with narration and dialogue.

Films by Preston Sturges or Woody Allen prove time and again, as director Sidney Lumet remarks in his wise and intelligent book, *Making Movies,* "that dialogue is not uncinematic." Their films are driven by verbal wit as much as by the dramatic action: "Men don't get smarter as they get older, they just lose their hair," wrote Sturges for *The Palm Beach Story.* "I don't want to move to a city where the only cultural advantage is being able to make a right turn on a red light," penned Woody Allen in the screenplay *Annie Hall.* The audience starts to expect another funny line or retort, and when Sturges and Allen deliver one, it helps to progress the experience.

Often the genre will dictate what will be emphasized in a movie. Action movies, such as *Terminator 2: Judgment Day* and *Lethal Weapon,* that are all about creating spectacle, are mostly picture and sound. Melodrama *(The Fugitive)* and farce *(The Producers)* rely heavily on plot for progression. Comedy can progress in many ways: through physical mishaps and plot devices as in *The Pink Panther* or Emir Kusterica's *Underground;* verbal wit, as in Woody Allen's films; the inconsistencies of character *(The Out-of-Towners);* or satirical irony, heightened characters in the service of a central idea *(Love Serenade).*

As I said above, a movie is many things and not just "a story in pictures." Film is indeed a visual medium, it would be ridiculous to deny that, but the eye can easily take a back seat to many other elements in a film—the plasticity of the medium is great. The pictures, the dialogue, the sounds, and the dramatic action interact synergistically, creating something larger than the sum of the parts. These variables are like the organs in the human body, competing for expression and affecting one another in complex and unpredictable ways, yet, utterly dependent on one another. What that sum of the parts eventually turns out to be for a film is often beyond anyone's vision, at any point in its creation; you can only tell what a film will be when it is completed. Which is precisely why filmmaking is such a wonderful and endless challenge.

Do Not Shortcut Process

The moving picture, the close-up, and the montage are some of the tools of film technique that are uniquely cinematic. However, in the character-driven screenplay, technique is never mistaken for substance. Subject matter and characterizations come first. Substance is best explored with words rather than pictures. The writer should not be afraid to use words and write an entire screenplay in dialogue form before examining how to make it visual. Once the characterizations and subject matter have been excavated thoroughly with words, the writer will be in a much better position to choose when to carry the story by the picture or by the word. By thinking that a movie is a story in pictures and just sculpting out a visual plan, the screenwriter will be working entirely in technique and actually avoid a much higher responsibility.

In a thousand-seat theater, an audience can literally be a hundred feet away from the stage, and in order to create an intensified experience the stage actor must be big. When it comes to film, the actor is blown up eight to ten times human size. Can you imagine if you took an actor ten times normal size and put him on the stage in a two-hundred-seat house? To grab the audience's attention, all that would be necessary is to blink the right way! The actor, like the storyteller, must always choose how much information to give, how far to go, in order to be effective at his or her job. For the actor enlarged eight times, speaking softly is highly effective. And with a face the size of a truck wheel, the film actor can just think a thought and the audience will get it. If a stage actor tried this, in most cases, it would be far less compelling and effective. Yet, in both media, the actor is obliged to create a character with layers, to enter a scene with a strong need, and to take action to get what he or she wants.

The same is true for the writer: Substance and form are the same for stage and film. It is the technique, the approach needed in order to communicate effectively, that is different. However this does not mean a screenwriter should write characters that are just reacting and looking and not talking—being oh-so-minimal. The screenwriter must uncover as much as possible about the characters and then choose what to present and how to present it to an audience. In the initial stages of the writing process, it is necessary for the characters to talk too much and go over the top with their reactions—screaming shouting, crying, and rambling on. This step is essential to create substance. Once accomplished, it is then, and only then, that the writer should start to cut, trim, reduce, and pull back the characters to adjust to the technique demands of the screen. It is always possible to pull back if there is too much, but it is difficult to create more if there is nothing there to begin with.

The problem with many screenwriters today is they do not dig deeply enough. They go right to the "result": characters speaking in one or two lines, just reacting, being mysterious and thoughtful, and so on. The writer's job is to excavate, discover far too much about a character, and then choose from that abundance of material and information what to use and how to use it to hold an audience's attention with clarity and a sense of dramatic progression, given the technical realities of film. If this excavation is not part of the process, the writer will create underdeveloped characters.

Discover the Subtext Before You Leave It Out

Screenwriters should understand that the subtext of a scene—the hidden thoughts and feelings of a character—can be communicated very effectively with a reaction shot or the close-up. However, the subtext must first be discovered and unearthed before it can be covered up or made minimal. Otherwise the characters do not truly have a subtext, they are just empty eggshells.

In the final scene of my last movie, *The Young Girl and the Monsoon,* two lovers confront each other on the waterfront, in a romantic, New York night scene. When we last saw them together he dumped her. She was furious and has since been avoiding him. The scene is about his effort to win her back, which he wants desperately to do. One of the issues that separated these lovers is that she wants to have a child. He already has a teenage daughter from his first marriage, which failed miserably and destructively, and he is reluctant to bring another child into the world. In the middle of this climactic scene he says to her:

```
              HANK
Do you still want to have a child?


              ERIN
What?! You've got to be kidding! (ERIN turns and
walks away, shaking her head in disbelief.) You've
got the worst timing in the world!
```

When we screened this moment I realized that the last line of this exchange was subtext that could be more effectively communicated in film with just a reaction. It did not occur to me when I wrote the script, as is often the case in the writing process, and so I was forced to revise it in the editing. Erin did not actually have to say, "You've got the worst timing in the world," she could communicate that idea with just the right look, a reaction, and the audience would get it. My editor and I recut the scene, taking out the last line of the exchange, and trusted the actress's reaction to say it all. When we screened it again the moment worked so much better. On stage this would not have been as effective. The writer would need the character to shout out her thought to keep the audience involved because the actress's reaction would not be seen as clearly. If the essential information is not delivered to the audience, they lose their concentration and drop out of the story.

In the character-driven screenwriting process, it is crucial to create the information first in words, before making the choice of how to communicate it—in picture or in word. The writer who follows dictums, such as the "story is only carried by the picture" or "dialogue is uncinematic," may avoid the difficult, yet very necessary process of discovering, through writing, and therefore words, the layers to a scene or character.

For every line of dialogue a writer uses in a final draft, at least twenty to fifty lines should be cut. These unnecessary lines are cut because the writer learns that they are unnecessary, but until those unnecessary lines are written there really is no way for the writer to know they are unnecessary. The information the writer gathers from the unnecessary lines is essential. If the writer does not know more about the characters than the audience, it will show in the scene—it will lack nuance. A writer needs to excavate subtext in initial drafts, and guided by the wisdom of craft, decide on how much information should be left to the performance, the reaction shot, the ellipsis, etc., given the power of the blown-up image on the screen.

7

The Picture: The Power and the Limitations

Film is a visual flow, and it is very difficult to express or capture that flow with words, which are the building blocks of a script. The writer must be aware of the demands of the visual flow, and even though it is impossible to exactly translate the written into the visual, the writer must take full responsibility for what is seen on the screen. It is the director's job to translate the written into the visual on the screen. In France for instance, the writer is often assigned to a director before a word of the script is written and the screenwriter works in service of the director. This process obviously mutes a writer's voice and vision, and as John Richardson writes in *Harper's* magazine, it is one of the problems with filmmaking today: "In the theater, the writer is king and directors know their place, and that's the way it should be."

In the early years of Hollywood filmmaking the director was king because all the films were silent, which meant they really were "stories in pictures." During the silent era, the montage was the primary tool used to tell the story; the director was the author of the images and their arrangement in the montage. But when sound arrived an entirely new movie was possible: one that was literary and driven by the word as much as the picture. But by the time this change had occurred, the director had long been declared king and everyone just kept to that tradition, even though the writer now gave the soul to the movie, not the director. In order to hold on to their power, producers and directors did everything possible to keep the "schmucks with Underwoods," as on old-fashioned studio chief once called writers, under their thumb. The directors, producers, and film executives guided the process, and writers, like interior decorators, just followed their clients' wishes. This process tended to homogenize scripts, which lost their specificity and complexity.

Savvy producers and directors know that if it is not on the page, ninety-five percent of the time, it will not be on the screen. When these wiser and more insightful executives hire a writer, they just "let 'em loose." They do not interfere in the process, because without exception, individuals, and not teams—of writers, directors, producers, and studio executives—write the best movies.

If the writer is specific in the writing process and creates layered characters and a unique and surprising world for the story, the translation to the visual flow from the written word will have a greater chance of having a single guiding intelligence and vision.

I believe all screenwriters should strive to be both writer and director. It is the only way to ensure that their vision for the film will be fully realized. Yes, the filmmaking process is collaborative; the final product is the result of the combined efforts of many artists and craftspeople. However, if the writer and director become one then perhaps the power struggle that has marginalized the script will end. Ultimately, every artist involved in the creation of a movie, should be working in the service of one thing: the script.

Pictures Cannot Communicate the Specific Thoughts and Feelings of a Character

Pictures involve light, composition, and color. The viewer experiences the action in a photograph indirectly, not as it is happening, but as it did happen in the past, as when someone snapped the shutter as a Vietnamese general fired a pistol at the head of a handcuffed traitor. A still photo can be compelling, but it is largely anti-dramatic. For something to be dramatic the action must happen before our very eyes, so we can experience a transformation in the "here, now, today." But if single pictures are pasted together and run at twenty-four times a second, creating a moving picture, suddenly the result is dramatic. By synchronizing the movement of single photos with sound, the picture is given an animating force and its effect is hypnotic—thus the magic of the moving picture.

As Neil Postman, critic, writer, and educator, notes in *Amusing Ourselves to Death,* "the name photography was given to the process of preparing a negative from which positives can be made by the famous astronomer Sir John F.W. Herschel. It is an odd name since it literally means 'writing with light.' Perhaps Herschel meant the name to be taken ironically, since it must have been clear from the beginning that photography and writing (in fact, language in any form) do not inhabit the same universe of discourse." Photography speaks in particulars, concrete objects—a green apple, Charlton Heston costumed as Moses, a red 1961 Chevy. Because a photograph lacks syntax, it is deprived "of a capacity to argue with the world," wrote Postman. If a photo shows an old man, it may evoke many things and suggest what he is thinking, but it cannot speak, in specific terms, of what he is feeling and thinking. To know his specific thoughts and feelings, they must be put in words, spoken through dialogue, or written as caption. Even if a montage of pictures is shown—an old man sitting on a bench deep in thought; an open grave; a view of the Atlantic from a rocky cliff; a young boy running on a sandy beach; the boy as he stops to examine an unseen object; a dead bird; the child's hand touching it; a reaction shot of the boy; a reaction shot of the old man—ultimately the spectator would have no specific understanding of the interior world of the old man. Ten different spectators could look at this montage and have ten different opinions about the specifics of this old man's hopes, dreams, wishes, regrets, and so on.

If the old man in the montage spoke several lines of dialogue, immediately before, after, or during the montage, there would be far greater certainty among the spectators about the thoughts and feelings of the old man because they would have more specific information from which to make inferences. One of the main goals of the character-driven screenplay is specificity, and the screenwriter should understand the limitations of pictures. If pictures are relied on entirely for characterizations, they will be more general and less specific.

The character-driven screenplay, however, is not incompatible with the use of montage, which is an important tool in filmmaking. Both pictures and words are indispensable to creating a movie. If a screenplay did not have words, it would have far less content; if it did not have the montage, it would have far less poetry and beauty. The trick is to have the proper proportion of words and pictures to create a synchronicity between them of content and poetry.

A common notion among many filmmakers today is that it should be possible to shut off the sound of a film and still have an audience understand an entire movie, simply by watching the moving pictures. And if this has not been accomplished, then the director has failed on some fundamental level. Nothing could be further from the truth. It is true that filmmakers like David Lean edited their films on silent heads (editing machines without sound capacity). It is indeed a good test of how well a director is orchestrating the moving pictures of a film so the pictures without sound can successfully suggest content. However, even when movies were silent, words were written under the image to give the movie greater meaning. Words provided complexity and specificity, two major goals of the character-driven screenplay.

Reliance solely on the beautiful, mysterious picture works against complexity of character. In order to have content, one must, sooner or later, propose or argue and consequently use words. It is dangerous to minimize the fact that the visual is an important part of the magic of a movie, but it is equally dangerous to underestimate the value of words in the formation of a good film.

EXERCISE — REPLACING PICTURES WITH WORDS OR WORDS WITH PICTURES: WHAT IS GAINED OR LOST?

Take a scene from one of your favorite movies that relies heavily on dialogue to reveal complex character. Some examples are *Secrets and Lies, Shakespeare in Love, It's a Wonderful Life,* and *My Dinner with Andre.* Try to cut out as many words as you can and express what is being revealed about character and setting just with the montage or images. What is gained and what is lost when you try to make this transformation?

Conversely, take a favorite movie that is primarily pictures (*Besieged* is a recent example). Take one or two favorite scenes and try to give the dramatic information with words instead of with images. What is gained or lost when you make this transformation?

When to Use the Picture or the Word

By carefully examining a scene or screenplay you can decide when to use pictures or words to carry the story. For instance, if I were to create a scene in which three people go to bed—a ménage à trois—or a scene in which someone participates in an assisted suicide, I would probably choose to carry the action with the picture rather than with the word. The content of these scenes dictates the treatment. What can be said about three people sleeping together and how they have come to this decision that hasn't already been said and is not another cliché? How can we talk about it with words without sounding like a trashy talk show? We can use words to describe the experience of facing the void of death, or life after death, issues steeped in the transcendental, but in film, pictures are far more effective in connecting the viewer to the mystery and mysticism of these metaphysical matters.

Talk show talk has co-opted our thoughts and vocabulary on many of these issues. It would be hard to talk about them without evoking the talk show, and in so doing, stall the audience's imagination. But if the story is carried with the picture we can reach people, on some level, in a way we can't with words. The montage can open up the mind of the viewer to a new way of thinking about a subject that either cannot be expressed, or has been over-examined by words.

A subject matter that has been trivialized by our culture, or one that deals with the metaphysical or spiritual realms of life, such as the questions screenwriter/director Terrence Malick tackles in *The Thin Red Line*, can be illuminated by the use of the image. Pictures evoke, suggest, create atmosphere, and foreshadow. The question of whether to use words or pictures should be predicated on the screenwriter's purpose.

To get a better understanding of when to use the picture and the word, think of the opening scene of *The Godfather*. The scene involves the undertaker Bonasera who asks Don Corleone, the godfather, to avenge his daughter's dishonor. The audience clearly needs words, not just pictures, to get the information necessary to understand the many layers of character and story. Coppola's purpose for the film was to go beyond the limitations of the typical gangster melodrama and to comment on the failure of the American justice system. He gave a Mafia story the dimensions of classic tragedy. Without dialogue—a great deal of dialogue by today's standards—Coppola would not have been able to accomplish his goal.

Making a Screenplay More Visual Yet Specific

The best way to make a screenplay more visual is to continually ask yourself if you have made the most of the visual opportunities in this moment, scene, act, or story. Is the work fully considered in terms of the visual? And if you do a scene without words will you be more effective in progressing your purpose?

When in the writing process you ask yourself these questions depends on many things: your way of working, the nature of your story, and your purpose. I have written screenplays for which I hear the dialogue first and I think of the visual after. In that same screenplay I may stop and find that some scenes are driven by the eye. My attention is first captured by the picture, not the words, and so I write the visual flow before I craft the dialogue. Other screenplays first appeared to me almost entirely visually. In my mind's eye I am haunted by images—an opening scene or an ending—and I allowed those images to lead me to story and character. Again, the process of writing a screenplay, because of its many elements, is chaotic, and it is hard to predict what will lead the writer—the image or dialogue.

Let's examine how a writer makes decisions about the visual aspects of a screenplay with an example. Suppose I want to write a story about a private detective who is down on his luck and has one last chance—a cliché idea for a character in a film, but it will help to illustrate the decision-making process. There are many strategies I could use to introduce the character. He could face the camera, break the "objective eye," and deliver a heartfelt monologue about his life—how he has one last chance to get back on track; or I could use the same monologue in an ironic way—creating a distance between the character and the audience. I could introduce another character who asks a lot of questions for an organically dramatic reason, thereby provoking the detective into revealing the same information; or the detective could walk down a rainy street as a narrator tells the viewer something about him. I could also introduce the character visually, without a single word, as follows:

```
INT. PRIVATE DETECTIVE'S OFFICE - MIDNIGHT

WILBUR BIGELOW, 44, sits at his desk in a shitty
office, examining a pile of stained documents. He
reaches for the coffeepot—it's empty. He examines a can
of coffee in his desk—it's also empty.

Wilber's POV: A trash pail at one corner of his desk.

He disentangles some trash and pulls out a used filter.
He places it in the coffee machine and hits the red
switch—weak coffee drips.

Wilbur's POV: An ashtray loaded with cigarette butts.
Wilbur dumps the contents of the ashtray and wipes it
clean. He places the ashtray on the hot plate to col-
lect the coffee drips.

CLOSEUP: His fingernails are dirty and bitten to the
flesh; his clammy hands shake. He lights a cigarette.

He lifts the ashtray filled with coffee to his lips,
shaking, and is delighted with his first sip of recycled
Java.
```

This sequence of pictures gives us a good deal of information about the character without a spoken word; it suggests he is broke, cheap, lazy, and possibly an alcoholic. It gives the viewers "space" to project their own interpretations and values onto the character and thus become co-creators. Some of the viewer interpretations of the montage may be confirmed later on in the movie, others may turn out to be false: Wilbur may in fact be kind, fabulously wealthy, and a teetotaler. If the assembly of pictures is presented in a fast tempo, the scene will be more humorous. If the sequence proceeds at a slower tempo—a long, slow build—it will create atmosphere and evoke tension. If each shot has deep intensity, a strong rhythm, slow tempo, and emotional weight, the effect will be different again: the montage will evoke the mystical or a sense of longing. If the rhythms are lighter but the tempo slow, and the visuals are not as dramatic, intense, and emotionally heavy, the effect will be lyrical or whimsical. Regardless of the combination of rhythm or tempo of the montage, it must grab the audience's attention.

Whether to use the visual or the word in the above scene ultimately refers back to the screenwriter's purpose. But if the visual choice is made, it must be original and compelling, and truly contribute to the progression of the movie.

A Case Study: Carrying the Story with the Image

A Short Film about Love is a wonderful case study because the screenwriters Krzysztof Kieslowski and Krzysztof Piesiewicz manage to progress the story by the picture and at the same time create a complex character, which is very difficult to accomplish. It is best to watch the film's opening scene (the first five minutes) before reading the analysis. However, if that is impossible, here is a synopisis:

Tomek, a lonely nineteen-year-old postal clerk and part-time student, spends his free time spying on his neighbor, Magda, an older woman in her mid-thirties, who lives in the apartment building across the way. Magda entertains a lot of men and Tomek observes her from a telescope in his small room. As the suitors come and go, he painfully watches Magda seduce and make love. Tomek finds many inventive yet secretive ways to connect to Magda—spying with a telescope, tampering with her mail, and so on. Finally, one of his schemes backfires and, in order to have a chance at a real relationship, he reveals to Magda that he has been spying, stalking her.

Furious at first, later amused, Magda accepts an offer from Tomek to have ice cream at a café. Magda is taken with this boy's innocence and cynically tries to seduce him, telling him that love is simply a matter of physical pleasure and not much more. Humiliated by Magda's seduction, ashamed at his inability to perform sexually, Tomek flees Magda's flat in a fit of despair and attempts suicide by slitting his writs.

Magda, feeling guilty that she might have hurt Tomek and touched by his sincerity, begins to obsess about him. The tables turn: Magda observes Tomek's empty apartment late at night from her flat. She rejects a lover and begins to desire a connection with this soulful young man—perhaps she just feels pity for him, a certain compassion, it is not clear.

The story ends where the film began, with Magda watching the boy as he recovers from his suicide attempt in his small bedroom. While at his side, Magda looks through the telescope he used to spy on her and she observes her empty flat from Tomek's perspective. This view triggers a fantasy for Magda: part flashback and part wish fulfillment, it is a vision of Tomek entering her apartment, comforting her in her isolation—the way she spends most nights.

This film "breathes with the audience," rather than pounds it with polemic. It is a chamber piece that evokes mood and atmosphere. Its slow tempo and intense rhythms focus the viewer's attention on what is not said rather than what is said, and elicits an emotional and transcendental response. Let's examine how the screenwriters use the visual to tell the story by analyzing the sequence of shots in the opening scenes:

1. With a handheld camera, we see a newly bandaged arm. A woman's hand moves towards it, as if to touch it. Another hand, that of an older woman, covers the first and motions for her to "keep away." The camera moves to reveal the face of a young man, Tomek, unconscious, gently resting on a pillow.

2. From a long distance away, we look in on an apartment through a window, at night. A beautiful woman plays solitaire and is alone. Our view of her is only partial. The woman moves to her refrigerator and her bare, sexy legs and buttocks, covered with only loose-fitting panties, fill the screen.

3. We cut back to an extreme close-up of the boy in bed. The light, from a source outside the room, illuminates his face.

4. Another long distance shot of the same woman in her apartment, amusing herself, dancing playfully to unheard music, idling away the time in the middle of the night, alone. Again the view is only partial and refracted by a crystal hanging in the lonely woman's apartment window.

5. Back to the boy in bed: the light from the hallway slowly, very gently, extinguishes. Apparently a door to his room is being carefully shut by someone.

6. Suddenly, in the middle of the night, shattered glass spills onto a hard wood floor in a large, shadowy room. The camera holds on the glass as Tomek enters the frame. He tiptoes about, having just broken into a building. Checking "to see if all is clear," he walks down a partially lit hallway.

7. A wider shot of the hallway. Tomek walks from the light into shadow into light with a greater confidence. A close-up of a flashlight sweeping through the darkness.

8. Tomek carefully enters another room and turns on the flashlight. We follow the light of the flashlight as it moves about, examining and exposing various shelves of computer monitors, typewriters, and other office equipment. Tomek reaches behind a shelf and extracts a small telescope. He puts it under his coat, turns off the flashlight, and exits the room into the darkness.

9. An extreme close-up of the focusing band on the telescope. Tomek's fingers twist it, adjusting focus.

10. From the point of view of the telescope, we see an apartment building across a courtyard. It is daytime, the view zooms in on a flat.

11. A close-up of the boy's face as he looks through the telescope. He is delighted with the results of his focusing. The camera moves to reveal a set of binoculars in his room. The boy dismantles the binoculars.

The above sequence of eleven camera setups takes approximately four minutes and fifteen seconds of screen time. For a film approximately eighty-six minutes long, that is a considerable amount of film time—nearly five percent of its running length. And it holds the audience's attention every moment of its play. What does this assembly of shots suggest, evoke, or foreshadow? And how does each particular shot add to the progression?

The movie begins with a wounded boy on a bed. The play of the two hands over his wound, one motioning the other not to touch, suggests a tension. This simple gesture foreshadows, and promises that there will be conflict up ahead. Since the scene begins in stasis, in a stable state, the stasis needs to be punctured for a progression to occur. New forces need to be unleashed, so a new flow can begin and we can witness the onset of an unstable state. This hand gesture unleashes the sense of unresolved tension, provides new information, and creates a progression.

The second setup of the film shows a woman viewed from far away. She is playing solitaire. The storyteller has triggered the viewer to wonder who she is, and why she is alone. Triggering this question in the mind of the viewer creates another progression. The audience gets a view of her bare legs and panties. This certainly grabs attention—she is beautiful and sexy. Film, like painting, loves to illustrate the ideal body and yet another progression occurs.

The third setup comes back to the young boy. Why does Kielslowski make this choice? Because he wants the audience to link the sexy woman with the wounded boy. Ah, the viewer thinks: this story is about the relationship between these two people—Tomek, a teenager, and Magda, a middle-aged woman. It may involve sex or some lustful desire. Why would the viewers think that? They were just shown a beautiful, sexy woman playfully dancing in her panties! What else would they think? With this inference the viewers experience another progression.

The fourth setup shows Magda again, from a cool distance—a telescopic view—dancing to music we cannot hear. This shot confirms the audience's suspicion—the story will be about these two people. What is the nature of their relationship? He looks like he is hurt and she is dancing. How will these two opposites come to relate? This musing is another progression for the story. At this point, the audience will trust the storyteller to eventually provide a reply to the questions posed in the setup, but the payoff does not have to answer these questions, only address them.

Fifth setup: Back to Tomek in bed, unconscious, wounded, possibly recuperating. Does his wound have something to do with the dancing woman across the way? Did she cause it? Did he get it from her? The storyteller is teasing the viewer: suggesting the two are tied together. But how? The web of questions triggered by the images in this setup increases the audience's appetite and so another progression occurs.

Sixth setup: Tomek, awake, vital, breaks into a building. This flashback is the beginning of the unfolding of the "present tense story"—the relationship between Magda and Tomek. With the presentation of the present tense story, a progression occurs. Why has he broken into this building? What does he want? And how is what he is looking for tied to his wound and to the middle-aged woman? Again, a web of provocative questions triggered by the screenwriter's choices continues to increase the audience's attention.

Seventh setup: Tomek walks down a hallway with more confidence, which indicates he is probably safe—the coast is clear. The camera comes in on a close-up of his flashlight. The viewers anticipate they will find out what he wants, increasing their attention.

Eighth setup: Tomek shines his flashlight on what he wants and extracts a telescope. This telescope is the payoff for the questions posed in the previous setup. A telescope? What does he want that for? The viewers move forward in their seats. Is Tomek a criminal? He was presented as clean-cut, not the cliché image of a criminal. Could he be a criminal? What an interesting and unexpected possibility. This reversal of expectation increases the audience's attention ever more, and hence another progression occurs.

The ninth setup immediately addresses one of the questions of the eight setup—why does this young man want a telescope? We see his fingers adjusting the focus. The audience is intrigued. The anticipation mounts. Another progression occurs.

In the tenth setup the reply is given with an image: from Tomek's point of view, the viewer sees a telescopic view of an apartment across the way. The audience wonders if the kid spies on the woman. Tomek grins with pleasure after zooming in on Magda's apartment and the viewer has an answer. But why? Since Tomek has been presented as unthreatening in the opening montage the audience identifies with him and projects positive values on him. At the same time, he is spying on a neighbor and the audience does not want to identify with that behavior. The push/pull creates a complex response from the viewer and the story begins to satisfy one of the values of the character-driven screenplay—complexity. The resonant, complex response elicited in the audience qualifies as another progression.

Eleventh setup: Tomek disassembles a set of binoculars. This is new and compelling information for the audience. Apparently this young man has been spying on Magda for some time—he is merely replacing one viewing glass for another. The plot thickens; a progression occurs.

In this sequence, each setup gives the audience dramatic information that suggests there is conflict up ahead, entirely by visual means. The viewer may not know the motive behind the character's actions at this point, but the inferences made by the images are clear. In the words of E. B. White, Kieslowski and Piesiewicz are "being obscure clearly." The subject matter of the film is about first love between a teenager and an older woman. What can be said about this subject that has not already been expressed in literature, poems, nonfiction books, or in the neighborhood gossip sessions through the centuries? The choice of carrying the opening story entirely in pictures is effective: it creates mood, atmosphere, and presents an uncommon impression of a common experience. The writers' purpose is to communicate the metaphysical resonance of first love. They accomplish this goal by progressing the story with images that allow them to be more impressionistic and poetic; to trigger in the viewer's mind clusters of interpretations and associations.

The picture is the poetry and beauty of a film. When used to carry the story, it evokes and suggests, but is not as effective as words to express the inner thoughts and feelings of a character. Those who rely too much on the picture for characterization will have less complex characters—words create complexity. However, without making use of the picture the screenwriter will not be as successful in creating mood, atmosphere, mystery, and the essential magic of a movie.

8

Sound: How It Can Carry the Story

The director Fritz Lang once remarked that in a scene with two "lovers" at a table in an outdoor café, if we can hear only the two talking, the audience will immediately think they are madly in love. If the din of other people talking, street traffic, the clanking plates in the kitchen, the flush of the toilet is heard as the two lovers speak, the audience will most assuredly assume that that these two people are not in love. Why does the audience make these assumptions? Because being entirely caught up with one another is what love is all about, and by allowing only the sound of the lovers' voices to prevail in the scene, the writer re-creates the "feeling" of being entirely caught up with one another. Allowing the realities of the world to seep into the scene, as in the second case, by bringing up the volume of the restaurant din, the audience is pushed out of the feeling of being in love. Sound can help guide the audience to know how to feel about the montage. If the screenwriter or director does not make a distinct, clear choice about the sounds of a montage, the audience has far less information with which to interpret the scene.

Sound is often overlooked by the screenwriter, despite its powerful influence on film. For instance, suppose a man, overcome by fear and panic, acts out and abruptly breaks off with his girlfriend. It is a cruel act, but his buttons have been pushed. When he comes to his senses several days later, contrite and remorseful, he tries to get her back. She is hurt and filled with outrage and will not take his calls. She decides to date other men. For her first date, she chooses her ex-boyfriend's colleague at work. One day, two weeks after the breakup, the three accidentally meet at a gallery opening. The ex-boyfriend watches his former sweetheart as she holds hands with his co-worker.

At this point in the scene, the screenwriter indicates that the sound of the din of the gallery fades, and the sound of an air vent, somewhere unseen in the room, increases in volume. As the scene progresses, the writer requests that all sound fade except for the sound of the air duct. What does this choice accomplish? It clearly expresses the feelings that are inside the man who wants his girlfriend back: the abandonment, the lack of closure, the stunning surprise. The sound choice evokes disconnection, alienation, and loneliness. The manipulation of the sound in the scene guides the viewer's interpretation of the montage.

Sound: The Writer's or Director's Choice?

The writer should not rely on the director to create the soundscape of a film. The writer should be as specific as possible in considering every element of a film, including sound, because when it comes time to shoot the script there will be plenty of interpretation. The job of the actor and director is to interpret what the screenwriter has created, just as the musician interprets a composition created by the composer. However, if you are as specific as possible when writing, you will have far better odds of having your script brought to life as you intended and you will also write a better screenplay. It has been my experience that you will also gain greater respect from both the actor and director whenever you pay close attention to detail for any element of a film, including sound.

Telling Story with Sound

During the writing process, the writer can use sound to puncture a scene and create a new flow by opening the door to unconscious discoveries. For instance, suppose I were to revise the scene between the two lovers in the café mentioned at the beginning of this section. It is the opening scene of the movie so it will provide the first impression of these lovers. I must grab the viewer's attention, surprise them, and at the same time reveal something deep and meaningful about these lovers both as a pair and as individuals.

When it comes time to write the scene I am blocked and don't really know why. Maybe, I am afraid that I do not have the skill to present the characters with originality, truth, and surprise. Realizing that I am burdening myself and blocking my unconscious because of ego demands, I decide to go for a walk in the park by the river.

In order to unblock myself, I decide to use sound as a possible way to create some new flow. I ask myself a simple question: "What do I hear happening, in my mind's ear, in the scene with the lover's at the café? For no rational reason, I imagine that I hear nervous tapping from underneath the table where the lovers sit. What could that be? In my mind's eye I discover that one of our lovers, a handsome young man who sits staring into the eyes of a beautiful young woman, is tapping his foot nervously, unconsciously, under the table. His girlfriend is completely unaware of this nervous habit, she remains transfixed in the warm fire of his bedroom eyes and focuses on how his two front teeth turn ever so slightly inward. His tapping is actually getting on my nerves. Why is he doing that? I want to tell him to stop. I trust this feeling and do not judge it, and if the opportunity presents itself, I will even use my emotions—frustration and irritation—in the scene. Using the emotions that I have as I create, often provides a great way to find a flow. Perhaps a waiter could walk into the scene and I could transfer the feeling of irritation that I am feeling to him and then observe what he does about that feeling. For instance, the waiter could trap that feeling of irritation into the action of serving these people; it might yield some interesting results. I imagine an angry waiter trying to be polite while serving these lovers, and how he would try to contain his anger with either physical or mental actions. I consider and reject the choice. Why? It simply just doesn't feel right.

Continuing with my discovery process, I notice in my mind's eye that our handsome young man has a slight bulge in his pants pocket, it looks like a tiny case. Intuitively, I immediately know what this is—it's a secret that he is keeping from his girlfriend. Secrets are great ways to puncture a scene and create flow. If you have one of your characters enter a scene with a secret, it can be a catalyst that will break the stasis of the scene and unleash new forces. I decide to use it. Our young lover is nervous about his secret connected to the little case in his pocket and that is why he is tapping. I dash back to my computer to revise the scene:

```
EXT. MANHATTAN, OUTDOOR CAFÉ—SUNSET
An outdoor café on the esplanade of the Hudson River.
Lovers of all ages, sip wine or drink espresso. IAN,
27, a handsome young man, and GRACE, 25, a beautiful,
spirited young woman hold hands, staring into each
other's eyes. We hear a tugboat move up the river as
the summer sky forms a warm canopy.

The SOUND of tapping under the table.

                    GRACE
    (Gently. Re: the tapping.) Stop.

                    IAN
    (Sincerely unaware.) What?

Grace reacts playfully. Ian's mood shifts.

NEW ANGLE. Ian nervously takes a tiny velvet case from
his pocket.

CLOSE-UP. A stunning antique ring. Grace is silent,
dumbstruck.

                    IAN
    It was my grandmother's.

Grace shifts her gaze to the river. She is scared and
happy. Ian waits on a razor's edge.

                    GRACE
    (She meets his gaze.) Yes.

                    IAN
    Yes?

                    GRACE
    Yes.

Ian kisses his fiancée; he accidentally sweeps the ring
off the table. Both are completely unaware it has fallen.

The ring rolls on the marble floor towards the river's
edge. The din of the café grows louder as does the
sound of the ring rolling on marble.

NEW ANGLE. The ring rolls into an iron grating: a drain
opening into the river.
```

```
SOUND. The slapping of waves against the pier.

NEW ANGLE. SLOW MOTION. The ring falls through air and
is swallowed by the river.

NEW ANGLE. The river in the foreground. The SOUND of
waves, the din of the café and passers-by. Through this
forest of sounds, we barely hear Ian and Grace, still
at their café table. NEW ANGLE. Ian and Grace are dots
on the horizon.

                    IAN
          Honey?

                    GRACE
          Yeah?

                    IAN
          I can't believe this...Jesus...

NEW ANGLE. A wide shot of the entire waterfront—Grace
and Ian cannot be seen. The SOUND of chairs scraping
the café floor.

                GRACE (OFF CAMERA)
          What?

The frantic SOUND of shuffled cups and plates.

                    IAN (O.C.)
          Jesus....

The SOUND of a table being uprighted—glasses fall and
break.

                    IAN (O.C.)
          JESUS!
```

This fun beginning for a movie all came about because I put my focus on sound and allowed it to carry some story. Ian and Grace at the end of the scene are off camera, we only hear what they say and do. The sound, at this point in the film, carries the story, not the image or the words. And by focusing on the soundscape of the scene, I was able to puncture it to create both a new flow and an entirely new, specific beginning to the screenplay.

EXERCISE

CHANGING
THE SOUNDSCAPE

Take a favorite scene from a movie and observe its soundscape. Then change it radically. What is the effect on the story, scene, and characterizations? Does this change suggest a new storyline or a new relationship between characters?

Setting Mood with Sound

Let's examine another example. Suppose you decide to write a scene between a dying mother and her son. It is noon, and the mother is on her deathbed. She is wealthy, so the room is well decorated. The son, who has come to be with his mother before she dies, sits at her side. There are many details to explore, but for the moment let's consider the sound in the room. Suppose the writer describes the sound of chirping finches and the laughter of children outside the window. From inside the house, in an adjoining room, through an open door, we hear a large gathering of people chatting politely, in the spirit of warm fellowship. What is being suggested to an audience about this woman, her son, and her death, with this soundscape? It certainly gives a pastoral feel to the scene, as well as a sense of love, kindness, gentility, and beauty; this woman attracts humanity rather than repels it.

But suppose the writer takes another tack and pens the following: We hear the old woman's death rattle, a shallow gasping for air. A clock ticks on the mantle and the son sits at the mother's side reading a newspaper. Through the window, in the far background, we see a workman hold a gun to an old horse's head. We cut back to the woman lying on the bed and hear the bang of the pistol in the background. This soundscape may spin the scene into the surreal or evoke dark humor or melodrama, but the effect it will have on an audience is very different than the previous choice. It suggests that this woman was a cold and mean-spirited person, disliked, unloved, and certainly not cherished, even in death.

Sound is a tool every screenwriter should consider at every step of the writing process. Like the visual element, it can tell the story, or lead the writer to a flow of more story, character, and nuance. It can suggest the inner life of a character or create a tempo and rhythm for a scene. It can also serve to bridge two scenes or acts.

Creating Irony with Sound

Sound can also be used to create irony by layering specific sounds at specific moments in a scene. The effect of this layering is to push the viewer out of the scene to give ironic distance. The scene will have resonance because it presents an incongruity between what is expected by the viewer and what is actually seen and heard.

Incongruity or a lack of harmony in a scene is the basis for irony. For instance, a visually ironic moment might play as follows: we see the vast expanse of the inside of a church; a woman kneels at the exterior of a confessional booth making a heartfelt confession. We cut to the inside of the booth and see a priest drinking a beer and reading the racing form. There is a discrepancy between what the viewer expects to see—a priest paying his full attention to the confessing woman—and what is actually happening—a priest getting drunk and reading the racing sheet. Discrepancy can also be created by sound: two lovers sit at a table, one proposes marriage to the other. In the tense silence as he waits for her response, we hear a customer farting. There is a discrepancy between the viewer's expectation that this is a solemn and important moment and the scatological sounds we hear. When the contrast between audience expectation and what actually happens in a scene is compelling and strong, there is irony.

Let's examine one last example of the use of sound from *Love Serenade,* a biting satire by Australian filmmaker Shirley Barrett. In this film, Ken Sherry, a smarmy disc jockey, has come to the backwaters of Australia to escape the city of Brisbane. Two sisters live in the house next to Sherry's, Dimity, a bit dim, and her perky sister, Vicki-Ann. When Sherry moves in, Vicki-Ann instantly develops a love "fever" and will do anything to seduce him. But Sherry likes Dimity more than Vicki-Ann, and the roller coaster ride begins.

Dimity comes face to face with the fishy Mr. Sherry for the first time at the Chinese restaurant where she works as a waitress. As Sherry enters the run-down, vacant restaurant, a buzzer, designed to alert the staff that a customer has entered the establishment, goes off. As Dimity takes the arrogant Sherry to his table, the buzzer continues, seemingly forever, in the background. Finally, with a perfect sense of timing, it stops. What do we hear next in this empty, quiet restaurant? The buzzing of a maniacal fly. What else do we hear? The cook in the kitchen whacking away at some chickens—whacking and whacking incessantly. Back in the dining room, the fly is electrocuted by an electric zapper. Finally, Sherry inquires if the "the prawns are fresh." Dimity, it appears, has never been asked this question before, and stumped, obviously lies: "Yeah," she says lamely. Sherry sniffs that she is lying and would like her to ascertain the facts with the cook. She enters the kitchen, we hear her murmur off camera to someone, who we assume is the chef, and then we hear a pot thrown across the room in a rage. Albert Lee, the proprietor and chef of the establishment, enters the dining room to address Mr. Sherry.

The essential sound elements of this scene are a buzzer that buzzes too long, a fly that is on the way to the lunatic asylum, its death by electrocution, the hacking in the kitchen, and finally, a pot tossed in outrage. Dramatic irony is added to the scene through the use of sound rather than the manipulation of picture or words. These sounds create a discrepancy between the viewer's expectations and what actually happens. The viewer expects a restaurant to be a place with some ambiance and professionalism. What actually happens in the scene is in stark contrast to these expectations. This incongruity creates a strong sense of irony, tension, and humor, and pushes the scene into the realm of satire.

When to Use Sound to Carry the Story

As always, the answer to this question depends on your purpose. Sound can be used to create variety and to suggest and create atmosphere. Sound should be used when it can help to break through the cliché and express something that cannot be described in words or by the picture. It can help to create unique and original scenes. In the example of the two lovers at the café, sound helped to create a sharper, newer way of viewing an all too familiar subject matter—a marriage proposal. But it is a tool that is often overlooked by the screenwriter that can provide yet another layer to a scene, adding richness and complexity. At every step in the writing process, scenes should be scrutinized to see how sound can contribute to the purpose of the screenplay.

PART 2

FINDING YOUR STRUCTURE

9

Dramatic Structure

Once the writer has excavated enough information from the unconscious imagination, he or she will next be faced with the task of making it cohesive and coherent. How does one arrange and proportion the material discovered from the unconscious flow in order to give it a beginning, middle, and end? What is needed is a central plan and guidelines to decide when and how to reveal certain information. The first step in creating a dramatic structure is for the writer to postulate a central dramatic question. It is the very foundation of any structure you build for a screenplay.

The Central Dramatic Question: The First Step to Building a Structure

Citizen Kane begins with a newsreel: *The March of News* documentary. A news executive, after watching the newsreel with his colleagues, complains that it feels incomplete and paces the shadowy, smoke-filled room, trying to pinpoint the problem. "All we saw on that newsreel is that Charles Foster Kane is dead. What we need here is an angle," he fires at his disgruntled reporters. "It isn't enough to tell us what a man did. You've got to tell us who he was," he continues. With this statement, Welles, rather baldly states the central dramatic question of the film: who is the real Charles Foster Kane? The audience is given a question to focus on—a context for the story. And despite its baldness, this strategy adds, rather than detracts, from the complexity and subtlety of the movie.

The central dramatic question certainly grows from the writer's purpose. But the purpose and central dramatic question are not the same. For example, I may have as a purpose to write a film about the complexities of farm life. The story is about a young boy and a wounded horse, and the central dramatic question is whether the boy can save his beloved horse. Using this question as an arc to frame the screenplay, I will write a story revealing the complexities of farm life.

One of the requirements of a narrative film is a controlling idea, a line of investigation, a theme to tie it together into a coherent whole. "It isn't enough to tell us what a man did. You've got to tell us who he was," proclaims the news executive in *Citizen Kane*. What could be clearer, yet more challenging than that—to tell us who someone is?

Culmination in One Dramatic Moment

Edward Ball, Professor of playwriting at Carnegie Mellon University, in his excellent book on script-reading techniques, *Backwards and Forwards,* postulates that every play (the same can be said for every screenplay) is really about one question and it takes a whole play to address or answer that question. For instance, the story of Hamlet hinges on the question of whether Hamlet will kill the king. The play begins with the appearance of the ghost of Hamlet's father, which breaks the stasis of the world and unleashes new forces.

Hamlet must now examine the question of whether or not he should avenge his father's death. Like *Citizen Kane*, in *Hamlet* we are shown, right from the top, completely on-the-nose, the dramatic question of the play. Shakespeare provides a framework for the audience, a context in which to track all of the action, events, and characters. If the audience is not given this question to ponder, they will eventually be bored to death after watching the prince of Denmark acting with ambivalence and neuroses for hours; they would have no idea why he is so torn and no context in which to understand his tortured conscience. Without the central dramatic question Hamlet's indecision would be annoying. With the central dramatic question, we see the action in a new light: Hamlet wants to kill the king, and, crippled by conscience, he cannot.

The *moment of the play* is when Hamlet kills the king. To make that moment resonate and have meaning and power, Shakespeare had to write the rest of the play. The moment provides the payoff for the whole play. What we were led to anticipate happens. For *Citizen Kane*, the central dramatic question is just as basic and clear: will our reporter ever find out what "Rosebud," the last thing that Kane said, means? "What were his last words?" the peripatetic news executive asks his assembled reporters. "Maybe he told us all about himself on his deathbed," he continues, "I'll tell you, Johnson, a man's dying words…" And from there on out the audience sits in their seat with a sense of clarity. The film will be about Rosebud, what it means, and how it tells us who Charles Foster Kane really was. The viewers put their focus where it counts, where the author has targeted the payoff; the moment when there is no real answer to the mystery of Kane. The substance of the story is what keeps the audience glued to their seats until this moment occurs.

To best understand what constitutes a central dramatic question, the screenwriter should consider the following: a screenplay is about one moment, and it takes a whole screenplay to make that moment work. Once the moment of the screenplay—its highest point of engagement—has been discovered, then the writer can naturally work backwards and infer a question that will encapsulate this moment. If the moment of *Hamlet* is when Hamlet kills the king, then quite logically, the central dramatic question of the play becomes "will Hamlet kill the king?" Once the moment is discovered, the writer can then look over the material and shape a beginning, middle, and end that will most effectively lead an audience to this moment. The idea is to shape a path that grabs the audience's attention and increases it steadily, until this moment occurs. When it occurs, the entire stasis of the story must come unhinged, burst apart, and new forces are released.

Posing the Central Dramatic Question

Here are some other examples of central dramatic questions:

1. *The Fugitive:* Will Harrison Ford (Dr. Richard Kimble) vindicate himself?
2. *Love Serenade:* As Dimity and her sister, Vicki-Ann, compete for the love of the fishy disc jockey next door, Ken Sherry, who will win what?
3. *Crimes and Misdemeanors:* Will Martin Landau (Judah) kill his demanding mistress, Anjelica Houston (Dolores), and live a guilt-free life?
4. *Full Metal Jacket:* Can Matthew Modine (Private Joker) become a real Marine, a killer?
5. *Twelve Angry Men:* Will Henry Fonda turn the jury around?
6. *Glengarry Glen Ross:* Who will win the prize for selling the most real estate?
7. *Mean Streets:* Can Charlie (Harvey Keitel) choose between his uncle's way, or the way of his heart?
8. *The 400 Blows:* Will Antoine, an unwanted twelve-year-old boy, ever find love?
9. *The Producers:* Will Zero Mostel (Max Bialystock) and Gene Wilder (Leo Bloom) get away with their scheme to defraud their investors and make a bundle on a sure-fire flop?
10. *The Unbearable Lightness of Being:* Will Daniel Day-Lewis (Tomas) give up his libertine ways and allow himself to become emotionally involved with Juliette Binoche (Tereza)?

The central dramatic question must be clear and simple, but not simplistic. "What is the nature of love?" is a very "simple" question, yet it has tremendous resonance. It is profoundly difficult, if not impossible to answer with any degree of certainty. It could take a thousand screenplays to explore all the sides of this question. Other examples of simple yet profound questions are: Why do people hate? Is there life after death? What is loyalty? How does one deal with irreparable loss? Does God exist? Is it ever correct to kill your own child?

I am not suggesting that a screenplay is a thesis. It does not have to prove its dramatic question, it only needs to provide a fully considered examination. The dramatic question is a question, not a statement; and if the screenwriter keeps the dramatic question a question, the screenplay will be an "exploration," rather than a proof. By keeping it a question the screenplay will have more of an open-ended focus.

Open-ended questions are a more effective way to explore. They allow breathing space and give license to discover. A writer who tries to prove a point (which is what a thesis statement will often lead him or her to do) will strip a story of its organic vitality and animating force, because the struggle to prove a thesis often closes the writer off from the unconscious imagination. Proving a point closes down the process of spontaneous discovery. Burdening yourself with trying to show the audience how clever, ironic, funny, or tragic you can be, or trying to make the audience "like" a particular character, will block you and lead you away from your real writing power—the unconscious.

Once you have settled upon a dramatic question, does it remain the same throughout the process of writing a screenplay? No, not necessarily. A central dramatic question is like most elements in a screenplay—character, world, and story—it will evolve, often into something you did not anticipate. For instance, I once began writing a play by asking whether one person can make a difference in the complex world of politics. As I proceeded to fully explore the fictive world and develop, get inside, and become the characters, the question began to change significantly. By the time the play was ready for production the question had evolved into whether one can be morally consistent, yet politically effective, in the complex world of politics.

Is a central dramatic question necessary to begin writing? No, it is not necessary; but the sooner it is formed, the better. Even if it is only a temporary one, a central dramatic question is important, otherwise you risk losing the psychological curiosity that is necessary to sustain the level of concentration to complete a work. If you are always spinning your wheels, just exploring this way and that, or writing one scene after another without a central plan, you run the very real risk of depleting all drive and enthusiasm for a particular project.

Referring back to chapter three to E. M. Forster's story of the king and queen, the explanation that the queen died of grief provides causation. By discovering causation, you also discover something else implicitly, a central dramatic question.

With a central dramatic question you have a direction that can be followed both by you and the audience. Once you say the queen died of grief, you have a way to pose a central question: Why did she die of grief? Or how did she die of grief? What is grief? How does society dictate that we deal with grief? There are obviously many questions and associations evoked by the causation—the emotion of grief. If you choose a central dramatic question that truly haunts you and powerfully holds your attention, it will most likely hold the audience's attention as well. It will also be strongly linked to your unconscious imagination and you will be able to tap into a vein, a powerful source of flow.

One of the most important lessons I ever learned as a playwright was when I decided to accept a commission to write the story of protégé Dennis Sweeney and mentor Allard Lowenstein. Sweeney was a political activist and Lowenstein a more mainstream liberal politician during the 1960s. The play was the love story of two men; how they came together and fell apart over a twenty-year period. When I finished the first draft of the commission I organized a reading. The script called for over sixty characters, and, doubling and tripling, twenty-five actors performed in the reading. It was a strange event, with only three people in the audience—a dramaturg, myself, and a friend—and nearly twenty-five other bodies facing us in a cold and dingy loft space in Manhattan's Hell's Kitchen. The reading proved that the script was overwritten and contained a dozen stories; it went this way and that way and lacked coherence. When the reading was all over, my friend turned to me and said exactly what I needed to hear, "That was great, very interesting, but I don't get it. What's it about?"

I was completely depressed and frightened to death because not only did I not know the answer to his question, worse, I hadn't even considered it. I ran home and began to strip, cut, edit, and search for the play's essence. But before I could do that, I had to finally take a stand and say to myself out loud, after writing a dozen options on index cards, exactly what my central dramatic question was. I came up with the question "can one remain morally consistent, yet be politically effective in the world of politics?" Immediately I was able to see how I could create a beginning, middle, and end to my play. Once I had discovered my direction it all became a matter of how I was going to play my cards. When would I show my hand? When would I keep them close to my vest? How should I arrange and proportion the scenes, the moments, the acts? And, because I was relieved of the burden of finding a central focus, I could now turn my energies to overcoming the cliché aspects of my script by giving it more specificity in terms of character.

When the revision was done, I had eliminated nearly forty characters and approximately an hour and a half of playing time. It was painful to lose some great material, but I finally had a coherent piece. When the next reading was done, I got an offer from a producer and the play went into production the following season. Was this offer for production mere coincidence? Not at all; I was given the offer because the play now made some sense, it was coherent and cohesive, and it had a rudder—a central dramatic question.

The Central Dramatic Question
Evolves out of a Central Emotion

The central dramatic question can actually be stated in many different ways, but it hovers around one thing—an emotion, in the case of E. M. Forster's example, grief. Every good screenplay has a central emotion. In *The Fugitive* the central emotion is vindication—to right something that is unjustly wrong. In *Mean Streets,* the Harvey Kietel character, Charlie, is crippled with guilt. He goes to church and holds his hands over a flame trying to do something about this overwhelming feeling that keeps him from readily accepting his uncle's dictates to cut Johnny Boy loose and to break from his epileptic girlfriend. In *Love Serenade,* however humorously played out, romantic passion is central to the screenplay. In *The Producers,* it is selfish greed; in *400 Blows,* it is abandonment.

There is a very odd book that a friend recommended I read: *The Thirty-Six Dramatic Situations,* written by Georges Polti in 1921. My friend suggested this book as a useful tool for screenwriting. Polti starts with the premise that "all conceivable situations have been used and that all modern plots are but variations and adaptations of certain original situations." Polti then goes on to discover and classify thirty-six dramatic situations. Unfortunately, the book never helped me with my writing; the dramatic situations, though accurate and interesting, were not useful in any practical way. But there is one concept that rang very true: Polti associates each of the thirty-six dramatic situations with corresponding emotional conflicts. For instance, one of the situations is called: "all sacrificed for a passion" and Polti describes an emotional state that we have all experienced. Whether it is the all-consuming need to watch the Sunday football game or break up a twenty-year marriage to elope with a student, most of us have, at one time or another, "sacrificed everything for a passion." A central dramatic question based on an emotional state gives a screenplay coherence, unity of purpose, and a lens through which to view a story.

A central emotion is vital to a screenplay because the reason we go to the movies is to have an emotional response. Working backwards, I began to apply this insight to my own work. I asked myself: what are the basic human emotions I am exploring in my screenplays? I looked at three of my screenplays. The first screenplay, *Dennis,* clearly deals with a central emotion: guilt. I looked at another screenplay, *Arab Bride,* and it too deals with guilt. I re-examined a third, *The Young Girl and the Monsoon,* again, its central emotion is guilt. Could it be that we write about the same thing over and over again—if not the same story and characters, certainly the same emotion? I believe the answer is yes.

I took this self-analysis and thought of a way to test its validity with my students. On separate occasions, I asked them to think of a time when they were angry, or filled with joy, fear, shame, pride, and so on. Starting with one of these emotional states, they were asked do a "free-write," a stream of consciousness exploration— essentially writing whatever came into their minds. The results were amazing. My students began to see that no matter what emotional state they chose, certain elements would reappear, such as rhythms and tempo of dialogue, types of characters, situations, and so on. The students began to see "who they really were" as writers, what interested them, and what they felt compelled to write about. The exercise gave them a good sense of their limitations and opened their eyes to what they could do best. All this self-knowledge made them better writers and hopefully saved them time in the future by not wasting time trying to construct something beyond their interest or abilities. Instead of trying to do many different things in a mediocre way, they could now do two or three things really well. The screenwriter/playwright John Patrick Shanley once said to me, "one of the most important things I learned as a writer was that the Bronx, the place I had been trying to leave behind in my writing and in life, was my greatest asset. When I wrote about this world my work suddenly was alive." Shanley became aware of his boundaries as a writer. Once he discovered them, he dove in and returned over and over again to the Bronx. For some reason, it was the landscape that most deeply tapped his unconscious imagination.

This self-knowledge should not limit you or stop you from taking risks and writing about things you want to know more about. It just represents a solid deposit in the bank that you can draw upon to help finance your projects and keep them viable, until they become what they need to become on their own, each time, in their own special way.

Each time you write a screenplay its central dramatic question will inevitably be different. You will discover it if, each time you plan your story, you simply ask yourself: what are the essential emotions of this piece? What specifically interests me about these emotions in the context of the world and characters of my screenplay? How can I take these discoveries and formulate them into a central question?

EXERCISE DISCOVERING THE EMOTIONS THAT HAUNT YOU

List three movies that you like very much. Ask yourself: what basic human emotion or emotions are central to each movie? Are there similarities between the basic emotions expressed in these three movies? If so, do you find these movies engaging because of what they have in common in terms of underlying emotional life? How can you use this self-knowledge to be a more effective screenwriter?

10

How and Why We Use Acts in a Screenplay

Why do so many students think a screenplay is always made up of three acts? As a test, I once asked students to analyze films with one-act structures *(Mean Streets* and *Vagabond)* and two-act structures *(Full Metal Jacket* and *Jules and Jim)*. Myopic in their drive to make every film into what they think all films should be—three acts, nearly all the students imposed three acts on these movies.

It is tradition in Hollywood to use a three-act structure, which is a structure that effectively serves the purpose of most Hollywood films: to assure the audience that the status quo will be maintained, that all will be restored to order. For many writers, professional and beginner, using a three-act structure is a knee-jerk response. Some films are best illuminated with one, two, or even five acts. The writer can make a choice about act structure, and like all the other elements in a screenplay, this choice should be predicated on how well it facilitates the writer's purpose.

What Is an Act?

An act is an arc, a line of action that leads to a climax or a culminating event. Traditionally, the best acts end with thematic or narrative questions left open in order to entice the audience to return for the next act. The climax can sometimes be followed by a denouement, which in a literal translation from French means "untying of the knot." It is the moment when the last suspense is eliminated. The denouement can also occur with the climax. When one act ends, and a new one begins, the spectator can literally feel the break, the leap into new narrative territory.

In traditional Arabic storytelling, the storyteller entered a café, grabbed everyone's attention with a story, and just as it reached a climax, he shrewdly gave the audience a choice to consider, such as how a certain character would behave, what outcome they would choose under the present circumstances of the story, and so on. And then the storyteller would bolt out the door, shouting that he would return the next day, leaving the café clientele on the edge of their seats. Often people threw things at him as he dashed away, furious at his manipulation. Essentially, this is what the screenwriter does when constructing an act. He or she takes a line of action that can be summarized in one dramatic question, and develops it until it reaches a climax.

An act is an arbitrary unit of dramatic time; it can be any length. Traditionally, in the linear three-act structure, the first act is roughly thirty minutes, the second sixty, and the third thirty. The first and third acts are generally shorter, by about thirty to fifty percent, than the second act. It does indeed make sense that the setup and resolution should move as quickly as possible since the most dramatically active portion of the three-act structure is in the second act when the protagonist actively pursues a goal. The first act or setup is generally less dramatic because it is backstory. The third act or resolution must move quickly in order to stay one step ahead of a well-informed audience. Since the audience already has so much information from the first and second acts, the third act need only give a little bit of information here and there for the audience to "get it."

In reality, there is a wide range of act lengths. These variations are perfectly fine as long as the attention of the audience is held and the writer's purpose is fulfilled.

Content Dictates Structure

Because structure limits what can be examined and not examined in a screenplay, it also communicates, in and of itself. Form invariably excludes certain content. As Neil Postman and his spiritual godfather, Marshall McLuhan, wrote, "consider the primitive technology of smoke signals. While I do not know exactly what content was once carried in the smoke signals of American Indians, I can safely guess it did not include philosophical argument. Puffs of smoke are insufficiently complex to express ideas on the nature of existence, and even if they were not, a Cherokee philosopher would run short of either wood or blankets before he reached his second axiom. You cannot use smoke to do philosophy. Its form excludes the content." It is the same for screenwriting: the form—the act structure—will include or exclude certain content or substance.

To find out how many acts you need, you must first have some idea of your purpose. If you follow a formula, you may or may not be able to say what you need to say, because the formula may or may not support the expression of your thoughts, feelings, and ideas. If your goal is to "break through" and express something specific and original, you must find your form each and every time you write a screenplay. Sometimes the nuances and details of your content will be best expressed in one act, other times five.

If you do not discover your structure each and every time you write a screenplay, you will fail on a fundamental level. It is in fact a lazy practice, not dutiful, to allow a formula to lead you to structure, which in turn dictates substance. This would be simply working on the level of technique—retreading an old tire.

The Big Question: The Essence of an Act

An act is a way to manage one "big question," and its implicit, related set of sub-questions. This is not to be confused with the central dramatic question. The central dramatic question is directly connected to the one big moment of the whole screenplay; it encapsulates this moment and is a question that covers the entire screenplay. Nor is the big question to be confused with the writer's purpose—the thoughts, feelings, and ideas she or he is trying to examine or express—the very personal reason she or he needs to write the screenplay. Because a screenplay may have several acts, it may have several big questions, but it only has one central dramatic question and one purpose. In the one-act form, as we will examine later, the central dramatic question and the big question merge; since there is only one line of action for the entire story.

The set of sub-questions related to the big question of an act must be tributaries of the big question. They should be directly linked in order to create clarity and cohesion. As long as an act fully addresses the big question and its related set of sub-questions, there is no set time or length to an act.

THE FIRST ACT OF *THE FUGITIVE*

An act is a line of action leading to a culminating event. The big question is broken into a series of *directly* related sub-questions.

An act is a line of action that leads to a culminating event: a climax. It is as long is it needs to be in order to give a well-considered examination of the big question.		**First Act Big Question** Can Dr. Richard Kimble prove his innocence to the American judicial system?		**Related Sub-Questions** 1. Who is Dr. Kimble? 2. How does he relate to his wife? 3. How did the murder occur? 4. Why do the police not believe Kimble? 5. Why can't he successfully defend himself? 6. How does Kimble handle himself under the pressure of police interrogation? 7. Will he be found innocent in a court of law?
	=		=	

In *The Fugitive,* the big question of the first act is: can Kimble prove his innocence to the American judicial system? The line of action of the first act addresses the big question. Kimble's immediate problem is with the local police and district attorney's office. He must prove his innocence in a court of law; and when he cannot, he is put in chains and sent to jail. The central dramatic question of *The Fugitive* is whether Kimble can prove his innocence, not only to the traditional authorities, but to everyone in his life, including the medical profession, the Feds (embodied in the antagonist, Detective Gerard), and society at large. He wants to clear his name across the board.

The big question of the first act of *The Fugitive* is broken up into related sub-questions: What is Dr. Kimble's life and world about? How does he relate to his wife? What does he do for a living? How did the murder occur? Why do the police not believe him? Why can't he defend himself successfully, even though they do not believe him? How does Kimble handle himself under the pressure of police interrogation?

There are obviously many possible sub-questions under the umbrella of the big question. The sub-questions should make sense to the author, first and foremost. Since complexity is an important tenet of the character-driven screenplay, these sub-questions should have substance, depth, and surprise. The screenwriter must then take each sub-question and translate it into a compelling, dramatic scene. Each scene in the screenplay should address one sub-question. Therefore, if a writer settles on a big question and fifteen sub-questions for an act, he or she will need to write fifteen scenes, at the very least, to fully address each sub-question.

CREATING STRUCTURE: THE CHAIN OF TASKS FOR THE SCREENWRITER

1. The unconscious imagination (flow) must be given a focus. The writer does this by discovering a purpose and using it as a guide for selecting what to use from the flow.

2. The flow selected must then be arranged and proportioned by the writer to make a good story. To do this the writer chooses a central dramatic question. The central dramatic question will give the writer a way to create a beginning, middle, and end.

3. The story must be broken into acts. Each act must have clarity. To do this the writer chooses a big question for each act.

4. Each act must be broken down into scenes. To do this the writer chooses sub-questions. Each sub-question is then translated into a compelling, dramatic scene. The number of sub-questions is often equal to the number of scenes.

"What If?" Questions on Index Cards

If I was paid a handsome sum to write sub-questions for the big question of the first act of *The Fugitive*—can Kimble prove his innocence to the American judicial system?—my sub-questions would be very different than those that exist because I would naturally be fascinated by different aspects of this story. I am a different person than the original writers; I have different likes and dislikes, different views of our existence, different themes, images, ideas, feelings, characters, and stories that haunt me.

I might choose to believe that Kimble had a lousy relationship with his wife. That she would get drunk and slept around. Perhaps he is a marvelous doctor, a great humanitarian, but one night his rage at his wife got the best of him and he struck her; he has been filled with guilt and shame ever since. Maybe on the night Kimble's wife was killed, he was on a date with another woman. And his lover is a wonderful person, someone he should definitely marry, but Kimble cannot give over to her. Maybe Kimble's wife lost their baby because of a prenatal accident, caused by one of her drunken nights, and there are cobwebs about that issue.

The changes I am suggesting for the first act of *The Fugitive* are declarative sentences, not questions. Eventually, when I go deeper into structuring an act, I turn these statements into questions. I change everything into a question because it creates a "what if?" possibility, a very effective way to conjure flow. I arrange and proportion my set of sub-questions according to their impact and intensity. I often write the set of sub-questions down on index cards and rearrange them, leaving them overnight, looking at them in the morning to access the new order.

It is important to orchestrate the acts so there is variety in the pacing, rhythm, and tempo. This strategy is similar to that of works of classical music, which are often divided into various movements, such as andante or allegro. Without the variety in pacing, the viewer will soon feel that the film is static and not progressing and lose interest. An intense scene should be followed by one that is less intense. Fast-paced scenes should be given counterpoint by following them with slow-moving scenes. A scene that is heavy in dialogue is often followed by a montage, to give the film some "breathing space."

Another strategy is to build an act like a fugue, slow and steady, using repetition. Or the act could also be a series of crescendos. A script is akin to a musical composition in many ways. I have actually asked students to sing a screenplay—a great exercise because it makes them aware that there is a tempo and rhythm to any structure.

I now make a new set of sub-questions based on the above statements. Who is Dr. Kimble? Does Kimble love his wife today? Did he ever love his wife? Why does he seem to be so guilty? Can he love anymore? How does he deal with his wife's death when he discovers it? There could obviously be many more sub-questions for the act, but for the sake of illustration I will limit them.

To address my new sub-questions I begin by opening the act with a scene in which Dr. Kimble performs a very difficult operation with great success. At the same time, I show that he is not open to receiving praise, which immediately raises a question in the audience's mind. Why can't he enjoy success? I can answer that question right away or just let it sit. I choose to let it go unanswered—a tease keeps the audience intrigued. With this introduction I have addressed the first question on my list: Who is Dr. Kimble? Now of course this is a huge question, and my entire screenplay could address this question, but I choose to present him in a nutshell: a great doctor and humanitarian, who is emotionally stuck. I have other storylines I want to introduce and I don't want to spend too much time on this one. I want the audience to know there are many threads to the story and give them a glimpse of each one—right from the top. How much dramatic time I give to those threads in the setup will tell an audience what to expect in terms of their relative importance.

If in the first act, I give twenty minutes of screen time to Kimble's skills as a doctor, and only five minutes to the murder of his wife, it would obviously lead the audience to anticipate more story about Kimble's professional life than about his relationship with his wife. The more screen time that is given to a character or plotline in the setup, the more payoff the audience will expect for that character or plotline.

Information: How Much to Give and When to Give It

Storytelling is always a matter of how much information to give in order to continually increase the audience's attention. If a writer gives too much dramatic information early on, the story will lose its mystery and the audience will become bored. It is not sufficient to just capture the audience's mind, you must also capture their imagination. If too much information is given, or if it is too literal, then the viewer's imagination will not be triggered. On the other hand, if there is not enough dramatic information, the audience's interest will drop because they will have no understanding of what is going on. They will have no context in which to track the events that follow. Too little information also stalls a sense of dramatic progression. The viewer must struggle too hard to make emotional and intellectual sense of a story—all is submerged, too subtle, lacks clarity, and a proposition has not been clearly set forth.

It is difficult to find the right balance. Subtlety is often the greatest weakness of beginning writers. Many beginners truly believe they are evoking and suggesting with great majesty, when in fact their subtlety is really creating a lack of clarity. A novice often thinks: "I shouldn't be too obvious, I want the audience to perceive how graceful, how subtle I can be." However, he or she learns, all too painfully, after a screening of the film, that the viewer is thinking just the opposite: "how pretentious, amateurish, unknowing, poorly examined, and unclear this is." A writer is better off writing too much and trimming, rather than underwriting and then being forced to excavate later on. The more information you have to begin with, the more ways you can trim, arrange, and proportion it. The less information you have to begin with, the less clever you can be in presenting it.

Returning to the revision of *The Fugitive,* the next thing I introduce is Kimble with a beautiful woman, at an atmospheric restaurant, having a marvelous time. After dinner, just as they are about to enter her apartment, obviously to have an intense round of lovemaking, Kimble stops suddenly and tells her he cannot go up tonight. She asks why not? Kimble is cryptic, "I just need to get some sleep. Been a long day."

Can Kimble love anymore? I addressed this sub-question by jump cutting to a strip joint. Kimble is getting very drunk as some hooker/dancer flirts with him.

Next is a flashback. We see Kimble, ten years earlier. He is with a vital, beautiful woman—his wife before she lost her youth—playing on the beach, obviously in love. Kimble produces a ring. She agrees to marry him. He is delighted. I have addressed the sub-question: did he ever love his wife?

Cut to Kimble doing a late night round with his patient. A resident notices he reeks of alcohol. Kimble does his best to cover up. We cut to scotch being poured in a glass. It is his wife, late at night at the Kimble's home. She has aged badly, and is hollowed out by her alcoholism. She and Kimble are in the midst of a fight. She is drunk, he is sober and tells her that she needs to stop drinking. As they argue we learn that she lost a child because of an alcohol-induced fall. But it is not so simple. Earlier that same night she had thought she was in premature labor. She had tried to find her husband for help but he was too busy with work, and she had to ask a neighbor to take her to the hospital. She never delivered that night, and upon returning home, began to drink because she felt neglected and unloved. Her drinking led to the bad fall. Both Kimble and his wife feel terrible guilt about the loss of the child. In these scenes, I have addressed the sub-question: why is he so guilty?

We cut back to Kimble downing a pint of vodka, out of control, while driving home to his suburban house. As he enters the house, he hears rumbling upstairs. Suddenly a one-armed man attacks Kimble. He struggles but is knocked unconscious.

When Kimble awakes, still drunk, he discovers his wife dead, brutally strangled. He dials the phone. We cut to his girlfriend in bed. Her phone rings. She answers and there is silence on the other end. Kimble cannot speak and hangs up. I have addressed the sub-question of how he reacted when he found his wife dead. We cut back to the girlfriend, she is confused and keeps saying "Hello?" She hangs up but seems to intuit something.

The police arrive and question Kimble. He is drunk and they note it. They have a record of him beating his wife. As they interview him at the station house, we see a flashback of the night he beat his wife and we learn another thing about the couple: they have not slept together for years. I hadn't planned on including this information, but I think about it, like it, and keep it.

I realize at this point in my process that the second act is going to be about Kimble and his girlfriend. This is another thing that I did not anticipate in my list of sub-questions. I am satisfied with my work because interesting discoveries are evolving from a conscious list of sub-questions. From past experience, I know this is a good groove to be in.

Great Structure Is Built on Great Stakes

As you can see, I took my sub-questions and arranged them to suit my big question and to hold the audience's attention. New sub-questions and directions popped up along the way; the ones I liked, I kept. I did not string the sub-questions together the way they occurred to me initially. I rearranged them, using my instincts. I had to make decisions about how much dramatic time to give to certain sub-questions. I chose to briefly present his relationship with his girlfriend before I got into the sub-questions of his wife and whether or not he loves her. Why? I gave more time to the wife's relationship with him simply because it illuminates Kimble's emotional baggage and has greater impact and resonance. In dramatic terms, Kimble and his wife, have greater stakes than Kimble and his girlfriend. They were husband and wife, they lost a child together, and they inflicted terrible pain on each other over a long period of time. There is greater jeopardy in a relationship with such a history or backstory because there is so much more to lose and no easy way out for both characters. When examining choices for constructing an act, a writer should always make choices that have the greatest stakes. Without high stakes, a scene will lack its full dramatic potential and simply lie flat, no matter how much "doctoring" a screenwriter does in revisions.

The biggest challenge when constructing an act is to make sure the big question grabs the audience's attention and contributes something original and truthful. It is crucial to not get lost in the subset of questions, and lose sight of the big question. Sub-questions must always relate back to the big question, giving it more complexity and resonance. This is not to suggest that one should be overly schematic; an act structure and its central line of action are not strictly an engineering problem. Digression is often of great value and can "fill out" an act. Again, it is a backwards and forwards process of how much or little to include and how clear, obscure, linear, literal, or suggestive a writer should be.

It is helpful to write the big question of an act on a piece of paper, and hang it on the wall. Allow for the possibility that it may change as the task of arranging and proportioning an act is executed. Like anything else, a big question can evolve, and if it does, this change should be embraced, especially if it will make the whole act better.

Each Act Provides More Information about the Characters

The second act of a screenplay introduces new complications for the major characters by placing more obstacles in their way. Essentially every act, no matter what its number or placement, is about creating more complications, finding obstacles to create more conflict, or increasing stakes and putting more pressure on the characters. However, in the character-driven screenplay, structuring is not just about new twists and turns of plot, it is about presenting new and ever more compelling revelations about the characters and the world of the story.

The priority is on imparting the ideas, feelings, and thoughts of the characters. To do this effectively, the writer must present the information in a dramatic way, through conflict and mental actions, such as seduction, confrontation, lying, etc. rather than physical actions, i.e., punching someone in the nose. As each act unfolds, the "reveals" about character and world accumulate, building steadily and reaching a climax. This accumulation of character and world reveals is the very essence of the character-driven screenplay. The screenwriter trusts that this tactic will be fulfilling to an audience; the accumulation of dramatic reveals "is" the story. The strength of the character-driven screenplay is that it allows an audience to get to know a particular set of characters and their world in a deep and meaningful way. It offers the intensified experience that many people seek when they come to the movies.

In *The Fugitive* the big question of the second act is whether Kimble will find the one-armed man by himself, through his own ingenuity and determination. It is broken into a set of sub-questions: What does he do with freedom, once he escapes the train crash? How will he outsmart the police? How will he track down the one-armed man? And so on. You will notice that these sub-questions have less to do with the character of Kimble and more to do with the physical actions necessary to overcome the increasing pressure of being a fugitive, such as running from the train, breaking free of his chains, jumping into rivers, and surviving death-defying falls. In my version, because of the changes to the first act, the second act will be very different. There will be much more material about Kimble's relationship with his girlfriend. We left the first act turning the audience's focus in the direction of this relationship, so we are now obliged to address it. Focusing on this relationship will give me the opportunity to dig deeper into Kimble's character, to show more of what is going on inside him, fulfilling the aesthetic intentions of the character-driven screenplay. I imagine a second act big question: Can Kimble and his girlfriend prove his innocence? Because the police believe Kimble's motive for killing his wife was to be free to be with his girlfriend, she is now in some way also implicated in the murder. She becomes a major character for the second act, significantly changing the focus from the 1993 version.

In the 1993 movie the third act begins when Kimble discovers that the one-armed has been hired by someone else. Kimble then tries to bring resolution to the big question of the act: who is the mastermind behind the one-armed man? In my version, it might not be so simple. We may discover that he can never find justice and he breaks with his girlfriend because he loves her too much to drag her further into his troubled life. He disappears entirely, to an unknown destination. This ending would be fitting for the character-driven form. It is open-ended, showing the complexity of life and the ambiguity of existence.

A screenwriter uses act structure to make the story cohesive and also to fulfil purpose. But the structure must be discovered along with the other elements of the screenplay. If a formula is blindly applied, the writer may eviscerate precisely what he or she is trying to express, because the "rules " of the formula may not allow for it.

11

The One-Act Form: Evoking Inescapability

If a screenwriter decides to use a one-, two-, or three-act structure, as we have noted, each choice automatically gives a film a specific feel and worldview. Let's examine what the one-act structure can do for a movie.

The one-act form has one central line of action. In *Vagabond,* Mona wants her freedom and pursues it without compromise until her death. In *Mean Streets,* Charlie seeks to meld the demands of his world with the demands of his heart. The line of action is never broken during the course of the movie in the one-act form because there are no act breaks to "break it," and spin the action in another direction. With only one line of action for such a long period of dramatic time, the spectator sinks, unconsciously, into a hypnotic state. A feeling of the preordained settles in like evening fog because there is no major shift in the trajectory of the main plotline. Since there is only one umbrella to hold over the entire story, there is a lot of room for the detailing of character and world. The writer is not forced "to squeeze it all in" because there is no pressure to get to another act, another arc of action.

Generally, with two or three acts, the screenwriter must make many more adjustments in plot for the story to be cohesive and maintain a dramatic logic. The alignment of plot becomes the greatest priority. Because of this impulse to hammer all events into a dramatic logic, the writer will often violate the truth of a character. In the effort to make two, three, or more acts fit together, the screenwriter will often "fudge" characters, forcing them to do something that is not true to their nature. For example, in *Rushmore* by Wes Anderson and Owen Wilson, Max Fischer is clearly set up in the first and second act to be a character who is self-destructively obsessive. He is thrown out of school because of this dark side of his character and he engages in a near murderous competition with Blume (Bill Murray) for a clearly inappropriate and unavailable love interest—his teacher, Miss Cross. In the third act, Max suddenly comes to understand that his obsessiveness is destructive and decides that Margaret Yang, a student his age, is a healthier choice in terms of love interest. Why does Max make such a sudden, unbelievable, and contrived change? Because it is apparent, that in order to make the third act into a successful resolution, the writers pushed him to make this change; they violated the truth of his character and forced him to service the plot. With the one-act form, the writer is not under the pressure to make so many variables, acts, and plot points cohesive, so there is usually a more truthful depiction of character.

In general, the simpler the story, the more complex the characterizations in a screenplay. And the reverse is also true, the more complex the story, the simpler the characters. When characters just exist and seemingly "hang out," they will reveal a lot about themselves. Because there is only one line of action, in the one-act structure, characters have more of an opportunity to just "hang out." The one-act form gives the viewers something often not available in real life—lots of time to spend, get to know, and bond with another person, in this case a character in a film. If characters are on a mad dash to the next plot point, they will show us less about themselves—they are too preoccupied. Just imagine meeting a person for the first time on the job—an air traffic controller. If you spent two hours together at work, what would you really learn about that person? Not much. He or she would be too busy working. If you spent two hours stuck in an elevator, you would probably learn a great deal more about that same person. This is precisely what happens when you simplify story: you allow your characters to breathe by creating an environment where they can expose more layers of themselves to an audience. Also, since the one-act form never has an act break, there is no visceral release for an audience that act breaks traditionally provide. The stasis of the act is never broken, evoking a feeling of inevitability—"that everything in life is already determined."

Examples of One-Act Films

To follow are examples of two profoundly resonant one-act films: Agnes Varda's *Vagabond* and Martin Scorsese's *Mean Streets*.

Vagabond

Vagabond is about a drifter—a young, ordinary woman. The opening scene is of a farm worker discovering her frozen to death in a ditch. The narrator tells us, "Her name is Mona. I know little about her myself, but it seems to me she came from the sea." The story takes place during the last months of her life. It starts with Mona bathing in the sea on a cool day. She appears like a force of nature, driven by something primitive and determined, and as mysterious as her namesake, the Mona Lisa. She espouses no grand ambitions or proclaims no great insights or belief systems, but is nakedly honest in her pursuit of freedom.

Freedom has its price and Varda lets us know this without ever making Mona's story an allegory, parable, or thesis. Because of the flashback in the beginning of the film, we know Mona has died, setting the context in which to view the last few months of her life, the body of the film. It soon becomes apparent her death is inevitable. She wants her freedom at the cost of having a warm bath, a steady income, security, health, constancy. She finds work where she can, sleeps in people's houses, and takes lovers for a night or two and then moves on.

We are never given the one character reveal about her personality or background that would explain Mona's drive toward self-destruction. The style of the script is naturalistic—things are scientifically observed. People tell us that Mona smells badly and needs a bath, we see her dirty fingers roll one cigarette after another, we watch her pitch her tent on cold days, yet the story has a terrible beauty. Characters project themselves on Mona. They judge her wandering as "withering," romanticize her behavior, or simply shrug with acceptance. Finally, when caught in a fire where she is squatting for the night, she runs for safety into the cold winter without her coat and slips in the mud. Freezing, wet, and muddy, she trips into a ditch; weary, shivering, she passes out. This is the climax. The story ends where it begins, and when we return to the same place we are faced with the same question we had at the start of the film: who is this woman? The irony is that after spending 105 minutes with her and hearing what many people have to say about her, we still do not know her, even though we have a tremendous amount of information about her many layers of character. A haunting, Rashomon tale, its hypnotic one-act structure illuminates Varda's overall purpose: to explore total freedom and its inescapable bondage.

Mean Streets

In Martin Scorsese's *Mean Streets,* Charlie says to Johnny Boy, "You don't fuck around with the infinite." And that is precisely what these characters do. Charlie, a practicing Catholic, with a heart too soft to be a petty hood on the streets of New York, is up against a monolith—the rules of Little Italy, which are manifested in the character of his uncle, a small-time don. Charlie is in love with Teresa, who his uncle disapproves of because she is "sick in the head"—she has epilepsy. Charlie has a self-destructive, out of control friend, Johnny Boy, who he also loves, and wants to save.

As with all one-act films, the central dramatic question and the big question merge. The central question of the film is whether Charlie will follow his heart or the rules of the mean streets. The audience waits for him to make a choice throughout the entire film. Charlie keeps all his balls in the air—Johnny Boy, Teresa, and his uncle—until the climax of the film, when Johnny Boy is shot and killed. It seems as if Charlie does not want to make a choice, but unfortunately he has to. The one-act structure works well for this story since it communicates the feeling of inescapability.

The audience knows, almost from the start, that Charlie, a man who should be a priest not a hood, is on a collision course, so the ending of this film is inevitable, inescapable, and predictable. The writers (Martin Scorsese and Mardik Martin) detail the characters and their surroundings with entertaining humor, which is a more American, optimistic approach than the cooler, pessimistic, and ironic tone that Varda uses to explore the world of *Vagabond.* Scorsese's superb technique integrates very well with the substance and form of his film.

This film has so much substance because the one-act form allowed for the luxury of developing the characters. Again, since the writers did not have the burden of getting to the next plot point, they had the dramatic time necessary to give more information and show the audience something unique, idiosyncratic, and surprising about the main characters. They did not push the characters around, they just let them be and allowed them to display who they are—to chat, to eat a meal together, to take joy rides in the middle of the night. The audience was allowed to have fun with the characters; they were spontaneous, impulsive, and unpredictable—not mere constructions used to serve a plot. Because the audience gets a chance to know the characters so well, when the movie does come to a climax, there is a far greater resonance. When the main characters meet with destruction, the audience grieves their loss more deeply, as they would with anyone they have had the chance to get to know so well.

MAKING A ONE-ACT MOVIE INTO A THREE-ACT MOVIE

EXERCISE

Take *Mean Streets,* a one-act structure, and revise it, using an outline form, so the story has three acts. This exercise should take no more than two or three double-spaced pages to accomplish. Revising a one-act film to conform to a three-act structure is a great exercise to bring greater awareness of how structure controls content.

Here is an example of a revised version of *Mean Streets* to show you how this exercise should work. Obviously, when you revise, use your own ideas and choices.

To make *Mean Streets* into a traditional three-act screenplay, the first act would have to happen in about thirty minutes of screen time. Deeper revelations of character and the world of the story would have to be cut in order to get to "the moment" of the first act when Johnny Boy is shot and killed for not paying his debts. The second act could be about Charlie confronting those who took part in Johnny's death and exposing his true feelings to the world. Charlie would stand up to his uncle and declare he wants to marry his girlfriend. He would have to pay the price for his rebellion. He could be gunned down, or almost gunned down, leading to action scenes. In the third act he would learn that in fighting the enemy he has become the enemy. He has only one option left, to get out, start another life with his girlfriend, in Montana.

This structure could yield interesting results. There is a lot of "spectacle value" (shoot-outs and fights) that the moving picture captures so well. And it would translate Charlie's problems into simpler, more black-and-white terms. It would make the spectator feel that change is always possible, that one man can create his own destiny, and that Charlie can see his tragic flaw and do something about it. It would bring more romanticism to the story. And it would uphold the status quo in terms of morality. But we would lose depth of characterization, certainly for Johnny Boy, and it would have a very different meaning than a one-act structure.

12

The Two-Act Form: The Open-Ended Resolution

Suppose we were to make *The Fugitive* into two acts instead of three. If we did, we would immediately have more breathing space for the characters, since they do not have to be pushed as hard to another act. If the writer examines only two big questions in two hours (the average length of a movie today), there are more opportunities for the author to expose the thoughts and feelings of characters, and observe the world of the story. And because the audience is given the visceral release of an act break, the viewer has the feeling that things can change, that we can make choices in life.

However, unlike the three-act form, the two-act structure steadfastly avoids resolving choices. Instead it communicates that all choices have consequences, and depending on the individual, these choices can be perceived as positive or negative. Making a choice unleashes new forces, and it is very difficult to predict what will happen once those forces are unleashed. The two-act structure implies that we are doomed to choose and it is unlikely that all will be restored to order, once we have made a choice. The two-act form forces the audience to resolve the story and discover and examine their own values.

If we were to cut off *The Fugitive* at two acts instead of three, it would go as far as the moment when Dr. Kimble discovers the true identity of the one-armed man and that he was hired by someone else to kill Kimble's wife. The dumbfounded, stunned Dr. Kimble, would realize how sinister and complex his problem is, and that if he wants to vindicate himself, he must continue to struggle on his own, even if the odds are against him. There is hope here. But the story is not resolved. Kimble may or may not vindicate himself with this new information, but the viewer would not be allowed to witness how things ultimately turn out. There would be many unanswered or unaddressed questions at the end of the film: Who could be the person behind the one-armed man? Will Kimble ever discover this person? Can justice become a reality for Kimble? Is there any justice at all in this world? What would I, the spectator, do if I were Dr. Kimble? What would I believe? How would I deal with all of this? Would I continue to fight to vindicate myself? Or would I just give up, escape to another country, and start all over again? And so on.

With the two-act structure, there is a bittersweet ending, Kimble has acquired substantial evidence and perhaps he can get Gerard off his back because of this information, but it is bitter because he has not seen justice. It is open-ended, and forces the audience to make a decision about what Kimble should do next and resolve the film for themselves as they walk out of the theater.

Examples of Two-Act Films

The two-act structure, a form used most often in theater today, gives the viewer set up and confrontation without resolution. Resolution becomes the responsibility of the audience. Viewers are forced to judge and reflect using their own values.

Jules and Jim

Jules and Jim, adapted by Francois Truffaut and Jean Gruault from the novel by Henri-Pierre Roche, has a two-act structure. Jules and Jim are close friends. Jim is French, Jules is Austrian. The first act quickly establishes their relationship with narration, montage, and a whimsical score by Georges Delerue. When Catherine, a haunting, independent woman, enters their world, we are introduced to the big question of the first act: will Jules succeed in winning Catherine's hand? Jules politely warns Jim that Catherine is his girlfriend and that he should make no advances. Jim respects Jules' wish and a tension is created between these two men.

Jim advises Jules that Catherine does not appear to be the marrying type, that she will never be happy in this world. Despite Jim's advice, Jules proposes to Catherine. Catherine is unstable, provocative, easily bored, and feels suffocated by the constraints of a committed and monogamous relationship. She is also exciting, charismatic, impulsive, and fun—she attracts and repels at the same time. The act ends with the answer to the big question. Jules announces that Catherine has accepted his proposal, but it may be a mixed victory. Evidently, for Jules, Catherine is worth the risk; he follows his heart, not his mind.

Truffaut creates an interesting bridge between the first and second act using a montage and narration about World War I. Newsreel footage of German and French soldiers in the trenches, being brutally gunned down on the battlefields, is intercut with Jules, a German solider, and Jim, a French solider, both writing letters back home to their lovers. Jim confesses to his mistress, Gilberte, "sometimes in the trenches, I am afraid of killing Jim." This bridge lasts for approximately three pages of script before we get into the second act.

The second act begins after the war, when Jim comes to visit Jules and Catherine and their young daughter, Sabine, at their new home in a small village on the Rhine. Jules and Catherine have been married for some time and we can only imagine what happened in the first years of their marriage; Truffaut does not show us this part of the story. The complication and tension builds in this act when we learn that Catherine is not satisfied with her marriage to Jules, she has had affairs, and she now wants Jim. Jules is passive and accepting; Jim, more assertive, falls in love with Catherine. The big question of the second act is put into place: will Jim win Catherine in a way Jules could not? Like all relationships with Catherine, the affair with Jim is rocky, but dramatic and exciting. Catherine breaks from Jim and returns to Jules with passionate embraces, tears, and kisses that are immensely seductive. Jules is hopelessly in love with Catherine and suffers much to keep her.

Catherine and Jim unite one more time, but Jim finally breaks off with Catherine, returning to his ever loyal Gilberte, arguing that he and Catherine "played with the very sources of life, and we have failed." Catherine is furious at being rejected. Time passes and Jim reunites with Jules and Catherine in Paris. During this reunion, Catherine is on edge; she is wild and reckless with her new car, weaving in and out of a deserted Paris square, like "a horse without a rider or a phantom ship." In a private moment when Jim tries to explain why it did not work between them, a furious Catherine pulls a gun on him. He grabs it and escapes. The climax to the act occurs a short while later when Jim goes for a ride with Catherine; she drives off a bridge, a willful act of suicide, and they die together. The film concludes with the narrator, an "objective voice," telling us that Jules' "friendship with Jim had no equivalent in love." Catherine, ever the boundary-tester, wanted her ashes "to be scattered to the winds from the top of a hill...but it was not allowed."

The two-act structure and gentle tone of the film, as well as Truffaut's vitality, humor, and deep compassion for every character in the story, all contribute to the power of this open-ended story with haunting resonance. The two-act structure allows plenty of room for character exploration. Each act has a clear line of action. The first act is "will Jules marry Catherine?" The second act is "can Jim win Catherine in a way that Jules could not?" There is no central protagonist per se, Jules and Jim blend into one protagonist, their goals are the same—to win Catherine. Catherine is the antagonist, her goal is to have a "pure" relationship, one free of hypocrisy and compromise, which is in conflict with Jules and Jim who are willing to settle for a relationship filled with compromise, contradiction, and sacrifice. "Will Jules or Jim ever find a satisfying and committed relationship with Catherine?" is the central dramatic question of the film.

The two-act structure works well here because it supports what the film is trying to communicate—the complexity and difficulty of making a choice when it comes to relationships, and how this indecisiveness entraps. We all want a partner that excites us, but at the same time we want someone who will be stable and committed. Life experience has shown many of us that this is nearly impossible to find in the same person. The two-act structure gives an open-ended feeling to the film. The author of the story does not want to judge and the two-act structure supports this ambiguity, illuminating the layers of contradiction that exist in love affairs.

Full Metal Jacket

Full Metal Jacket, with a screenplay by Stanley Kubrick, Michael Herr, and Gustav Hasford, is a very clean example of the two-act structure. The big question of the first act is baldly stated within the first ten minutes of the script when Sargent Hartman shouts to his recruits, "If you ladies leave my island, if you survive recruit training, you will be a weapon. You will be a minister of death praying for war!" The big question is whether these recruits will make it through basic training.

Two recruits are given more screen time than others: Private Joker (Matthew Modine) and Gomer Pyle (Vincent D'Onofrio). Private Joker clearly has "issues with authority." He mimics John Wayne in the middle of one of Sergeant Hartman's tirades, rebelling against the power structure. Joker is quickly punished by Hartman, which tells us to watch the development between these two characters; their opposing natures and goals foreshadow conflict. Next is Pyle's turn: the sergeant hammers away at him, shouting, "Wipe that grin off your face, soldier!" Pyle can't, and the sergeant proceeds to choke him. The action is from Joker's perspective and he is the emotional center of the film.

A major progression occurs in the first act when the sergeant assigns Joker to the task of training Pyle. Joker's training style is the complete opposite of Hartman's; Joker is kind and patient with Pyle, and there are positive results. The kind, peace lover (Joker) helps the spastic misfit (Pyle) find his strength. However, the authors do not want this relationship to be a simple matter. The sergeant discovers Pyle hiding a doughnut in his footlocker, and instead of punishing Pyle, he punishes the entire squad. Later, in a brutal gang attack, Pyle is beaten by all the recruits. The last attacker is Joker, who gives Pyle the most brutal beating of all. Their relationship is clearly complex: Joker has rage as well as compassion toward Pyle. This action unleashes new forces in the story, and Pyle becomes emotionally isolated from his squad. The pressure of the isolation forces Pyle to break from reality; he starts talking to his gun.

The sergeant discovers Pyle has a natural talent as a marksman and is delighted. The story progresses as we see the recruits begin to operate without the aid and instruction of the sergeant; their training is finally showing some results. The final sequence of the act occurs when Joker has fire watch for the evening, and discovers Pyle in the bathroom, holding a semi-automatic weapon with live rounds. Joker tries to disarm Pyle but does not succeed. The sergeant appears and demands that Pyle give him the gun. The sequence ends abruptly when Pyle kills the sergeant and commits suicide—the climax of the act. This climax leaves open the question of how this training experience will affect Joker.

The length of the act is approximately forty-seven minutes. The most resonant aspect of the first act is the characterization of the drill sergeant; he is specific and surprising. Unlike the cliché of the genre, he is not a tough guy with a heart of gold, he is a tough guy with a heart wrapped in a full metal jacket—undiscriminating, lacking compassion, a precisely honed killing machine, yet effective at his job and powerful.

The setting of the second act (approximately sixty-six minutes) is the war zone of Vietnam. Joker is up against an antagonist—the army as a whole—that manifests itself in many characters including the editor of *Stars and Stripes;* Animal Mother, the Marine killing machine; Cowboy, the ineffectual officer and leader of his squad; and a passing general who notices the peace symbol on Joker's helmet and demands that he "get with the program."

The loss of Sergeant Hartman is unfortunately felt in the second act and the collection of new characters diffuses the story. The magnetic character of Hartman galvanized the story, gave it clarity and sharpness. But Kubrick wants to examine how an individual navigates the world of the Marines, so he is willing to sacrifice a highly magnetic character to fulfill his purpose. One of the difficulties of screenwriting is that you often have to sacrifice a favorite scene or character, to keep another, even if it weakens some aspect of your script.

The big question of the second act is clearly presented at the beginning of the act when a soldier observes that Joker "ain't been in the shit, because he ain't got the stare. The thousand-yard stare." The question is: will Joker see real combat and will he be changed by it? Joker navigates the world of the Marines for much of the second act as the Joker we knew from the first act: brash, rebellious, and still out of touch with the killer side of himself.

This "plot-free" strategy allows us to learn many details about men at war—how they twist the truth about combat, fake body counts, dehumanize all in their path, participate in a form of madness—all part of a monolithic killing machine. This stasis is finally broken when Joker's squad is ambushed by a sniper who begins to take out, one at a time, his fellow men.

A progression occurs because the war has finally become a personal matter for Joker. His tactics must change, he can no longer stand back and be a wry, ironic observer; he is "in the shit." When Cowboy, the squad leader, is shot by the sniper, Joker "wants pay back." The act climaxes when Rafterman, a photographer who has never seen combat, shoots the sniper; she is revealed to be a petite, pretty woman. The sniper lies in front of Joker, dying, suffering a slow, agonizing death. The denouement centers around the question of whether Joker will kill the mortally wounded sniper. Animal Mother advises "fuck her, let her rot." "We can't just leave her here," Joker replies, reacting to her suffering. "Cowboy is wasted, you're fresh out of friends," retorts Mother. And, to make matters more complex, the sniper speaks up in English, barely audible through her death wheeze, "Shoot me."

Finally, Joker fires a round wasting the sniper and making his first confirmed kill. He has become a soldier. But there is an ambiguity to his action. Has he killed the sniper to put her out of her misery? To avenge his friend's death? To perform his duties as a Marine? To win the approval of his fellow soldiers? Has Joker and his squad treated the sniper with less respect and dignity because she is Asian and a woman? Is Joker unconscious to his misogyny and racial prejudice? Kubrick does not answer these questions. The authors force the audience to resolve these matters for themselves, and there is no easy answer. The two-act structure helps to communicate this ambiguity.

13

The Three-Act Structure: Order Is Restored

The three-act structure is based on something that became popular in the theater over a hundred years ago: the well-made play. The well-made play, according to Edward Wright, director and author of *Understanding Today's Theater* is a "name given to those plays written in the mid-nineteenth century which followed a set-pattern or formula in their construction." He goes on to say, "it now has a derogatory meaning."

This three-act formula can be traced to a French playwright, Eugene Scribe, who from 1815 to 1861 wrote or collaborated on over five hundred plays, and whose purpose was to entertain the masses. He clearly sacrificed depth of characterization for plot and suspense. His formula dictated that every play should have a clear setup about the main characters and their world, followed by many logical but unexpected plot reversals with continuous and mounting suspense. There should be a big scene that is anticipated from the beginning of the play; and then a logical and believable resolution in which all is restored to order and the status quo—morally, socially, and politically—reaffirmed. This dependable structure served Scribe's purpose, and so in that sense he was a success.

Scribe's student, Victorien Sardou (1831–1908), also a very popular French playwright (*Cleopatra, Odette, L'Affaire des Poissons*) took Scribe's rules for structure and made it into the formula we know today as the three-act structure, outlined by Syd Field in his book *The Screenwriter's Workbook:* Exposition, inciting moment, rising action, turning point, falling action, climax and denouement, and conclusion. Field translates Sardou's concepts into the formula traditionally followed today: Exposition becomes setup (pages 1–15 of a screenplay); the inciting moment is transformed into the first turning point marking the end of the first act (between pages 25–30); rising action, turning point, and falling action are reworked into Field's concept of the second act which is the "act of confrontation" (pages 30–90), in which the protagonist pursues an objective, meeting one complication after another, until the second turning point at the end of the second act (pages 75–90); the climax and denouement are in the third act (pages 110–115); the conclusion makes up the last five pages (pages 115–120). There is essentially no difference between the linear three-act structure most commonly used today in filmmaking and the concepts put forth by Scribe, and later made into a formula by Sardou, over a hundred years ago.

The demands of the linear three-act structure conflict with some of the major strengths of the character-centered screenplay, such as in-depth characterizations; questioning the order of things; and expressing the complexity of the world we live in and the consequences of the choices we make. The linear three-act structure, as it has traditionally been used, tends to cover up all of these complexities and prevents them from being successfully communicated. The three-act structure communicates that change is inevitable and when it does occur, it will always be for the good.

Movies such as *The Fugitive* are indeed entertaining and successful, largely because of the successful application of the three-act formula. But *The Fugitive* TV series presented a far more complex story, with a more layered protagonist. Although it is possible to write a linear three-act screenplay that has complex characters, as we will see with the example of *The Godfather*, it is very difficult because the formula demands that the story be plot-driven, linear, literal, and a precise amount of pages. If the character-driven screenwriter chooses to use the three-act structure, it is best to discard the above formula. Woody Allen was very successful in doing this in *Crimes and Misdemeanors*, which we will analyze later in this chapter. He used the three-act structure but without a linear cause-and-effect plot. Instead, he used contingent causation and created subplots that were polyphonic.

Finally, as a skilled craftsperson, a character-driven screenwriter should be able to successfully execute any type of screenplay—character or plot-driven. Although the trend is clearly moving in the direction of the character-driven screenplay, the screenwriter should have a solid understanding of the principles of the linear three-act structure. This knowledge will help to avoid the traps inherent in the linear approach, and bring greater complexity to story and character, as in the case of *Crimes and Misdemeanors*.

Examples of Three-Act Films

Following are two examples of powerful three-act films: Francis Ford Coppola's *The Godfather* and Woody Allen's *Crimes and Misdemeanors*.

The Godfather

The Godfather is a classic example of how to use the three-act structure in a character-driven way. Its running time is 171 minutes, which means it should have approximately the same amount of pages in its screenplay form. The story is told from the point of view of Michael Corleone (Al Pacino), who is the emotional center of the movie. The three big questions for the three acts are as follows: 1.) Will Michael play a part in the Corleone family business? 2.) What specific role will he carve out for himself? 3.) Once committed to leading the family business, what type of king will he be? The central dramatic question is what price must Michael pay for being a part of the family.

There are many linear plotlines that directly intersect one another to push the story forward. There is the plotline of Michael, his involvement with the family and his girlfriend, Kay. There is the plotline of Don Vito Corleone (Marlon Brando) and his attempts to hold onto and consolidate power within his family, and among the five other Mafia families, his competitors. There are two other plotlines about the Don's sons, Sonny (James Caan) and Fredo (John Cazale), and how they try to be effective and valued members of the family. The last major plotline is about the Don's daughter, Connie (Talia Shire), and the difficulties she faces in her marriage to an abusive man. The screenwriters, Francis Coppola and Mario Puzo, intersect these plotlines, with great craft, to create dramatic progression and payoff for each one. Despite the linearity of the structure, which often takes away from the complexity of the film, these plotlines add resonance and fill out the story because the characters in each are so well developed and layered.

The first act begins with a wedding. This choice gives the screenwriters many opportunities to set up the world of Don Corleone: his responsibilities; his family members and their conflicts; the difficulties he faces with the law and competing families; the statesmanship he must possess in order to keep his family and friends supportive of his leadership. The Don is a king. He is a man of principles, he espouses the values most of us identify with as good and honorable: loyalty, courage, generosity, and respect. "A man who does not spend time with his family can never be a man," warns Corleone.

At the wedding, the Don waits for his son Michael to arrive. He will not allow a family portrait to be taken until he does. Michael makes his appearance with his girl-friend, Kay Adams (Diane Keaton), a woman who is clearly outside the world of the Corleones. Michael tells Kay the truth about his family: they can be ruthless and threaten with murder and violence in order to get their way in business. Michael tells her, "That's my family, Kay, that's not me." This information sets up Michael as a man who is aware of the differences between the right and wrong behavior of his family; he has an outsider's perspective. A question lingers in the viewer's mind at this point in the film: will Michael grow in this awareness or will he become just like his tribe?

Approximately forty-six minutes into the movie, after Don Corleone has been shot by a rival family, the first act ends and the second begins. The plotpoint that spins the action into the second act is when Michael comes out of Radio City Music Hall with Kay, while on a date, and discovers his father has been gunned down. Don Corleone's shooting marks the end of the first act because this event breaks the stasis of the world of the story. With Corleone disabled, there is a power vacuum in the family. The king has been shot. Who will now lead the family and the kingdom? Michael, upon discovering his father's attack, immediately runs to support his family during this crisis. Michael's action breaks the stasis of his character. He is no longer the loner or outsider of the family. New forces are unleashed. Once his father's life is in jeopardy, Michael discovers that he needs to be part of the family. He must do something about those feelings; come to terms with them through action. The love his father and family have given him must be returned.

Michael's reaction to his father's attack rings true, and therefore his transformation does not seem contrived; it springs from a basic human emotion—the loyalty we all feel toward our clan. We now learn that Michael's posturing in the first act, stating he is not his family, was his way to get attention. He now runs to help his family because he knows, on some level, that this is his moment to shine. Michael, it seems, needs to be a powerful man; he has a thirst for it. Before his father was shot, he could be powerful by being provocative and creating an image of himself as one who stands alone, strong, outside the family. Now that his father is wounded, he has another way to consolidate power. He can demonstrate to the other members of the family his leadership skills and fill the vacuum left by his father.

Michael is called into action in the second act, and the Big Question is what role will Michael play in the family, now that he has committed to them. Michael breaks off with Kay and protects his father, who is left alone in a hospital bed, vulnerable to the henchmen of a rival family. "I am with you now," Michael whispers in his father's ear, as his father lies in critical condition. Michael, during a family meeting in the Don's absence, shows he clearly has the best judgment among his siblings. Michael proposes there is only one solution to the family problem: Sollozzo, the family enemy, must be killed. It is the only way to end the war started by the attack on his father, he reasons. When his brothers, Tom (Robert Duvall) and Sonny agree with Michael's assessment, Michael goes one step further: he will personally kill Sollozzo.

Michael, after careful planning with other family members, succeeds in assassinating Sollozzo, along with a corrupt police captain. This action further defines the role Michael will play. He is an effective leader. After killing Sollozzo and the corrupt cop, Michael must go into exile; he must lie low until the shock waves of his bold action have subsided. While in exile in Sicily, Michael finds a bride. Soon, however, his past catches up with him, and his wife is assassinated in an act of revenge. The second act continues with the plotline of Sonny; he is ineffective as a leader of the family and is eventually gunned down. The deaths of Sonny and Michael's bride break the stasis of the act. With the loss of the brother who was leading the family in the Don's absence, there is clearly another power vacuum and Michael is again pulled back to provide stewardship for the family. Also, when Michael's bride is murdered, he loses the opportunity to start his own family, and another stasis is broken. The second act ends in approximately one hour and twenty minutes. The first and second acts require approximately two hours and five minutes, far longer than the standard Hollywood formula—thirty minutes for the first act, sixty minutes for the second act.

The third act, the act of resolution, begins with an act of closure. The Don calls for a meeting of the five warring families. Since his son, Sonny, was gunned down, the Don wants to call the war off. He proposes a peaceful solution, but declares that he will not forgive anyone, if his youngest son Michael is ever hurt. Also in the spirit of resolution, Michael reconciles with Kay and achieves his goal of starting his own family. After the Don announces his semi-retirement, Michael becomes the official head of the family.

Pumping new energy and youthful vision into the family business, Michael goes to Las Vegas to acquire a hotel and casino. Michael accomplishes this goal with a ruthlessness that seems to indicate that he is indeed like his family. This action addresses the central dramatic question about the price Michael will pay for being part of his family; he will become like them—just as ruthless. The climax of the act is when Michael, in a very premeditated and bloodless fashion, arranges for the murder of his brother-in-law, Carlo, who has betrayed the family and set up Sonny to be gunned down. Taking the law into his own hands, Michael witnesses Carlo's brutal death by strangulation. This is the climax of the act because it confirms that Michael, despite all of his strengths and positive qualities, has radically transformed. He will now murder not only outside his family but also inside it. In a sense, Michael is finally, completely and irrevocably, made a part of the family by killing Carlo. He crosses a line into a territory that extinguishes all the outsider awareness that we saw in him in the first act, when at the wedding, he told Kay, "That's my family, that's not me." The denouement to the act is when Michael lies to his wife, Kay, about murdering Carlo. With this action, Michael sets the stage to isolate himself emotionally from anyone in a trusting way. The trust he gave Kay in the first act is gone. Michael takes the last step of this rite of passage: he becomes "a man." He is the king, but he is totally alone.

The Godfather is a classic family drama. Its characters are fully developed and layered and elicit a complex response from the audience. The viewer is attracted and repelled by their actions and values. The actions of the characters as well as the plotlines all grow from a basic human emotion. In the film, melodrama ascends into tragedy.

In the end, like *Henry IV, Part I, The Godfather* is the story of a prince, Michael Corleone, who like prince Hal, must learn to do his duty. Like Hal, who proclaims, "I am not yet of Percy's mind, the Hotspur of the North; he that kills me some six or seven dozen of Scots at a breakfast, washes his hands, and says to his wife, 'Fie upon this quiet life! I want work,'" (*Henry IV, Part I,* II, 4, 103–107), Michael declares at the top of the movie that he is not like his family. At the end of the movie this proves to be utterly false. The adolescent, heroic posturing that gave Michael an individualistic, outsider identity in the first act is completely destroyed by the end of the third act.

As we can see *The Godfather* has a linear three-act structure. By adding so many plotlines and taking the time to fully develop the characters, the screenwriters created a lasting film. *Crimes and Misdemeanors* also employs the three-act form, but Woody Allen did not use a linear version. By doing so, he created a film with complexity and ambiguity.

Crimes and Misdemeanors

In this film the screenwriter and director, Woody Allen, uses the three-act structure to combine elements of melodrama and tragedy. There are two main contingent plotlines that run parallel to each other, never intersecting until the end of the film, and then, in only a very minor way. The characters are complex and they wrestle with many warring characteristics and needs. Allen uses the restorative qualities of the three-act structure in an ironic way. At the end of the film, on the surface, it appears everything has been restored to order, but the audience is aware that this is indeed not the case. The two main characters, Judah Rosenthal (Martin Landau) and Cliff

Stern (Woody Allen) have become disillusioned with themselves and the world they live in. All cannot so easily be brought back to equilibrium.

The central emotion of the film is guilt. Its central dramatic question is whether the eyes of God are always upon us. If someone commits a crime, will he or she, in one manner or another, be caught and made to suffer the consequences of his or her actions?

The two main plotlines concern the story of Judah and his unhappy mistress, Dolores Paley (Anjelica Huston) and Cliff's desire to win the heart of Halley Reed (Mia Farrow). The characters of Judah and Cliff—combined—are the protagonist of the film. Sometimes two or more characters will meld together to be the emotional center of a story, as a group, they perform exactly the same function as the traditional, single, protagonist. The two plotlines are tied together by theme: is there a higher power that governs our universe and does it always bring forth justice?

The first act (forty minutes) begins with the setup—through flashbacks and flash-forwards—of Judah. He is a highly respected doctor, citizen, and fundraiser; ironically, he is an ophthalmologist who turns a blind eye to his own behavior. The act begins with a benefit dinner, where Judah is the honored guest. Within the first five minutes of the film, much like *Citizen Kane,* the audience is baldly told the central dramatic question when Judah, during his guest of honor speech, tells the assembled crowd that he was raised in a religious family which taught him "the eyes of God are always upon us."

The inciting moment of the first act for the plotline of Judah is the moment when he stumbles upon a letter his mistress sent to his wife, with the intention of exposing their two-year affair, which he intercepts and keeps a secret. This moment immediately signals to the audience the big question of the first act for this plotline: how will Judah handle his mistress' demands? The second plotline of the first act begins with the setup of the character Cliff. Cliff, who has a cold and loveless marriage and likes to go to the movies with his niece, is an unsuccessful documentary filmmaker with a strong social conscience. He despises his brother-in-law Lester (Alan Alda), a highly successful yet soulless television comedy producer. The inciting moment for the plotline of Cliff happens when Cliff is offered a job by Lester, to be his biographer. The big question for this plotline is established: what will Cliff do about the lack of love and support in his life? Cliff reluctantly accepts Lester's offer, and while working on the project, he meets Halley, a producer hired by Lester, and is immediately smitten. Cliff convinces Halley to look at his labor of passion, the biography of a profound yet little known intellectual, Louis Levy. This documentary awakens in Halley a whole new respect for Cliff. Cliff succeeds in seducing her with his work, but Lester remains strong competition.

The act continues with Cliff's discovery that his divorced, middle-aged sister, while making love to a stranger, was tied up and defecated on. Upon first glance, this scene seems to come out of left field. What has this strange scene got to do with that plotline of Cliff? This is a wonderful example of digression and how important it can be to the character-driven screenplay. This scene does not have any direct relationship to the two main plotlines, but it is directly connected to the central dramatic question—are the eyes of God upon us? Because it is directly related to the theme, it does not feel out of place in the film. Thus, this digression fills out the movie and adds complexity and resonance to the story.

The first act ends when Judah asks his brother for advice on how to handle his mistress. Judah's brother, Jack Rosenthal (Jerry Orbach) suggests that Judah hire a hit man. Judah is horrified by the suggestion, but finally, after much painful and guilt-ridden deliberation, asks Jack to arrange for the murder of Dolores. This is the major event of the first act and a turning point that leads us to the second act. It unleashes new forces that must be brought to equilibrium and raises the stakes of the story. With this turning point, we have the answer to the big question of how will Judah deal with his mistress. He hires a hit man and will solve the problem with murder.

The major action of the second act (forty minutes) deals with two new big questions: first, how will Judah deal with the consequences of ordering the death of his mistress and two, will Cliff and Halley become a couple? In the second act, Judah begins to suffer a great deal of remorse as he tries desperately to face what he has done. In a sense, he is propelled through the second act by his feelings of guilt and remorse; his consistent goal throughout the second act is to find some way to alleviate his pain and suffering. In other words, he has a strong set of complex feelings that he is trying to do something about. The first major event of the second act is when Judah is informed by his brother that Dolores has "been taken care of." He visits Dolores' apartment and finds her dead on the floor. But at the same time, he continues to lie to those close to him, especially his confessor, the rabbi, Ben (Sam Waterson).

The audience begins to wonder if he will come clean or not. Judah lies to the police about his knowledge of Dolores, which indicates he does not have the strength of character to take responsibility for his actions. Finally, when Judah's brother threatens to kill Judah if he does confess his crime, Judah feels trapped. He uses this threat as an excuse to not confess and take responsibility and live with the consequences—a living hell. Jack's threat to his brother, Judah, is the turning point of the second act; it increases the stakes for Judah, and unleashes new forces that will need to be contained, dealt with, and somehow brought to equilibrium.

In the second act, Cliff's storyline progresses when, coming to terms with his loveless marriage, he makes a real pass at Halley. He impulsively kisses her and openly declares his feelings. This declaration raises the stakes in their relationship: Halley must commit or reject him. She rejects him, giving the excuse she is not over her divorce and that she must resolve her career ambitions. This plotline ends on the same thematic note as the Judah plotline: people use lame excuses to avoid examining their lives. It also answers the big question of whether Cliff and Halley become a couple.

The third act (twenty-seven minutes) begins with Judah drinking heavily. He must unburden himself of the crushing weight of his feelings of guilt and remorse. The big question of the third act for Judah is what can he do to come clean since he has rejected the possibility of confessing his crime. Since Judah will not take responsibility for his actions, will God or some higher power intervene and do it for him and bring about justice?

Judah, quite accidentally, and ironically, at the conclusion of the third act, meets up with Cliff at a wedding. They are total strangers and Judah confesses the murder to Cliff in a very ambiguous and complex way. Judah talks about "a great murder story" he has to tell, but Cliff thinks Judah is just another unhappy drunk at a party talking too much. What appears to be happening—a drunk talking too much—is quite different than what is really happening in the scene—a murderer is truly confessing. This resolution, though ironic, does provide payoff: what was anticipated to happen—Judah confessing his foul deeds—does happen. However, at the same time, there is no catharsis because Judah, ultimately, is not taking responsibility for his own actions. The resolution for Judah's plotline is not only ironic, it is complex and ambiguous.

Cliff's plotline in the third act comes to a very ambiguous resolution as well. Cliff's big question of the third act is what will he do to secure Halley's commitment now that she has rejected him. Cliff is fired by Lester because he created a biography that would obviously meet with the egotist's disapproval and outrage. This act of self-destruction raises the stakes again, and Cliff asks Halley to marry him. Here again, there is ambiguity because his proposal seems like a desperate measure. Halley returns a love letter to Cliff in order to bring closure to their relationship. At the conclusion of the act, Cliff, like Judah, must live with a painful burden that is not easily resolved. His worst nightmare is realized: he has lost Halley to Lester, and his wife is leaving him for another man.

Besides using a polyphonic structure, Woody Allen uses other strategies for creating complexity. Cliff's hatred of his brother-in-law is layered and complex: He has contempt for his brother-in-law's values, but at the same time, he is envious of his power, status, and privilege. Halley clearly has a war going on inside of herself since she admires Cliff but chooses Lester. Although she appears to be able to love both men, she chooses the most superficial of the two—something quite surprising and unexpected. Professor Levy maps out a great philosophy of hope and understanding, yet commits suicide. Judah is a loving husband, good provider, and an unselfish giver to the community, but at the same time he is a liar and murderer. These rich and complex characterizations of believable people, who have a perpetual tug-of-war within themselves, adds depth and resonance to the story. Their renderings slowly accumulate to contribute to a powerful impact.

Allen mixes types and styles in this film—another strategy often employed by the character-driven screenwriter. The subject matter of the story is quite serious and profound, and the leading characters are men of privilege and power. Both major characters possess a tragic flaw to which they are blind—Judah cannot accept responsibility for his actions and Cliff cannot see his self-destructive side. These flaws bring both of them down. At the same time, Allen mixes into the tragic fabric of the drama not only comedy and verbal wit, but also melodrama. For instance, Halley's sudden reversal and decision to commit to Lester, a man who does not seem the least bit appealing, seems improbable and melodramatic, as does the sudden and unexpected death of Cliff's spiritual godfather, Louis Levy. Similarly, Allen injects flashbacks for Judah that have a fantasy, dreamlike quality, weaving these scenes in with the more predominate realistic style of the movie. This mixing of types and styles adds a richness and density to the story and Allen performs this alchemy without losing clarity.

Allen's strategies support his very ambiguous view about the questions raised in the drama. He seems to think that we do in fact live in a godless universe, one that is unfair, yet at the same time, he believes that man is struggling to imagine a merciful god. In short, life is unfair, hard, and out of our control, yet we must struggle, as hard as we can, to be responsible. His purpose—to give expression to this profound and complex idea—is well served by the strategies he employs.

The character-driven screenwriter should not try to avoid the traditional three-act structure. The idea is to take responsibility for structure—to weave it in organically with the content and make it support and effectively express the purpose. Therefore, any dogmatic proclamations abut the number of acts to use or their approximate length would violate this goal.

EXERCISE
MAKING A THREE-ACT MOVIE INTO A ONE- OR TWO-ACT STRUCTURE

Take your favorite three-act movie and imagine it as two acts, and then as one. Write a brief synopsis (two to three pages) of each revision. List what is gained and what is lost with each revision. How does revising a three-act story change the story and the characters? Which act structure will you select for your next screenplay and why? (See example of *Mean Streets* on page 89.)

PART 3

CRAFTING YOUR SCRIPT: STEP BY STEP

Finding the Story

Emily Dickinson once said that a writer is like a carpenter who builds a house in the hope that it will become haunted. To find a story, follow something that haunts you, allow it to lead the way to trigger flow and free up your unconscious imagination. It can be anything, a character, situation, idea, or another story you need to make your own. It can begin in the ear, with dialogue overheard on the street, or in the eye, with a montage or image that evokes a story. There are many ways to discover story and here are eight possibilities:

Begin with a Character

One day I was walking down a Manhattan street with my stepfather, an effusive stockbroker who came to America from Egypt thirty years ago. He was ranting, as usual, about how "the country was going right down the drain!" How the younger people at his office "had no discipline!" "Princeton, Harvard, Yale. MBA, Ph.D. Piled High and Deeper. All Daddy's contacts. They don't produce! I am a producer! I tell you, talking to them is like having intercourse over the phone!" he shouted. As he vented, heads turned and I did what writers do—I listened and observed.

I found his ranting very funny; it bordered on lunacy. His emotions controlled him and he was not capable of strategizing because that would require self-control. This trait made him trustworthy, on a certain level, since he consistently called things exactly the way he saw them. Someone who can inspire trust or be very convincing is magnetic. Magnetic characters are highly dramatic because they are so engaging. At the same time, because he was so out of control, he was equally untrustworthy since he couldn't keep a confidence and could be brutal with his honesty. He used this brutal honesty to puncture pretensions and bring the other person down to create a level playing field. These warring characteristics made him complex. I imagined if I put a character inspired by him in any situation, he would create drama.

As a character, he also gave me a vicarious thrill. I reasoned that if he was capable of giving me such a thrill, he would provide the same for an audience. I often never say, as most of us don't, many of the things I feel and think because I do not want to offend or hurt someone. I want to be liked, promoted, rewarded, etc., so I try to behave "appropriately." My stepfather just blurted out anything that came into his head and it provided a catharsis for me (and for my imaginary audience). I imagined if I put him in situations where one must be polite, observe clear boundaries, there would inevitably be conflict because he would do the wrong thing. In general, characters that do the wrong thing are far more interesting than the ones who do the right thing. Whenever I wrote his character (or, more precisely, the character he inspired) I found myself laughing, another good sign—if I was delighted with him, an audience would be as well. And for some odd reason, I could just become him. I could actually stand up and act him out; my body language and voice would change and a certain madness filled my eyes.

It is a very good sign if you can act out a character and transform yourself without thinking about it. Good dramatic writing is acting on the page; it is giving the actor something to do. As mentioned before, many of the great playwrights have studied acting or have been actors, such as Shakespeare, Molière, David Mamet, and Sam Shepard. Many writers talk about becoming their characters, as if by a flip of a switch they can behave, walk, and talk like one of their creations. Mark Twain, who lectured to make his living after he went bankrupt, used his touring as an opportunity to test his characters with audiences. He would act them out, so he could hear how they "sounded out loud." Dickens was known to act out all his characters for family and friends. Willy Russell, author of *Educating Rita,* noted that when he stumbled upon the character of Rita he knew right away that he had something because he could just be her. Whenever he reads from his work it is amazing to watch—he becomes Rita.

With my screenplay *Arab Bride* I found the story by imagining my mother's first date with my stepfather. My mother is a combination of Princess Grace and Anne Mera. Just when you thought you knew her as Princess Grace, she would change her tone and let some of her Queens accent bleed into the conversation. She loathed pretensions, and liked to puncture them with her Queens accent. On another level, she was ashamed of her working-class accent, and to deflect attention from it, she used it offensively.

I thought of my mother's life at the time she first met my stepfather. She was divorced with five children, barely making ends meet, trying desperately to support a façade of upper-middle-class life, and feeling like an outsider in a wealthy section of New York suburbia. I thought of my stepfather at the time they met: also divorced, and despite great success, he too felt like an outsider, a foreigner in America. It was a fertile combination: my mother, aristocratic impersonator, and my stepfather, outraged that people thought of him as a second-class citizen because of his accent and Arab background. The glue that could bond them was the fact that they both felt marginalized and had internalized shame. When the character inspired by my mother did her Princess Grace act, she could give her husband what he wanted—to be perceived as a Brahmin, part of the country club. And my stepfather could give my mother what she desperately needed—emotional and financial support. In order to bond and connect deeply, both characters would have to drop their camouflage and game playing which was something very threatening to them both. This threat provided the stakes for the story.

Arab Bride sold to Hollywood Pictures literally one month after I completed it. It was a wonderful turning point in my life, allowing me to give up my day job at Time Warner and become a full-time screenwriter.

Make a Found Story Your Own

Another way to start is with a story that needs to be made your own. One time I overheard a true story about something that happened at the turn of the century in Maine. A very pretty thirteen-year-old girl fell in love, had an affair, and became pregnant. Her lover ran off and her parents decided it was best to put the child up for adoption. They found a very respectable family in Boston for the adoption. For years, this beautiful young woman, who remained in her hometown, was courted by many eligible bachelors, but never fell in love again. One day, she met a man, who was passing through town, working on the railroad, and they immediately fell in love. He was considerably younger, but her family and townspeople were delighted that she was finally going to settle down. Two days before the wedding, the young man's parents arrived from Boston to meet their future daughter-in-law. To everyone's horror, the young man's parents were the same people who took the future bride's illegitimate child away, twenty-two years before. This young woman's fiancé was her son.

When I first heard this story it stopped me in my tracks and to this day I honestly do not know why it haunted me. Obviously Sophocles did a good job with this same tragedy centuries ago with *Oedipus Rex,* but I needed to make it my own. For years it remained in the back of my mind, gestating. It came to life when I met a young actress, Bai Ling *(Red Corner).* Bai Ling came to study in my screenwriting workshop in New York, and when we became friends, she told me stories about her childhood experiences in China. Somehow, even though she seemed much too young, I had a strong hunch she was perfect for the main character. There was something haunting about Bai Ling, similar to how I imagined the character. She seemed forlorn and abandoned and this quality came through in her work on the stage. When I first told Bai Ling about the story she burst out laughing, thinking it was too farfetched and melodramatic, but as I continued to talk, she could see my passion, and that made a difference. I confessed I would use her as my inspiration to create the main character. She politely told me she was honored and I took that as permission to proceed.

Because Bai Ling is a Chinese immigrant, I decided I wanted to place the story in contemporary Chinatown in New York. Not having a clue where I was really headed, I did a huge amount of research on China, spent hours with Bai Ling asking her questions about her recollections of the small town in China where she grew up, read dozens of books, spoke to Chinese-American friends in New York's Chinatown, and was introduced to many immigrants who told me their stories. I wanted to ground my story in a contemporary situation and be well informed about the world of my main character. Eventually a story began to emerge out of this research. I cannot go into further detail because the project is presently in development, but the important thing to note is that the story became my own story once I gave it a contemporary setting with a complete change of ethnicity and backstory for the main character.

Based on this experience, I now try and take people that I know from my own life, whether or not they are actors, and I imagine them as my leading characters, plugging them into the roles that I am writing. Eventually, the person I use as a prototype dissolves and the real fictional character emerges, and usually he or she has absolutely no resemblance to the person who inspired the creation.

Let the News Lead You

The director Fritz Lang collected newspaper articles for many years, and he claims that is how his masterpiece *M* was created. News stories have long been a source of fiction. Many argue Truman Capote did his best work—*In Cold Blood*—when writing about a news story. Norman Mailer's *Executioner's Song* was based on the news stories of Gary Gilmore, a convicted murder who fought a bizarre battle to have the state execute him by a firing squad rather than the traditional electric chair or gas chamber. One of the major difficulties with this approach is unburdening yourself of making something historically accurate. History and fiction are mortal enemies, and if you use news as a starting point, it should be just that, a beginning, a way to start an imaginative flow, rather than the chronicling of current or past events.

Many years ago, while in rehearsal for a one-act play I had written, an actor came to me during our break and mentioned that the underpinnings of my play were similar to the story of Dennis Sweeney and Allard Lowenstein. Although I did not know their story, I did know of Allard Lowenstein, who was a maverick congressman from Long Island during my childhood, and a hero to many. The actor brought in an article on the relationship of these two men and I was instantly haunted by their tale. For weeks I felt compelled to read the story over and over again.

Briefly, Sweeney, a former protégé of Allard, walked into Lowenstein's law office one day and shot him dead. Their relationship went back over twenty years, beginning when they first met at Stanford University. Lowenstein was from a wealthy New York family and attended the best private schools; Dennis was from a working-class family in Portland, Oregon, and won a scholarship to Stanford. Both men reached their peaks during the politically turbulent 1960s, and in 1980, when Sweeney shot Lowenstein, Allard was clearly "out of the loop," had lost his power base. At the same time, Dennis, who had left the political world to work as a carpenter, had literally gone insane, hearing Allard's voices through the crowns on his teeth.

My instincts told me I understood their connection, that of teacher and protégé, and I felt I knew how they were driven to work for causes like the Civil Rights movement in 1963, in Mississippi. Their story had the elements of a modern tragedy, something I had wanted to do for a long time. I immediately began researching both men and their world. Three years later, after reading volumes about the early Civil Rights movement, interviewing people who knew both Lowenstein and Sweeney, traveling to Washington, San Francisco, Seattle, Portland, Los Angeles, Mississippi, Baltimore, and Boston, I collected a lot of information about the time periods, the characters, and their world.

I wrote dozens of drafts of the play because it was very difficult to find a way to distill such a complex story and history into a single, workable narrative for a two- or even a four-hour play. What caused me the most trouble was the burden I felt to be historically accurate. The day I decided to trust the information I had absorbed to guide and inform me, but not feel compelled to explain, illustrate, chronicle, educate, meet anyone's political expectations, or be well liked by those who I had interviewed, was when I finally wrote a draft that was alive and true. A storyteller has no obligation to prove the factual truth of anything to anyone. Although it is a useful strategy to write what you know, it is equally valid to write about something you want to know more about.

Begin with an Image or Montage

Another tactic is to find a story by letting a montage that haunts you lead you to it. There is an old anecdote about the movie producer Dino De Laurentis that helps to illuminate this method of finding a story. One day De Laurentis called a screenwriter into his office and with a thick Italian accent tells the story of a man who is sailing by himself across the Pacific in a small boat because he needs to take time out from life and discover a new direction. One day, out in the middle of the ocean, he looks into the horizon and a parachute suddenly appears in the sky. He grabs his binoculars and sees that it is attached to a capsule. He looks for ships that might be there to pick up this capsule. There are none. He decides to head for the capsule. An astronaut comes out of it and his life raft does not inflate. The astronaut climbs to the top of the sinking capsule, holding on for dear life. The sailor shoots off a flare to warn the astronaut he has been sighted and help is on the way. But the sailor is not sure his flare has been seen. Here De Laurentis stopped. The screenwriter, very much taken with the visual tease and the passionate way in which De Laurentis told it, asked what happened next? "That's notta my problem, thatsa your problem," replied De Laurentis.

Starting with the visual is not only about starting with a single image, although that too is possible, it is about starting with a montage, a series of moving pictures that progress and suggest a larger story. The montage that haunts you does not have to be the beginning of a story, as is the case with the De Laurentis example, it can suggest a world, a character, or any part of a story.

Adapt a Novel, Play, or Short Story

Surprisingly there are many novelists and short story writers who will negotiate the rights to their work for almost no upfront monies, although a legal agreement should be made with the authors. Many authors, especially if their work is not widely recognized, are willingly to negotiate "back-end" deals, in which they will receive compensation only if the screenplay is made into a film.

There are many problems with adaptation and I would need the large part of a book to adequately address the issue. That aside, the lesson I learned about adaptation is the same one I learned when writing from news articles: trust your own integrity, your own truth. Since writers must wrestle with the demands of craft every day, they are very sensitive to others' work and they do not want to extinguish an author's voice. Adaptation is taking another writer's work and making it your own. In order to do that successfully, to give the adaptation vitality and vigor, the writer must impose his or her own view of the story on the previous author's viewpoint. If the screenwriter is equivocal about this imposition, the work will suffer. Screenwriters cannot worry about pleasing people when it comes to adaptation—they must take another author's work and ruthlessly put their stamp on it.

An excellent example of an adaptation and a gem of a movie is *The Heart Is a Lonely Hunter,* which was adapted from Carson McCullers' novel by McCullers and Thomas C. Ryan. It is a simple story with complex, layered characters. The screenwriters were able to translate the novel into dramatic action that has a strong sense of progression. The story is compelling not because of what the characters say, but what they do not say—what is left out by the screenwriters and left to the audience's imagination. This strategy is called ellipsis and can be very effective at suggesting and evoking in film. In many ways, the film was a better media for this story than the novel.

A screenwriter friend once gave me some odd but valuable advice about adaptation. He suggested that before I begin an adaptation project, I should have someone else read the book and tell the story to me. Based on the story that I hear, he suggested that I then complete a first draft of a screenplay, without ever reading the novel. I took his advice when I was being considered for a writing job; I asked the producer and development executive to just pitch the story they wanted me to adapt from a novel and not send me the book. They found this strange but agreed. I took a few days to think things over and came back to them with how I would approach the project (in Hollywood, until you are on the A List, you must audition as a writer). When I got the job I paid another writer friend of mine (I think writers give the best notes) to read the book and tell me the story out loud. I spent hours talking to this writer and asked hundreds of questions about the character and world. The writer answered me as factually as he could, only giving answers he felt could be supported by the text.

Once I completed a draft, I finally read the novel. I was amazed at the similarities. I must admit that I had to make many revisions to my first draft, but I had discovered my take on the story first and then used the information from the novel to layer the core. In essence, this strategy allowed me to work the best way a writer can—from the inside out. When I handed in the screenplay, my executive was delighted with the results. As is often the case in Hollywood, he was fired six months later and any project he had promoted was automatically shelved, put into "turnaround." I was well paid, but the movie was never made. Such is the common experience in Hollywood.

Begin from a Portrait or Photograph

One exercise that has been successful with my students is to take photographs by Diane Arbus, Richard Avedon, or any great portrait photographer, and lay them out on a table or a floor. I ask students to pick one that speaks to them, haunts them. With picture in hand, they must then write in the first person, speaking the way the character in the photograph speaks, about what was happening during the exact moment the photograph was taken, including their inner thoughts and feelings. After completing several pages of automatic, free association writing, they are asked to review another series of photographs of objects: a dusting feather, an alarm clock, a gun, a bottle of vodka. The students are asked to select an object that is important to the character. Once an object is selected, the students must write again in the first person, telling why this object is so important to the character. Breakthroughs usually occur at this point in the process. I then ask my students what story can be made from what this character is saying and doing.

Start with a Feeling

Using the following six emotions—anger, joy, guilt, fulfillment, shame, and revenge, recall a time in your life when you were the most "filled" with each of these feelings. Reflect on that time for at least fifteen minutes, alone, in a quiet place. Recall everything through your senses: what do you see, smell, hear, touch, and taste in your mind? Write automatically, recording on paper whatever comes to mind when you meditate on the emotion. Let one line of automatic writing lead you freely, uncritically, to another. Be fearless, none of this has to make sense, it just has to feel true as you write it. If you remind yourself that you are entirely free to throw any ideas out, you will unburden yourself and have a more trusting relationship with your unconscious, the most powerful source of story.

The automatic writing should last at least thirty minutes for each emotion chosen. Do not take your pen off of the paper, or your hands off of the keyboard, once you have begun. Write in the first person at least to start, although it may lead to the third person, or some other approach. Write simply, honestly, and make each line coherent. Write until you get to a breakthrough. You will know you have a breakthrough when you will feel a strong shift of emotion or energy; you will lose a sense of time and feel very alert. When this shift hits you, it is usually your best work. After a break of a day or a week, collect all six examples and reflect upon them as objectively as possible. Can you discern similar stories emerging from all six examples? Similar themes? Similar characters or ways of saying things? Any similar obsessions? What do the similarities tell you about what interests you as a writer, and what worlds and types of characters do you like to write about? How can you use any of this information to help you shape a story?

Reveal a Secret

Write a secret on a piece of paper—something you have never had the nerve to discuss with absolutely anyone in your life. Write about all the thoughts and feelings associated with this secret for at least a half-hour. Once you have finished, burn the pages you have written. Make it into a ritual. Do this every day for five days. Use the same secret, each day, exploring different layers of it, or choose an entirely different secret. On the fifth day save your paper, do not burn it. Ask yourself if any of the material you have written can be used to create a story, looking at what you have written about the secret.

Continuing with this exercise, use this material to imagine a story that is about a relationship: a girl and her teacher, a husband and wife, two lovers, etc. Write a brief synopsis of five possible plots that would change this relationship. Let these five plots stew for a while; do not review them for at least a week. When you do review them ask yourself: can I use any of these plots to create a screenplay?

Once you have found a story to work on, you are ready to take the next step in the process of creating a screenplay: the pitch. As mentioned earlier, screenwriting is a backwards and forwards process. It is about freeing up the unconscious, mining it, and then examining the extracted material in a more logical, conscious way. The process is similar to making bread: the materials are mixed, the flour rises organically, and then it must be kneaded, shaped, and allowed to rise again.

The pitch is a key element to the conscious side of the screenwriting process. It acts as a reality check. Very simply, once you have discovered the elements of your story, if you cannot get them to hang together in an interesting way by pitching it to someone else, then you are in trouble. There is something wrong somewhere with your central dramatic question or subject matter. It is important to know if the subject matter is as compelling to others as it is to you and that you have clarity on the central dramatic question, before executing an entire screenplay.

The Pitch

I believe it is absolutely vital that all screenwriters develop the skills necessary to pitch their projects. For many writers the skills are excruciatingly difficult to learn, but pitching remains an essential tool. Pitching requires you to get to the heart of an idea and understand the big picture. After finding a story that you want to write about, you need to conceive of boundaries for it by deciding where to place your parentheses around the story. A pitch is a tool that will help you do that.

A pitch should be no longer than five to seven minutes and should be done by speaking out loud to another person. You can make notes of course, but the real value of the pitch is in the actual pitching experience, which creates a visceral understanding and awareness of your story, which will serve as a valuable anchor. It is quite possible that everything you say in a pitch will never end up in the final draft of your screenplay as things evolve. The actual writing of the screenplay is a substantial amount of work, and if you just go ahead and write one without solid preparation, both in characterization and story shape, you will have to make many revisions. And since most people have only a certain amount of energy for a particular story before they burn out or get bored with it, a pitch helps to conserve the enthusiasm you need for executing an entire screenplay.

A Shaping Tool

Developing your pitch is an excellent way to manage your ideas for a screenplay. A screenplay consists of many scenes that need to be strung together to create something larger than the sum of its parts. A pitch is a way to test the summing of the parts before you actually write it in screenplay form, because weakness of dramatic logic or structure quickly become evident. Writing a screenplay is like trying to find your way through a dense rain forest. A pitch can provide a satellite map of the rain forest and an outline (which we will explore later) gives an aerial shot from just above the tree line. When you start writing the screenplay, you are on the ground, in the thick forest, and if you don't have these two maps, the pitch and the outline, you will get lost and may never find your way.

A pitch is essentially what you tell your friends when you have seen a really great movie and you want to share your enthusiasm. You give them a sense of its basic plot, characters, actors, some of the great moments of the film, and maybe bits of dialogue. To begin a pitch you should first lure someone with a tease, such as "Did you ever think what it must be like to have sex with someone in your office? It doesn't just happen in the oval office. Maybe your girlfriend has just dumped you and you are hurt and vulnerable, or maybe you found out that your lover is two-timing you. Sometimes we grab onto anything to fill the hole left by a loss." The pitch then continues with the narration of the story of a lawyer and his secretary, who both liked to skate close to the edge. They were having sex in his office at least twice a day. They would simply close the door, in the middle of the day and well....Then something happened. The lawyer discovered his office was bugged. And he didn't know who did it—his wife, someone in his firm, his secretary's husband, a disgruntled client, or someone who he beat in court. It could've been any of these people.

You may notice that I tied the tease to the current events of that time in the Oval Office. The tease piggybacked on the power of that story to draw in the listener. However trite it may seem, it's a good strategy. Giving a pitch is not about being elegant and complex, it is about being simple and shameless in your effort to grab the listener's attention. I learned this while giving a pitch in Hollywood. A producer asked me to take the concept of the film *The Man Who Came to Dinner* and change it into *The Woman Who Came to Dinner.* He had a producing deal with a well-known actress and thought this screenplay would provide an excellent vehicle for her talents. Written by the Epstein brothers, *The Man Who Came to Dinner* was based on the Kaufman-Hart play about a pompous New York critic, Monty Woolley, who accidentally slips on ice, breaks his leg, and is forced to stay with a Midwestern family during his recovery, driving them crazy with his arrogance and grandiosity. At the time we were pitching this project in Hollywood, *Jurassic Park* had just opened and everyone was taken with its blockbuster success. When we sat down to discuss the project with a studio executive, my producer introduced me in this way: "James has a really great story to tell you. Just like *Jurassic Park,* this story is about a dinosaur that descends upon an unsuspecting Midwestern town."

As bizarre as it sounds, my producer was doing exactly what he should have done by using whatever he could to pull in his listener. And what could grab a studio executive's attention more than something that is currently making a huge box office? Even if everyone in the room knows it is a clear manipulation, as long as you say it with a "wink in your eye," it'll work. A pitch is about breaking the ice and giving the listener a sense that you want to have fun—play—and you want them to play along with you.

A good way to test a pitch is to walk into bar and have a drink with a stranger. Give only the first half of your pitch and excuse yourself to go to the bathroom. If the stranger asks you to continue with your story when you return, then you know you have a good pitch. The more questions the stranger asks, the better your pitch.

After the tease you should start to talk about the "high points" or great moments of the story. Give your listener a clear sense of the main characters right away by using a well-known personality or star. For instance, in the first tease, I could have said the lawyer was like a younger Henry Kissinger, a modern-day Gary Cooper, or John Kennedy Jr. Or create a hybrid character in the listener's imagination such as, "Tom Hanks meets Truman Capote," or "Elizabeth Taylor meets Mother Teresa." Sum up the pitch so the listener gets an idea of the big picture: "It's about how you never know if anyone is watching, especially with all the cheap, endless technology out there today. It's the guy in the next work station who'll screw you and turn you in to Big Brother, not because he wants to rule the universe but simply because he is bored with his pathetic little life and needs some adventure. And that adventure could be you."

What Is the Movie About?

As Sidney Lumet explains in his book *Making Movies,* "movies will define themselves as I make them. As long as the theme is something I care about at the moment, it's enough for me to start work. Having decided, for whatever reason, to do a movie, I return to that all-encompassing, critical discussion: What is the movie about? Work can't begin until its limits are defined, and this is the first step in the process. It becomes the riverbed into which all subsequent decisions will be channeled."

The same is true for the screenwriter as it is for the director: work cannot begin until limits are defined. Once you have discovered the main elements of the story, you must decide on a theme—what these elements are about. The theme must be something you care passionately about and are haunted by "in the moment."

Purpose, as I have defined it, is your personal reason for writing a screenplay—what you want to express or examine, theme is an interpretation of what your screenplay is about. For example, in *Before the Rain,* the writer's purpose was to write about his homeland and the destructive strife he saw there. The central dramatic question is: Will our hero make a commitment? And the theme is: War is a virus. The writer needs to know all of these things in order to bring coherence and shape to a screenplay.

But again, with a pitch, it is only a beginning, themes will evolve and change the focus of the story. You may start with one interpretation of your initial story elements and soon learn, as you execute an outline or screenplay, that your initial hunch was not right, not interesting, or not good enough. Each new interpretation (and there are hundreds, perhaps thousands of interpretations of this nature until the screenplay is finally completed) adjusts the limits and boundaries, shapes and focuses the story, and leads you deeper and deeper to the center of your truth. This is inevitable. However, without some defined limits to begin with, you will never get to a deeper, more informed, more truthful interpretation of your work The screenwriting journey will be stopped short, and the final destination will never be discovered.

Here are a few examples from Lumet's *Making Movies,* of that critical question: what is your movie about?

- *The Pawnbroker:* How and why we create our own prisons.
- *Dog Day Afternoon:* Freaks are not the freaks we think they are. We are much more connected to the most outrageous behavior than we know or admit.
- *Twelve Angry Men:* Listen.
- *Network:* The machines are winning. Or, to borrow from the NRA: TV doesn't corrupt people; people corrupt people.

When I start a screenplay I go around for days pitching it to unsuspecting cab drivers, people at the gym, my friends, and family. I try to give a tone to the pitch that approximates the tone and feel of the screenplay I want to create. If I want to write a funny story, I obviously try to make the pitch funny; if I want to write something that is to be taken as being absolutely real, I pitch it that way. I have gone as far as pitching something as "an absolutely true story," which was, in fact, absolutely made up. Writers naturally embellish—okay, lie—it is an occupational hazard. When we tell stories, our first requirement is to get the listener to enter into the world of the tale. When you are pitching, you can immediately tell if something is weak; people will fidget, their eyes will glaze over, and their body language will read "bored."

Finally, the pitch can help to give you a sense of the act structure. Look at the completed pitch and ask yourself: how I will divide my screenplay up? What are the big questions I can use to break up my idea into manageable chunks? Do I need one, two, or three acts? In the beginning, stay open. Try not to force yourself into any choice about act structure until you have tested several possibilities. You just never know. Sometimes you will discover that what you really want to say, your purpose, is best expressed in a one-act rather than a three-act form.

Once you have conquered the problem of a pitch, it is time to get unconscious again, to explore and discover. It is time to do a free-write. The free-write is like a children's playground. Children will play more freely if their playground is surrounded by a fence or a stone wall with clear boundaries. The pitch provides the boundaries; the stage has been set to free up the unconscious imagination and you can now play freely with the free-write.

The Free-Write

When I first started writing, I read dozens of books on screenwriting that suggested doing character profiles to learn more about my characters. I dutifully answered the questions these profiles asked, such as what are your characters' ethnic backgrounds? Are they introverted or extroverted? What would they do with a million dollars? What type of shoes do they wear? What is their favorite dessert? After I answered the questions I found that I was no closer to the character; it just didn't work for me. I spoke to other writers and all of them told me that profiles never work for them either. Creating a character profile is a nice intellectual exercise, working from the outside in, but creating a character for a fictive world is an intuitive process.

Objectively answering questions about your characters does nothing to free up the unconscious imagination. Yes, you should know a great deal about your characters before you try to include them in a screenplay, but you need to know them from the inside out rather than from the outside in. So I decided to make a very simple adjustment to the character profile that made all the difference: I asked students, when doing their profiles, to answer anything about the character speaking the way the character speaks, using dialogue, not prose. This forced the students to intuitively get into character and practice being their characters. By talking like them, writers eventually got a strong feel for their characters.

The free-write helps the writer to prepare. The writer must prepare just like the actor, who prepares so that when they are thrust into a scene, they can just be in the moment, stay spontaneous, and discover. Uta Hagan, renowned actress, teacher, and author of *Respect for Acting,* always told her students that an actor must strive to be "as free as possible" when on the stage. The same holds true for the writer, who must be as free as possible when finally sitting down to write a scene. You must have extreme confidence about your characters to be this free. The free-write helps to develop that confidence. Only after you have done sufficient preparation with the free-write, you should figuratively, not literally, discard it all and go about spontaneously writing a scene. The work you have done with the free-write will stay with you and add layers to your work, making it fully considered.

The Magnetic Character

The free-write is a tool to develop character. It brings a deeper understanding of a character to the writer and it will do the same for the audience. It is a way to discover more information about characters, and from that information, create a more compelling, engaging, and dramatic story. If the information is just so-so, or prosaic, then it is not of much use to the writer. The free-writing process is like panning for gold: you spend hours shifting through sand and pebble to find a nugget here and there. If the writer is working a river that is not connected to a mother lode or a vein of gold, then the work will be for naught.

A magnetic character must be developed from a character that has been discovered, using the free-write. Magnetism is intangible and difficult to achieve; however, we all know it when we see it. If the true value of a screenplay resides in character, then it stands to reason that the more magnetic the characters in the story, the stronger the screenplay will be. The writer needs to learn the following about what makes a character magnetic:

- The first thing to look for is intensity. The magnetic character is intense, aggressive, and demands attention. This demand for attention does not mean the character should necessarily be over the top. The composed intensity of Al Pacino's character, Michael, in *The Godfather* is a great example. Great actors have deep intensity, subtle or overt, that they pour into the characters they create. Magnetic characters are the same. They are intense, ultimately, because they want something badly. They are driven people.

- Intensity is a quality in characters that leads them to galvanize any exchange they have with other characters. Magnetic characters arouse, excite, stimulate, ignite, and stir up trouble wherever they go. They scare people or excite them positively. This fright, or contagious enthusiasm, raises the level of adrenaline in the individual or the audience and this increase of adrenaline creates a charge that eroticizes the character. Magnetic characters are very sexy. Hannibal Lecter (Anthony Hopkins) in *The Silence of the Lambs* is a classic example of this type of character; his energy, however extreme, eroticizes his relationship with Clarice Starling (Jodie Foster). Or, on a less creepy level, in the scene when George (Jimmy Stewart) and Mary (Donna Reed) both listen over the telephone in *It's a Wonderful Life*, Jimmy Stewart's energy charges the scene and makes it highly sexual.

- Magnetic characters have a clear sense of what they want and present a formidable obstacle to anyone who gets in their way: Blanche DuBois *(A Streetcar Named Desire)*, Louise Sawyer *(Thelma and Louise)*, Guido *(Life Is Beautiful)*, or Max *(Rushmore)*, are all very clear about what they need to accomplish. They may be ambiguous characters but they never operate from a place of ambiguity. They intuitively have clarity on the right thing to do and when to do it. They follow their instincts, spontaneously, in the moment. They have clear expectations of others, and if these expectations are not met, they have equal clarity on how to respond to a letdown.

- Because magnetic characters have such clarity about their own feelings, standards, and values in life, they can be very convincing. They totally believe in what they are doing since, by their very nature, they would not do anything that they, themselves, did not believe in one hundred percent. As a result, like pied pipers, they can lead others to follow them because their confidence inspires trust. There must be some vulnerability in magnetic characters, otherwise their confidence will be just off-putting and bombastic. This vulnerability is sometimes exhibited in a tragic flaw. Charles Foster Kane was crippled in childhood because he was so cruelly abandoned by his parents and he is blind to his need to control. This flaw is evident to the viewer, yet not to him. Such a flaw and backstory elicits a compassionate response from the audience who suffers with the character. There is obviously a wide range of vulnerable spots a character may possess, from the outlandish buck teeth of *Austin Powers,* and the brewing self-destructive rage of Louise (*Thelma and Louise*) to the outsider status and oddly oversized nose of Max Fischer in *Rushmore.*

- There must be something a bit exotic about a character to make them magnetic. Exoticism is a relative concept. Your characters need only be exotic in the time and place of their story to be considered exotic. They do not need to be "fish out of water," just a bit odd. Exotic can also be eccentric, as in the case of Mr. Chips (Robert Donat), in *Goodbye Mr. Chips.* Magnetic characters are intriguingly unusual and their differences must excite, stimulate, or elicit curiosity from others. John Singer (Alan Arkin) in *The Heart Is a Lonely Hunter,* Karl Childers (Billy Bob Thornton) in *Sling Blade* and Alex Murphy in *Robocop* all intrigue viewers on some level. Another effective tactic to employ to give your characters an exotic feel is to give them a secret. Characters who have a secret such as Hannibal Lecter, or Hamlet, will immediately elicit curiosity from other characters in the story as well as from the audience.

Using the Free-Write to Develop Magnetic Characters

The free-write is similar to free association or journal writing. In order to write a character for the page, you must first find the character, which means you must find a way for you (the writer) and that character to become one. Ideally, the writer knows they have "cracked" a character when they can get up and walk and talk like the character. Often I play in my room, imagining my characters are having lunch with someone important, or that they are on the phone with their girlfriend after a big fight, or they are talking to a crowd after winning some big award. If I can act like them in any circumstance then I feel I really have found them; and only then can I write them.

I know I have my characters when they are no longer controlled by me and I can plug them into any story or situation and they just take off. Now, when I say I act out my characters, it does not mean that you have to be a good actor to write unforgettable characters. All that is necessary is to find a way that makes you truly believe that you are your characters while playing them. No one else has to believe your performance, that's what actors are for. Cole Porter did not get famous by singing his own tunes. He got famous because other people sang them. But he had to hear songs in his head first, and I am sure, in order to do this, he sang them to himself, somehow. The same is true for the dramatic writer. A screenplay is written not to be read, but to be performed; it is interpreted by the actor and director. And a screenplay is written with the spirit of performance in mind, so it will come alive when it is time to perform it.

When you do a free-write you learn about the major characters by asking them hundreds of questions. But remember, you must answer those questions speaking the way the character speaks; if you respond to those questions in your own voice, you will not be working from the inside out. In the process of interviewing, the writer must respond to the questions using the character's voice, while simultaneously translating these spoken words onto the page as dialogue. The writer may have to create as many as fifty pages, typed single-spaced, on a character before they are truly prepared to write the character into a scene.

Example of a Free-Write

The following is an excerpted example of a free-write done by a student. The student needed to create the character of Ben Shepherd for his screenplay, *Fresh Air,* and used the free-write to deepen his understanding of the character as well as to find new story.

Interviewer: Ben, let's start with the basics, where are you from?

Ben: Brooklyn, New York. I was born in an area called Sheepshead Bay, went to Lincoln High School, and then on to Baruch College, where I majored in the exciting and dangerous subject of accounting.

Interviewer: What was it like growing up in Brooklyn?

Ben: Not bad, I didn't get a chance to do as much as I would have liked. I played baseball since I was seven until I got hit by a pitch once and my mother took me out of the league. I played violin. I was pretty good at it although if I picked it up now it would sound like a cat in heat. Mom was Mom. Cooked a hell of a potato pancake, made her own homemade applesauce that was pink and not cream color by the way. Dad was a hard worker. He worked in a deli for fifty years, had a heart attack, and passed five, was it five, five or six years ago. Dad was funny. The man was funny. A wit drier than the Sahara Desert. One day my grandmother, eighty-six at the time, was opening up a birthday present and everyone was calling out "I wonder what it is, I wonder what it is." Dad yells out, "bowling shoes." The man was funny.

Interviewer: Were you close with your father?

Ben: Dad was my best friend. You usually hear women say that about their mothers, but that's the way it was. I could talk to him about anything. He came into my room one day when I was fifteen. He sat down on the edge of the bed, wiped his brow with my sweatshirt, and said, "We're gonna talk about sex. I want to get it all in before your mother gets home." Get it all in, he said. I didn't get the joke until ten years later and I still laugh at it. Dad did that. He told me jokes that will last forever. Like he was giving me a gift.

Interviewer: What happened on the day he died?

Ben: I got to the house after my mother called. My mother was screaming for him to wake up but the paramedics were just standing there. I knew. I knew when she called. I knew before she called. I started yelling at him to wake up. Susan pulled me into another room. (Susan is Ben's wife who recently passed away).

Interviewer: How did you meet Susan?

Ben: In a furniture store. I was there looking for a sofa and she was looking for a chair. She asked me if I worked there and I said yes. I spent the next half-hour helping her pick something out. I even acted like I knew the other people that worked there. Then she figured it out, thought I was insane, and I begged her to go out with me. She said yes, as long as it was a public place. She's gone but I still talk to her every day. The kids do too. I encourage it. When it's a guy thing I talk to Dad, anything else, I give Susan a ring.

Interviewer: Susan was a big loss for you.

Ben: Like someone stealing all your insides at once.

Interviewer: Any new prospects of romance?

Ben: I don't think about that. I want to concentrate on the kids and my career.

Interviewer: If you could buy one thing for yourself, what would it be? It doesn't have to be practical at all.

Ben: You mean it could be a roadster?

Interviewer: You're very quick-witted.

Ben: When you're brought up not to hurt anybody and you get the crap beat out of you as a kid, you develop a sense of humor.

Interviewer: The jokes keep you from being hurt again.

Ben: Yes, Doctor Freud. Should I lie on the couch? I couldn't take another loss right now. I worry every day, more about the kids than anything else. I'm vulnerable right now. Nobody gets too close, I can't get hurt, right? Right.

Interviewer: Sounds like you don't trust people.

Ben: What's to trust? When I was an accountant, I was promised to be made manager. Was I? No. The doctors with Susan, "We don't think it's anything, probably stress." She had cancer. "The surgery went well." Do you see her here? I believe nothing of what I hear and only half of what I see.

This method is particularly effective because it is both conscious and unconscious. The writer, as the interviewer, is consciously asking questions of the character, Ben, as acted by the writer unconsciously. The writer is working primarily from an unconscious place when doing this type of free-write, however he or she is also forced to consciously probe for the relevant information needed to fill out story and character as planned in the pitch.

The Uncommon Reaction to the Common Experience

Once a free-write is completed for a character, the question becomes: What can I extract and use from the free-write? How do I know what to use and what not to use? And how can I make a choice compelling? Is there any way to revise a choice so that it will present a fresh perspective to the viewer?

Many possibilities for scenes, moments, plotlines, immediately spring to mind for the free-write example above. You can easily picture a scene in which Ben tries to pick up his wife in a furniture store. Or a scene when Ben first discovers his father's death. Or a moment when he is talking to his dead wife, Susan. There could be an obvious storyline where Ben meets another woman and must take the risk of opening up to her again. But don't settle for the obvious. Try to go beyond the cliché or obvious choice. It is okay to start with the obvious choice, and you often do, but then stop and ask yourself if there is somewhere to go with this that excites you because you cannot recall seeing it done before.

Try to work with what the character says or does. For instance, Ben says he is trying to concentrate on his career and his children. How many times have we seen the Hollywood story about a dad who has to get in touch with his feelings and be more connected with his family and friends? Knowing this, suppose you do the opposite. Suppose Ben, after Susan's death, was actually too good of a father and everyone comes to him, including his children, asking him to change his ways, to become more selfish because his selflessness is driving them insane. With this choice we have turned an expectation on its head.

Try to "go against" your first choices or play with expectations and see where it leads you. Don't be afraid to constantly play devil's advocate with yourself at this point in your process. The more possibilities you come up with the better. Keep searching, playing, discovering, until you come up with choices that surprise you, fill you with enthusiasm, and lead you to someplace you never anticipated. As Charles Bukowski, poet and author, remarked, "look for the uncommon reaction to the common experience." Bukowski was on a cruise and overheard a young boy, looking out at the ocean, tell his dad that "it was ugly." We have all been conditioned to think that an ocean is beautiful and here was a child who saw it otherwise; he said the "wrong" thing. It was compelling because it made everyone take a second look at the ocean and "see it anew," which is what the word "revision" literally means. Revise all your choices, look at them over and over, and seek the uncommon reaction so that the spectator can see what you see anew.

Building a Bond with the Character

When the writer has made a complete exploration of a character with the free-write, then he or she should figuratively, not literally, toss away every page. Everything discovered about a character in a free-write—the backstory, hidden thoughts, and feelings—is meant to inform and prepare the writer, so that the story and character-izations are well considered. Holding onto anything discovered in the free-write to just plug it into a screenplay will violate one of the writer's most important responsi-bilities—to be spontaneous when writing a scene. If a writer just lifts what he or she discovered in a free-write and plugs it into a scene, it will show; the scene will not feel fresh and alive.

Use free-writes to discover your character's idiosyncrasies and quirks, to bond with your characters, and to find out what you respect about them. When a character reveals something you like, dig deeper and ask more questions. Don't let your character off the hook, but at the same time, don't lose your compassion—your ability to empathize with the character rather than judge.

A free-write is similar to going on a retreat with someone. You take the time to sit down to dinner, walk along the ocean, and get to know each other better. If there are questions about the character's world that you truly cannot answer, such as what is it like to be a working lawyer or how does a surgeon mentally prepare for surgery, then go outside the free-write and ask people who are lawyers and doctors about their world. Then return to the free-write with that information and use it to help embellish your character, always using the character's voice.

Personalizing the Character: Anchoring the Unconscious

When doing a free-write, you are exploring a character. You will often get more mileage out of doing a free-write if you can personalize the character. Most writers create their best characters when they are based on someone they know. Mark Twain used his mother Jane as the basis for Aunt Polly and Huck Finn was modeled after Tom Blankenship, the town drunk in Hannibal, Missouri, where Twain grew up. Many of the aristocratic characters Tolstoy created for *War and Peace* were based upon counts and countesses he actually knew. Mario Puzo confessed that for the model for Don Corleone he unconsciously used his mother who was always con-cerned about her family, and ruthless if she felt betrayed. When the Don spoke he would hear his mother's voice.

Personalizing a character does not mean using the biographical facts of another person's life, and then slipping a new name over that person—fictionalizing what is factual. Instead you meditate on that person, and in the process, actually create a dif-ferent character. It is alchemy. The magic is that the more specifically you personalize a character, the more specific, original, and distinct your fictional character will be. I have actually used friends to personalize characters I have written, and when my friends have watched the play or the movie they "are in," they have never once noticed or recognized "themselves." Usually after the lights go up these friends will remark on how much they liked certain characters and of course they're talking about the ones based upon themselves.

Many students are leery about using personalization to create a character. It feels like they are not creating, just reporting and that they are robbing the soul of a real person. Such notions should be dispelled. It is the business of the writer to be a highly skilled observer of life; personalization is really just testing the writer's powers of observation. If writers are not observing life, in excruciating detail, they are not doing their job. Because writers are required to be great observers, they are often accused of "betraying" the confidentiality of relationships between lovers, friends, co-workers, parents, and so on. On some level, this is true. This is what they are required to do. Simply put, using a real person to personalize your characters is ultimately just a good way to free up the unconscious imagination in a free-write.

Grounding the Free-Write with Research

While you are doing your free-write, move about the world you live in and do some research; you can't come up with everything shut in the house writing. For example, in chapter three, I wrote about an idea for a screenplay about Fredrick, a wealthy businessman. While working on a free-write for the character Fredrick, I would probably take breaks from my free-write and walk up Fifth Avenue and choose the building I think Fredrick would live in, noticing every detail. I would process it through my senses: how its looks, how it feels to the touch, what sounds are around this building, what smells are evident, what the people are like going in and out of it. Eventually I would go to a very expensive restaurant that I think Fredrick might regularly visit. (If it is not in my budget, I use my credit card—after all, it is a necessary research expense.) I would ask a woman friend to join me for dinner. I would dress the way I think Fredrick would and talk about him during our dinner. I would give her examples of how I think he would treat a date or a wife. I would try to find out what intrigues my friend about Fredrick. I would act like I am Fredrick and she is my wife and we are at dinner. She asks me questions about him, and they interest me because they are things I hadn't thought of. I either answer them on the spot or I make a mental note of them. After dinner I would ask my friend to come with me to the Pierre Hotel. We go to the ballroom and there is a very big benefit going on for some charity. There are lots of very wealthy socialites there. I look around the room and find people who I think would be friends of Fredrick. If I have enough nerve, I would go up to them and chat and eventually ask questions about their lives.

Through this process, I would absorb the taste and smell of Fredrick's world. When I go home that night I would try to behave like the character of Fredrick. I would make a cup of tea the way he would, draw a bath the way he would, imagine what his ritual is for undressing before a bath, and finally, I take a stab at singing the way I think he would in the bath. I would discover his favorite song. Before I go to bed I make some notes on the key things I discovered. I remember things people said to me during the night and I write them down. They may eventually be a trigger for a scene or help me to re-enter the fictive world at some point in my process.

In your effort to crack open your character, it is absolutely necessary that you are obsessed, detail-oriented, controlling, and self-absorbed. Ask your family and friends to please understand that you are leaving the continent like Admiral Byrd and exploring dark Antarctica. You are hypnotizing yourself, shutting out almost everything else for the sake of conjuring up your characters and their world. As a writer you must commit to this process. It takes intense concentration. There is no other way. It has its cost. But you must be willing to pay it. You must want it badly enough to make it your first priority.

Getting to the Hard Questions

After the first phase of the free-write of gently getting to know my character and going out into the world to do research, I continue my free-writing on Fredrick. I start to ask him the hard questions. How can he justify his act? Does he think he is entitled to do anything he wants because of his wealth? Why hasn't he shared more of his money? And so on. I do not accept the first answer. I probe and probe until I finally hear something that I think is utterly truthful and surprising. These truths are the core of a character and very valuable. As I do all my questioning, I try to stick to my agenda, but I stay flexible and let Fredrick's answers lead me to new questions on the spot.

If I get bored with my character, I try to remain courageous and hang in there until I reach a breakthrough. If that does not seem to be happening, I drop my character entirely. I have learned from past experience, that if I simply cannot play or become a character or if one doesn't turn out as interesting as I had thought, then I will probably never be able to "crack" the character and use him or her in my story. If the story still holds me, I find a new substitute to personalize the character and begin a whole new free-write. Is this an insane amount of work to be doing? You bet it is. But it must be done. You must be persistent if you are ever to come up with characters that are alive, true, and complex. Sometimes it can take days and many, many pages of exploration before your character "comes alive." And when it happens, it is the most amazing thing to witness. It is birth.

Variations on the Free-Write

If you can only write about your character in the third person, then begin in that manner, but your character must eventually begin to speak using his or her voice. If you are blocked in your effort to do a free-write, a great way to unblock and create some flow is to find an object that means a lot to the character. This object can be anything, a hairbrush, an old Chevy, a pair of tap shoes. Ask the character why this object means so much, record an answer, and then ask if it could possibly mean something else. And something else again. Try to get past the obvious choices or responses. Usually it is the fourth or fifth answer that your character gives to a question that is the most interesting choice. Always push your free-writes until you get to the breakthroughs, where the gold is buried.

The free-write provides a way to have a greater frequency of breakthroughs or moments of flow. Once you have accumulated enough of these "breakthrough moments," then you must become conscious, look for patterns, and reflect on what they may evoke. From these patterns you begin to assemble a narrative; you begin to see what really haunts you. This self-knowledge is invaluable. It will lead you to write what you can truly handle. And what you can truly handle is always your best work. You will discover your subject, your world, your themes, and the type of characters that can best express what you unconsciously need to express. You might learn that you are interested in working-class people or people who are wealthy and privileged. You might find that you are interested more in satire than in tragedy or for some reason you always have the color pink in a scene: on a character's clothes, on a wall, in a painting. You may discover that you are more interested in archetypes rather than "layered" characters; that you are obsessed by spiritual questions rather than political ones; that the theme of betrayal is one that haunts you; or that your writing comes most alive with the theme of romantic love. The free-write provides you with meaningful direction, by leading you to worlds, characters, and interests that are organic to you.

When you have done enough free-write exploration for your major characters you are ready for the next step: an outline. It is time to get conscious again. To be a critic and kill your favorite creations because of the demands of your medium—film.

The Outline

The outline is an opportunity to address the arrangement and proportion of your screenplay; to deepen characterization and the specificity of the world; and to unearth more story and characters to find an unexpected plotline or two. An outline is an expansion of your five- to ten-minute verbal pitch, in which you have already given an extremely broad summary of the storyline. The outline helps you to discover if your storyline has a dramatic logic that will not falter when given a deeper examination and whether the central purpose will fill out an entire screenplay and not collapse on itself.

Limit your outline to seven to ten pages of written material (typed single-spaced on standard 8½ x 11" paper) broken into steps of dramatic progression, which will be explored in greater depth in this chapter. At this point of the screenplay sculpting process, the writer needs to think in practical terms. Ten to twelve reels of film need to be filled in order to complete an entire film, assuming each reel is ten minutes of screen time. The outline provides a detailed plan for filling that time. The best way to handle this challenge is to keep the outline simple by noting the progression of the scenes in very clear, distinct steps.

A Step Outline

A step outline sketches the progression of the film one step at a time, with one- or two-line descriptions of what happens next, abbreviating whenever possible. For example, a sample from a step outline for the story of Fredrick might look like this, with each step written on a separate index card:

1. **Chloe gets away with stealing.** Establishing shots of nursery school. Chloe plays blocks with other children, and, when the coast is clear, steals a child's favorite doll and lies about it to a teacher. Everyone is convinced she is innocent.
2. **Fredrick learns he will die soon without a new kidney.** Fredrick sits, half-naked, on an examining table, as a doctor delivers the news: his kidneys are beyond repair, his only hope is a new one. The waiting time for a new kidney is three years. The doctor estimates he has only six months. Nothing can be done to change the rules of the waiting list. It is first come, first served. No exceptions.
3. **Terrance may or may not be a good father.** Terrance strips his surgical scrubs, dashes through the hall, passing a dazed and upset Fredrick, and exits the hospital into the street. Thirty minutes late, Terrance runs to the nursery school to pick up Chloe who has been waiting with her teacher. The teacher reassures Terrance his daughter is a little doll.

4. **Fredrick's lawyer proposes they steal a kidney. Will Fredrick agree?** A party for wealthy socialites. Fredrick is with his wife. He orders a martini. She warns him about his health; he is getting drunk and it could seriously damage his kidney. Fredrick doesn't give a damn; he is on self-destruct. Raymond, a partner in a prestigious law firm approaches him. They are school chums. Fredrick confesses his troubles, Raymond pulls him aside and makes a proposal: he can arrange for a kidney within a week. How? Steal one, of course.

You may notice that the step outline is, at times, written almost in code. For instance, in the fourth step of the outline, it states that "Fredrick doesn't give a damn." There is no indication or description of how this is to be specifically accomplished in the writing. The fact that Fredrick doesn't give a damn may be made clear to an audience by dialogue, a reaction shot, or a montage; there are obviously many choices. But remember, a step outline only sketches the number of segments or scenes that need to be written in order to complete the screenplay. The specificity of those steps, the exact nature of their execution, should be left to when you are actually creating the scenes, which should not happen until all the planning is done with a step outline. The specifics of a scene should be discovered when writing the scene, otherwise the scene will lose spontaneity. You will notice there is a heading to each step in the outline in bold. This heading summarizes the essence of the scene, and how it adds to the overall progression of the screenplay.

When the step outline is completed the screenwriter should have a good sense of how well the entire screenplay will hold together and if it progresses with clarity, increasing the interest of the audience with every step. The step outline is a tool that will pinpoint weak characterization or storyline and ineffective arrangement and proportioning of the events and scenes of a screenplay.

Getting Practical with Index Cards

An excellent way to create a step outline is on index cards. Choose different color index cards for each act, each big question. Estimate how long each step of the outline will take in terms of film time. For instance, in step one above, I estimate it will fill two and half pages of a screenplay and take two and a half minutes of screen time. Write a step and its description on an index card, noting the essence of the scene, what it's about, and how it progresses the action of the story.

Write the estimated screen time each step will take on the index card and then pin it to the wall with a tack. Once all the index cards for one act are pinned to the wall, in a vertical row, step back several feet and try to "get the big picture." You may notice that if you add up the screen time for the first act, it would come to three hours! Certainly one could write a movie that runs three hours, but there are practical considerations. If you want to sell the film in the open marketplace, you had better keep it to no more than two hours, the average length of most of today's commercial screenplays.

There are other utterly realistic considerations that are best not ignored by the screenwriter at this point in the process. If you intend to shoot your film independently with a small budget, look at the number of locations and the number of extras. Perhaps you have too many of either, which will exceed the film's budget. For example, if the screenplay calls for a car chase scene in front of Tiffany's in Manhattan, on a Saturday afternoon, with crowds in the hundreds, for budgetary considerations you may want to change it to a chase down an alleyway in a less populated section of the city. Perhaps there is a character that lives in a very expensive, downtown Manhattan loft. You may want to think this through one more time, and find a rationale as to why this character may actually live in a one-bedroom apartment in Brooklyn that would be cheaper to shoot. Oftentimes, when forced to deal with these practical considerations, you may be surprised to discover how it injects more truth and specificity into the creation. Our first choices for location or action are often either the obvious choice or a generalized one. Practical considerations frequently and inadvertently force the writer to go beyond the obvious first choice.

When assessing the step outline, the writer may learn that many scenes can be cut simply because they "are about" what has already been said or expressed in some way. A film audience has very little patience for repetitiveness. Remember that film is a powerful medium and the audience can get the point with just a glance, reaction, or montage. The outline may indicate that new, unplanned characters are popping up in the story. For example, I may discover in the outline above that the assistant to the unscrupulous and desperate lawyer is becoming a very important character, certainly in terms of the plot, because of how she controls the lawyer and his world. Since this character was not originally planned for, I make a mental note to develop her later in a free-write. Upon reflection of my step outline, I may discover that I don't know much about the inner workings of a law office. So I make another mental note to do some interviews with people in the field. I may also begin to realize that I need to have a greater depth of understanding about the world of a hospital and organ donation. I make yet another note to do a day or two of research on that subject. Perhaps I notice that breaking my story up into two acts does not seem to work very effectively; it's just a feeling at this point, but I trust it. I go with this feeling and decide that there is one more big question that needs to be examined within the framework of the story, and therefore one more act needs to be planned. I adjust and accept this evolution and plan for a three-act screenplay.

The step outline will open up lots of questions and shed light on many of the weaknesses of a screenplay. Heed them. Solve them. Once you have finished your outline, completed any necessary and additional free-writes and research, reworked plotlines, thrown out entire characters and replaced them with new ones, and developed a clear sense of the arrangement and proportioning of acts, you are at last ready for the scene-by-scene writing. If you are totally prepared, and have taken a little break, you will be filled with the enthusiasm you need to meet the challenge of writing a full screenplay, and at the same time have an enormous database to draw upon that is "fresh in your mind." All the preparation and planning have helped to get you past the obvious choices.

How to Create
a Great Scene

You have already done hours of free-writes, tapped into your unconscious imagination, consciously developed your purpose, and refined your story and characters with the pitch and outline. You have done a great deal of preparation and now you are ready to execute a first draft, by fleshing out your outline with a scene or several scenes for each step of the outline. Creating scenes takes much longer than any other step of the process because, first of all, a great scene often needs to be revised many times before it has resonance. Secondly you simply have many more pages to fill usually—between 105 and 120.

Screenplay Format

Since we are getting to the point where you will actually start to "type up" a screenplay, let's discuss the most commonly accepted screenplay format.

1. A screenplay should be typed on white 8½ x 11" paper with the following margins: top: 1 inch; bottom: ½ inch; left: 1½ inches; right: 1 inch.
2. A slug line that describes the place, time of day, and whether the scene is interior or exterior, begins at the left margin and should end at the right margin. It should be typed in all capital letters.
3. A general description or action line that describes what the characters are doing begins at the left margin and ends at the right margin. The first time you mention a character in a general action line, the character should be in all caps.
4. The character name should be in all capital letters at 2½ inches from the left margin. If you fold your page in half, the name should begin at the fold.
5. The dialogue should being at 1½ inches from the left margin and end at 6½ inches from the left margin.
6. Parentheses descriptions (of reactions, emphasis, or physical action) go in two places. If they start the dialogue they should begin at 1½ inches from the left margin and end at 5 inches from the left margin. If they come within a dialogue then they should be on their own line and begin at 2½ inches from the left margin.
7. The Title Page (the first page of the screenplay) should be formatted so that the title is centered on line six. The first scene of the screenplay should begin on line twelve.

8. The cover of a screenplay should have the title and author's name centered. And at the bottom left-hand margin, the contact information: author's name, address, telephone number. It should be simply typed. Do not add any illustrations, drawings, or other unnecessary nonsense. It should be on a pale blue or green 65-pound card stock.

9. The font for the entire screenplay is 12 point Courier New.

10. The entire screenplay should be single-spaced. There should be a line space between a general action or slug lines and the name of a character and between the end of one character's dialogue and the next character's name line.

All new scenes of a screenplay must begin with the following noted on the slug line: whether the scene is an interior or exterior one, abbreviated in capital letters: INT. (interior) or EXT. (exterior); followed by a two- or three-line description of the location, also capitalized (i.e. MARTHA'S BEDROOM or MOUNTAIN PEAK); and lastly, the time of the day, again capitalized (i.e. DAWN, DUSK, EARLY MORNING). Do not write CLOSE-UP, PAN, MEDIUM SHOT, or any other camera angle unless it is absolutely necessary to effectively communicate the nature of the scene. If you do envision a change in camera angle just write NEW ANGLE on a separate line.

It is important that your screenplay read well since it will be viewed first by all of the gatekeepers: development executives, agents, directors, producers, stars, etc. Cluttering up a screenplay with descriptions of dozens, if not hundreds, of camera angles will work against it being a "good read." Remember your goal is to make your screenplay extremely readable. Also, overdoing your general action lines or descriptions in general is not a good idea; it will make your screenplay a "bad read" and also signal that you are not a professional. You should not use two pages to describe a really seedy room in the East Village, Manhattan, instead you can do the following, which is far more effective and professional:

```
INT. APARTMENT - LATE AFTERNOON            (Slug line)
The East Village. A shitty one-bedroom flat.
(General description or action line)

            JOHN            (Character's Name)

     (Anxiously) Begin dialogue here.
     (Parentheses description) (Dialogue)
```

Here is an example of how to write a montage incorporating sound and character descriptions.

```
RALPH, 37, dirty and tired, enters the kitchen as his wife
BARBARA, 36, in a threadbare dress, labors over the stove.
She ignores him and is very tense. We hear water boiling
in pots; a Kitchen-Aid grinds away, working a batter.

Ralph sits at the table, waiting for his meal to be served.
Barbara fixes a plate and grabs a butcher's knife.
```

```
Hesitant and stricken with terror, Barbara lunges the
knife into Ralph's chest. She does a bad job of it; the
knife doesn't pierce his chest, but hits his breast
bone and snaps in two.

Ralph rises, a madman, in shock. Barbara runs for her
life out the door. Ralph pulls the knife blade out of
his chest and dashes after Barbara.
```

You will notice that the descriptions are written in separate paragraphs. A new paragraph is begun when the action breaks into a new action, when there is a new beat. The sound descriptions are incorporated in the framing paragraph of the montage—the paragraph that sets up the montage (usually the first one). Again, changes in soundscape and camera angle should be noted in the rest of the montage only if it is essential for the reader to know because it significantly alters the mood or action.

When a director looks at this scene, he or she may break it down into as many as thirty camera angles. If the screenwriter wrote the specifics of camera angles, it would go on for pages and the tensions of the scene would not be effectively communicated to the reader; the drama would be lost to tedious technical instructions.

It is also important to avoid, at all costs, writing too many reactions. It is insulting to actors and directors and it is also a sign of an amatuer. Reactions should be written only of absolutely necessary.

Questions to Ask Yourself Before and After You Write a Scene

Upon first examination, it would seem that if a screenplay is made up of many scenes strung together, and, if a step outline provides a solid road map showing how the scenes are put together, then in order to make a screenplay all that is necessary is to create great scenes, one by one and place them where planned. Unfortunately, that is not the case. Ultimately, no one can really know how all the scenes of a screenplay will play together until they have been created and experienced as a whole. How different scenes will eventually act upon each other is unpredictable and after completing a first draft, a writer may discover that some of the best scenes of the screenplay need to be cut because they do not add to the progression of the movie; they misdirect the audience from the writer's purpose, or somehow repeat information. The duty of the writer is to stay one step ahead of the audience and not fall behind for a second. If a writer communicates something more than once through dialogue, pictures, reaction shots, or a montage, it will usually detract from the sense of progression.

Most screenplays, especially among beginning writers, show weakness first in characterization, and second in creating active scenes. There are basic laws to writing a great scene that are like the laws of thermodynamics—irrefutable and immutable. This chapter will examine these rules in great detail and to overlook them would be sheer folly.

Before I begin to write a scene I always examine it as I was trained to do—as an actor. When you think of a scene in this way, you are addressing practical concerns. Every actor knows that you cannot just walk into a scene unprepared; an audience or camera crew are waiting for a performance. I still have nightmares of playing unprepared before a packed house: wandering about the stage, improvising, sweating, dry-tongued. Yet many writers will do just that—begin a scene without the proper preparation: without the slightest idea of the character's previous circumstances, vague about what one character wants from another in the scene, lazy in the choice of actions, content if there is no event, and settling for virtually no stakes at all.

There are dozens of questions that writers should ask of themselves and of their characters and world before executing a scene. And the writer should try to find an uncommon response for each one of these questions. Again, it is a backwards and forwards process. The writer needs to be fully prepared before executing a scene, and, at the same time, be entirely in the moment when in the scene. This means that all preparation should be tossed away and used only if it organically arises in the midst of writing a scene. Preparation is a way to focus the imagination, to drive it toward greater specificity and link it to the unconscious; preparation, however, is not the scene. The scene is the scene, and it should be an act of spontaneous imagination, not a chance for writers to display how well they have done their research; it should be a given that all writers have done their homework. A writer should not feel a burden to work all the preparation into a scene while in the actual midst of writing a scene. The best work is usually written in a fever. Yet, if a writer has not fully prepared before falling into that fever, the work will be less interesting, less considered, less layered, cliché, and dull.

I have written the basics of a great scene in the form of questions. Before you begin to write a scene, ask yourself if you have given some consideration to the challenges that each question poses. Some of these questions are really asking the same thing from a different angle. A writer needs to examine the scenes from all angles in order to make them great. All of these questions should be asked before executing a scene. But they need to be asked again after writing a scene.

1. Are the Characters in Conflict?

Although the above may sound like a silly question, I don't know how many times I will ask students, after they have read some of their work out loud, "Where's the conflict in this scene?" They look at me agape, because when they examine it, there really is none. Drama is conflict. Without conflict there will be no drama. So there must always be conflict in every scene.

The Obstacle

Traditionally, conflict occurs when two characters have goals in opposition. However, there can actually be conflict in a scene when two people do not have opposing goals. For example, suppose two lovers both truly want to get married, yet there seems to be something blocking them from doing it. These blocks, or obstacles, provide conflict. Suppose they are both already married. In this case, they are blocked by an "external obstacle"—their legal and moral obligations to the institution of marriage. Suppose at the same time, they have both experienced really horrible marriages in the past, this emotional baggage would be another thing blocking them from getting married, an "internal obstacle." With these two obstacles in place, there could be tremendous conflict even though the two people have the same goal—to get married.

I prefer to think about conflict as an obstacle that prevents a character from getting what he or she desires. This obstacle can be external, internal, or interpersonal. The obstacle is more interesting if it is not a physical thing—a mountain, a car, a radar gun, but rather another person and his or her needs and actions, or some internal block or societal interdiction. All great scenes have conflict that exists on all of these levels simultaneously: internal, external, and interpersonal.

Three Levels of Conflict

Suppose John and Mary both want to get married. But John has an internal conflict, he is really gay and is hiding it from himself and Mary. This internal conflict can easily apply its force whenever he is in a scene with Mary. He must find a way to deny it at all times and keep it from influencing his judgment or revealing itself in his behavior or dialogue. Second, suppose he is a Pentecostal Christian but Mary is not, and the pastor of his church has warned him that, in order to have a successful marriage, he should not be "unequally yoked to a non-believer." John, who is very religious, takes this advice seriously. This scenario would provide an external conflict for John, in the form of a societal or community interdiction.

Finally, let's give John an interpersonal conflict with Mary: she has promised to convert to his faith, but told him today that she can no longer keep that promise, and John feels betrayed by her reversal. This overwhelming feeling of betrayal is a very potent obstacle between Mary and John. John must overcome it to keep from pushing her away with his anger. At the same time, this interpersonal conflict gives him an objective in the scene: he wants Mary to make a commitment today to go forward with the baptism and initiate herself into his church.

Now, let's propose three levels of conflict for Mary in this scene. Suppose her inner conflict is that she feels rejected and angry because John does not seem very sexually interested in her. Mary who is no youngster and was married before, has enjoyed a full sex life in the past. She finds no sin in sex outside of marriage. For her, lovemaking, with the right guy, is great fun. She has withheld her feelings about this matter because she does not want to lose John; she loves him deeply. A possible external conflict for Mary could be that she is taking the bar exam tomorrow. She has failed it once already and does not feel the least bit prepared, after spending years juggling a job and law school at night.

Finally, Mary's interpersonal conflict is that she wants John to sleep with her—here, now, today. She needs to make love to feel connected and supported because she is nervous about the exam. Mary is convinced that if she lovingly leads John into experiencing more sexual pleasure he will come around. Mary wants something here, now, today, and there are strong expectations attached to her objective: she fully expects that her actions will bridge the gap she has with John on the matter of sex.

As you can see, this scene is fully "loaded" before it starts. There is conflict on all three levels for each character and expectations attached to each level of conflict. When a scene has various levels of conflict it results in complexity and resonance. It also makes the writer's job easier because a fully loaded scene is more likely to just take off on its own and "write itself." The scene will lead the writer rather than the writer having to push or force it.

In the opening of *The Godfather*, Bonasera, an undertaker, asks Vito Corleone for help. Bonasera's daughter's boyfriend tried to "take advantage of her," and when she resisted his sexual advances trying to "keep her honor," she was brutally beaten, suffering a broken nose and jaw. The perpetrator received a suspended sentence and Bonasera doesn't think that justice was done. He wants Corleone to murder the boy in revenge. Corleone refuses and then remarks that Bonasera has not paid him the proper respect in the past because he has never come to him in friendship. He has never invited the Don to his house for coffee or asked his counsel, despite the fact that Corleone's wife is godmother to Bonasera's only child. The Don understands that Bonasera has never really needed Corleone—the undertaker has made a good living in America and up to now the system has worked for him. But the Don wants respect. Bonasera capitulates, calls him "godfather" and asks Corleone to be his friend. The Don grants his wish, he will bring justice to the situation for Bonasera.

This scene has great complexity and works wonderfully because all three levels of conflict exist for each character. The external conflict for Vito Corleone is that today is his daughter's wedding day, and Sicilian tradition dictates that you cannot refuse a favor to anyone on that day. His internal conflict is that he feels disrespected and has been slighted in the past by Bonasera. The interpersonal conflict is that Corleone has to give a guy he doesn't really like, Bonasera, what he wants, and at the same time maintain his self-respect. Bonasera's external conflict is that he must play by the rules of the family, not the rules of American law that he wants to play by. Bonasera has invested himself in the American justice system and it has failed him by not delivering the proper order to his life. His internal conflict is obvious, he has a thirst for revenge; he is haunted by the brutal beating of his daughter. His interpersonal conflict is also clear, he wants help from Corleone on his terms, not on the terms of "the family," which dictate that Bonasera not only pay respect, but also enmesh himself with their corruption, "their business." In a sense, Bonasera has the same interpersonal conflict Corleone has: he must get what he wants without losing his self-respect. But Bonasera cannot get what he wants on his terms. Corleone and the monolith of the family is too big an obstacle to overcome. So Bonasera must adjust his tactics. He kisses the Don's hand, submitting, and declares Corleone his godfather, and in so doing he loses his self-respect, the cost he must pay in order to get revenge.

The three levels of conflict shape the scene, giving it texture, variety, and complexity. Every moment of the scene has a certain tension because there is so much going on for each character and so many land mines that can go off. The screenwriters Francis Coppola and Mario Puzo were successful in bringing all of these layers of conflict to the scene, and they did not just lie there dormant, which can sometimes happen. The conflicts shape, twist, and give nuance to the actions, dialogue, and reactions of both characters, and in the process reveal the web of connections and expectations both Corleone and Bonasera have about each other, themselves, and the world.

Warring Conflicts

As you may notice, in the Bonasera scene, the internal, interpersonal, and external conflicts are clearly at war. Warring conflicts within one person usually create great scenes and provide maximum complexity. In *A Short Film about Love* (discussed in chapter seven), the young man Tomek looks across the courtyard to see a lover enter the older woman's (Magda) apartment at night. Magda is a middle-aged adult, so there is nothing unusual about a visit from a lover. But the young man is wild with jealousy, masochistically watching her pleasure herself with another man. While Magda and her lover are in the midst of foreplay, Tomek calls the gas company and reports that there is a leak in Magda's apartment. A short while later two technicians from the gas company arrive, pounding on the door of Magda's apartment, interrupting her lovemaking. Tomek watches from his window as a confused Magda runs to get her clothes, trying to get control over the situation. As the gas attendants leave the apartment, satisfied that it has all been a big mistake, Tomek breaks out laughing, gleeful, childish, releasing his tension over his twisted practical joke. As his laughter subsides, he pauses and bangs his fist against the wall. Angry and ashamed of himself, he sinks into greater depression and isolation. Achieved entirely through visual means, this scene has tremendous complexity because of the warring conflicts within Tomek. He is filled with jealousy and wants to control Magda's world and so he makes the phony phone call to the gas company. At the same time, he is delighted with his own ingenuity and the success of his ploy, and is filled with glee. On top of all that, he knows his behavior is wrong and is utterly ashamed; he has hurt the one who he claims he loves and has crossed a boundary.

All of these feelings grow out of the conflicts within Tomek that are at war with each other. Each one of these emotions strongly pull at Tomek and compete for expression, causing him to take action. The feelings, in and of themselves, have clarity because they spring from a basic human place and the result of this stew of warring feelings is great complexity, resonance, and spontaneity.

Before you begin writing any scene, you should have already found original and compelling possibilities for each type of conflict. They are basic to any good scene. Again, never settle for your first or second choice. Go beyond them and you may discover that your first choice was the best. But going beyond the first choice and returning to it makes the first choice even richer, because it will be fully considered.

2. What Does My Character Want?

No great scene was ever created without a character wanting something as if his or her life depended on it. If your character is passive and unclear about what he or she wants, you will have a weak scene. A scene is only as strong as the character with the weakest need.

Objective

What a character wants is called an objective. I much prefer the word objective to intention, because it evokes greater specificity. Borrowing from Uta Hagan, an objective is the overall goal that a character has—here, now, today—in a scene. The objective must be accomplished in the scene, not off camera, or anyplace else. For something to be dramatic, the struggle must be witnessed in the present tense, before our very eyes.

The objective is the "why" of the scene.

In the opening scene of *The Godfather*, Bonasera wants the Don to avenge his daughter's beating. To achieve this objective he must first explain his tale of woe, then make his proposal and entice the Don. When the Don is not in agreement, Bonasera must persuade him. When the Don asks him specifically what he has in mind, Bonasera proposes his plan to avenge his daughter by killing the ex-boyfriend. When the Don points out Bonasera's previous independence, Bonasera must submit and declare his allegiance. To explain, to propose, to entice, to persuade, to confront, to reveal, to submit, to declare, are clearly the major series of actions in the scene. Working backwards, you can ask why this man behaves this way, why does he take these specific series of actions—here, now, today. And the answer that you come up with, the "why" of it all, is his objective.

Line of Action: An Active Verb

A good scene can always be boiled down to one issue. Will she marry him? Will he avenge my daughter's dishonor? Is he going to get the job? Everything the characters do in the scene, which of course relates to what they what, is derived from this one line of action. Every scene must have a clear line of action for it to have clarity. A scene will only be clear if it has a clear "line of action" that comes out of a basic human emotion—love, betrayal, joy, jealousy, desire, ecstasy, etc. Going back to the scene with John and Mary, if John enters the scene and knows exactly what he wants (Mary's conversion to his faith), the scene will have clarity and a clear line of action. The line of action that drives the scene is John's attempt to get Mary to convert. The rest of the conflicts are loaded in John providing nuance in the scene and they can express themselves at any moment and turn the action in another direction.

A character can only pursue one line of action at a time in a scene. This line of action should be simple-stupid clear. The line of action is given specificity and nuance by the internal, external, interpersonal conflicts in the scene; they spin, shape, and bend the line of action into something unique. For instance, John's line of action is to get Mary to convert, but his internal conflict of being secretly gay will specifically affect what he chooses to say, the points he will emphasize, and the points he will do his best not to emphasize.

In the opening of *The Godfather,* Don Corleone wants something that clearly comes from a basic human emotion: he wants respect. Various characters enter his dark chambers, each with a very clear line of action. Johnny Fontane, a popular singer who has been refused the lead in a new war film by the head of a Hollywood studio, wants the Don to use his influence to get him the role. Johnny is part of the family and he has been slighted and so it now falls to a male member of the family to intercede and protect his interests. Fontane's line of action is clear because it is based on a human emotion: ambition. Luca Brasi, the stuttering, simple, hit man, pledges his loyalty to the Don. Luca's line of action is also clear: He wants security, to belong, and to have a place in the family. If your scene is unclear, then you should examine its line of action. Each character should have an arc—line of action—that grows from the character's guts; it should give us a way to understand and track what is driving a character.

Actions: Mental and Physical

In order for a scene to have a clear line of action, it must have characters with clear objectives. If characters are true to their objectives, they will take action—both physical and mental—in order to achieve them. In the modern narrative, the actions tend to be mental actions, not physical ones like jumping through a window, driving a car down a street, or blowing up a bridge. A mental action is best stated as an active verb—to seduce, to manipulate, to plead—and is usually portrayed with words, not pictures. But since pictures are the magic of a movie, a mental action can be made physical in a montage.

In *The Truman Show,* we see Truman furtively rip pictures of female models from beauty magazines. We watch as he tries to construct a composite from different parts of the models' faces. When we first see this behavior, we have no idea what he is doing or why—there is a mystery to it. Later, it is revealed that he had a true love who "left for Figi," abducted by a man posing as her father. Truman's objective behind this behavior is to reconstruct a composite of his true love.

These actions could have been executed in dialogue, generated from a conflict with another person, but it would have not been as effective and it also would have violated the author's intention to dramatically express and give us a feeling of the oppression and fear this man lives under. If Truman just "talked this out" with someone, then it would diminish the specific feeling that the author is trying to communicate that he is an emotionally isolated and trapped man, even though he is surrounded by lots of "friendly" people. When writing your scene, if you can translate mental actions into montages, without losing complexity, then definitely go in that direction, unless, of course, it violates your purpose.

3. Is My Character's Objective Linked to Desire or Need?

What a character wants can be broken into two parts: desire and need. When placing a character in a scene, you should use desires and not needs to shape the character's objective.

In *Rushmore,* Max Fischer desires Rosemary Cross, an older teacher, but what he really needs is Margaret Yang, a fellow student with whom he can have a real relationship. In *Shakespeare in Love,* Will Shakespeare's desire is to break his writing block; what he needs is to find true love to get over his block. In *The Godfather,* Michael Corleone desires to show his love and support for his father while he recuperates from an attempted assassination. What he needs, and certainly does not desire, is to take over for his father, to assume the throne. His criticism of the family and rejection of playing any part in the business masks his unconscious need to be the top dog. In *Happiness,* Bill desires the eleven-year-old Johnny. What he needs is intense psychiatric intervention.

Always begin a scene by getting into the characters' shoes and imagining what they desire. Form an objective from that place, rather than asking what they need. In real life, most of us never know what we need because we operate from our desires, not our needs. If your characters go for what they need and not what they desire you will often lose nuance and idiosyncrasies. Suppose Max's objective in *Rushmore* is to win what he needs—Margaret Yang. Besides being a boring choice, we would never see the side of Max that is the most engaging—the dreamer. If he didn't try hard to win his desire, the schoolteacher Rosemary, the audience would not get a glimpse of how he builds coalitions, usurps authority, and can be so wonderfully undaunted.

Often, a need can be an obstacle to an objective. Michael Corleone's duty to assume the throne is clearly an example of that. His desire is to break out of the family. His duty (need) draws him back in. A character is most alive, alert, engaged, vulnerable, driven, specific, and complex, when going for what he or she desires. So locate the desire, not the need.

4. Am I Confusing Condition with Objective?

A condition is something your character already had in a scene, like polio or cancer, a learning defect or a limp. A condition is not a need or a desire. Don't confuse these concepts.

One of my students, a very good writer, read scenes from his screenplay about several characters who had cancer and lived together in an alternative healing facility. His major character, a very funny man, seemed to go from scene to scene just being funny. After the reading, I asked the student what this character wants. "He wants to find a cure for his cancer, or at least find ways to prevent it from recurring." he said. "Okay. Great. But what does he want in the moment—here, now, today?" I asked.

It is a given that anyone who has cancer wants to be cured and does not want it to recur, but this is not a desire that is specific and in the moment. People who have cancer still want revenge, to fall in love, or to take control of a business meeting. Cancer is a condition they must deal with and it may or may not affect how they pursue their objectives in a scene. A condition is not an action or an objective. A condition is an affliction, a state of being. Don't fall into the trap of playing the character's condition in a scene. Make sure your character has a basic and truthful human desire at all times, and that he or she pursues this desire, with a specific objective in mind.

In *My Left Foot,* Christy Brown is born with cerebral palsy and can use only one limb—his left foot. Cerebral palsy is his condition. Despite his condition, he takes actions, and pursues objectives in life, just like everyone else. In the opening of the film, while waiting to receive an award for his writing, he has a flask of whiskey hidden in his pocket and wants desperately to have a sip through a straw, but a hired nurse objects. Brown deflects her attention by asking for a light for a cigarette:

> **NURSE**
> But Mr. Brown, you know that smoking is not good for you.
>
> **BROWN**
> I didn't ask for a fucking psychological lecture, I only asked for a fucking light.

Brown is a character fiercely determined to get what he wants; he is not his condition. He is a complex person that has moment-to-moment, as well as overall objectives. A condition is descriptive not dramatic. If a writer has the character playing a condition in a scene, the scene will be passive, inactive, and not compelling.

5. Have I Made a Positive Choice for My Character?

Always try to find choices that are about your characters going toward something they want rather than avoiding something they don't want. If characters exist in a scene because they are trying not to do something, then they will be less active and specific.

For example, let's think of a scene about a young man who wants to leave his hometown. He has outgrown it and is unchallenged by what it has to offer. If the writer makes negative choices for his character—avoiding boredom, escaping drudgery, wanting to run away—the scene will be weaker and less effective. A positive choice is one that operates out of a character's desire, with expectations and a specific goal in mind. By changing the negative choices—avoiding, escaping, wanting to run away—into something more positive and specific—going to New York to study acting, starting a software company in San Francisco, or climbing Mount Everest—the character will be more active and have greater humanity, with clear and achievable objectives. "Escaping" is general, not specific, and hence less doable. If an objective is less doable it cannot evolve into a clear line of action and the scene will lack focus.

Will Shakespeare in *Shakespeare in Love* comes to life and galvanizes the scenes he is in because he has met his true love and acts on his feelings to declare his love to her. We find out that Will has had some bad relationships in the past, including a marriage that went sour. If the writers were to make negative choices for Will, like not wanting to "make the same mistake again" or wanting to avoid rejection, then we would never have the great scenes that exist in the movie. Instead positive choices were made for Will: he sticks his neck out, becomes very active and specific, pursues the woman he loves, and seeks her love in return. Of course, Will's past marriage has its ramifications in the scenes; he is most likely very careful about sticking his neck out because he has been badly burnt in the past. But the feeling of wanting to protect himself and avoid rejection, is just that—a feeling. A character cannot play a feeling, but must take some action to deal with a feeling. If the objective of the character is specific and clear, so will be the actions.

Trapping Emotions in the Actions

All characters need a full emotional life if they are to be fully realized. However, if your character just plays the emotion and does not find a way to put it into a container—an action—then the scene will be less effective. If your character is filled with grief over the loss of a child and simply plays this emotion in a scene, you will have a weaker scene. You will have a better scene if you take that same character, a mother who has lost her daughter to AIDS, and trap her feelings in a strong action—initiating a campaign in her neighborhood to raise money for AIDS research.

Trapping emotion in an action is a way to create counterpoint. When we see a character trying not to cry by trapping that feeling in cleaning the house or calling a friend, it is counterpoint. Counterpoint adds resonance and increases the complexity of the characterization. Finally, trapping the emotion in an action often gives the audience "space" to experience the emotion. Again, if a character tries hard to keep from crying, the audience will cry instead. Since it has not been done vicariously for them, they must do it to make the viewing experience complete.

Characters Do Things for the Best of Reasons

All of us, most of the time, do whatever we do in life for the best of reasons. Sergeant Hartman in *Full Metal Jacket* is a fully realized character because he does what he does for the best of reasons. He wants his recruits to be the best soldiers they can be to live up to the rigorous standards and traditions of the Marines. To ensure that this happens, he must ride them hard and demand a great deal from them. If he had wanted to break the spirits of the recruits just because it gives him a thrill or to show his superiority, then the scenes would be less interesting and less layered. Basically the character would be judged by the writer and judging a character is a sure way to make him or her one note. It is important to not stand outside characters, but to get under their skins, and rationalize like they do—finding positive reasons for everything they do.

Even if the results or outcome of your character's action is pure evil, it is the writer's responsibility to make that character human by providing motives for the actions that the character would be proud or at least not ashamed of. Sergeant Hartman is proud that he is performing his duties well by making good soldiers out of the unfocused recruits, and consequently there is a clarity about his actions. His job of hammering these boys into top-notch fighting machines is also a calling, mission, or cause. Giving such a positive choice to the character will not only make the character more human, but also more magnetic.

6. Have I Asked a Compelling "What If?"

It is best, in terms of process, if a writer has no idea what is going to happen in a scene before writing it. A scene should be written in order to discover the answer to a very intriguing and compelling proposition—a "what if?" If this "what if?" is thrilling, engaging, tantalizing enough, the writer will thirst and ache to write the scene, and become fully engaged in the activity. There will be no writer's block; the flow will be swift and pure. What if Mary senses something askew in John's defensiveness? And what if John feels he must confess the truth to Mary about his involvement with other men and his preference for a male rather than a female lover? What if Mary is also filled with sheer lust, and plans on seducing John, here, now, today? With such clear propositions in place that spring from basic human emotions focused around a line of action, a writer can literally burst into a flow, dive deep into the unconscious, and discover. A writer can create this kind of excitement before executing a scene, by making choices on all three levels of conflict for each character, choosing a clear line of action for each participant of the scene, and then letting the chips fall where they may. If a writer knows what is going to happen before writing, then the scene will often feel contrived because it will not be as organic or surprising to the writer and therefore to the audience. A writer should hone his or her truth meter—that small voice inside that can be heard only when the mind is still—and trust it during the execution of a scene. If, after writing a scene, the writer is not surprised by the discoveries within it, then it is time to start again and continue revising until something pops as a true discovery.

7. What Is the Worst Thing That Could Happen?

In order to make a scene more dramatic, you should not only ask present tense "what if?" questions, but you should ask questions with the greatest stakes. You need to ask: what is the worst thing that could happen? Kurt Vonnegut told young writers they should learn to think like a "hack"—someone who does not have a passionate connection to the work and who will write just about anything for the money. To accomplish this, he suggested continually asking what is the worst thing that could happen. If a man is arrested for stealing a bag of flour in a small town in the rural South, what is the worst thing that could happen? He is given a punishment that does not fit the crime: a lengthy prison sentence in a maximum-security penitentiary. What is the worst thing that could happen after that? He is made to work on the chain gang. What worse thing could happen? The chain gang must clear the roads in his hometown. Embarrassed to be seen as a convict, he manages to avoid being identified by keeping his head low and turning into the shoulder of the road. What again is the worst thing that could happen? He has left a favorite dog Smokey behind. Smokey comes running across the town square and recognizes his master; barking, leaping, licking, he alerts everyone in town to who this man is.

Asking what the worst thing is that could happen is what most hacks do. But hacks are effective and employable because they are great craftsmen. Learn from their craft, and ignore whatever else they do. The difference between you and them is that they make cliché choices and don't stick to the truth of a character or world. They generalize and avoid complexity and do not treat their subject matter with the same personal, deeply felt attention that you do.

Here are some examples of applying the question to some recent films. Young Will Shakespeare in *Shakespeare in Love* has no money, and a play, for which he has been commissioned, is long overdue. What's the worst thing that could happen? He has writer's block. But at least he finds his true love. What's the worst thing that could happen? She is forced to marry a lord and neither of them has any legal right to go against this arrangement.

In *The Fugitive*, Dr. Kimble comes home to find his wife dead; can there be anything worse than that? Yes. The murderer is still in the house and tries to kill him. Can it get any worse than that? Sure. The murderer escapes and Kimble is falsely accused of the murder.

How about *Happiness?* Bill, the pedophiliac good Dad, lusts after his son's eleven-year-old friend. He decides to drug him by lacing ice cream sundaes with a sleeping potion so he can rape the friend. What's the worst thing that could happen? He almost gets discovered by his wife while lacing the ice cream. What's the worst thing that could happen yet? It turns out that the boy "hates chocolate fudge." What's the worst thing that could happen? He isn't in the mood for anything else. Not even a drink. "But there must be something," Bill, the pedophiliac good Dad, asks, not giving up on pursuing his desire. "Do you have any grape Hi C"? replies Johnny. What's the worst thing that could happen? Trish, Bill's wife, informs him that they are out of it. Asking this question will lead the writer to choices that have greater stakes. And when the stakes are high, a scene is more resonant.

Hone Your Truth Meter

Before executing a scene ask yourself: what is the worst thing that could happen given the character and situation? Write down at least six choices. Pick the one that most aptly answers this question without seeming overly contrived or false. You are not trying to create a melodrama, (unless, of course, that is your purpose), you are trying to find the most compelling choice for your scene. Your choice should organically suit your characterization and vice versa. If you make a choice that violates the truth of your character, then you have failed to accomplish the most difficult task a writer has: to merge narrative and character. Narrative and character should flow truthfully into one an other, so that there are no gaps and no obvious rupture of either truth—character or story. You are required, at the very least, to have people believe what is happening on the screen, in the moment.

If you do not meet this requirement, your audience will fall out of the scene. And if you want your work to be lasting, your audience should still believe after they have seen your movie. If their belief holds up after a second viewing, you may have created a classic. If they look at it again in twenty-five years and still believe, then you probably have written a film that will stand the test of time. I say "probably" because the final test happens long after we will have gone to the grave. But, in the meantime, striving to be absolutely honest with your characters and their world, is the only way to create permanence in your work.

8. Why Is Today Like No Other?

Remembering Stanislavsky's dictum (Here, Now, Today—What if?), you should make a decision, before you execute a scene, about why this moment in time is unique and extraordinary. The best way to do this is to ask the question: why is today like no other? If a scene takes place on an ordinary day then things just tend to remain ordinary. *The Godfather* begins on an extraordinary day—Don Corleone's daughter's wedding day. *Hamlet* starts on an out-of-the-ordinary day when the ghost of Hamlet's father appears. *Saving Private Ryan* begins on D-day.

I am not suggesting that you only begin a screenplay on a special day, I am suggesting that every scene be rooted in a unique time and place, a once-in-a-lifetime type of choice. One of the most powerful scenes in *A Short Film about Love* is when the young man openly declares his love to the older woman. It is like no other day because we truly get the sense that it is the first time he has ever been in love. If you are about to execute your scene and realize that today "is just like every other," then stop and reconsider. There are very few great scenes that occur on ordinary days. Finally, as with all matters of choice for your scene, use discretion. Every world and set of characters has its own reality. Don't violate that reality or your truth meter by making choices that are contrived or unbelievable. You must create a day like no other that is truthful to the world and characters of your story.

9. Has the Stasis Been Broken?

Every scene begins in stasis—a stable state. Things would stay as they had been up until this point if something does not happen to unleash forces that break the stasis apart. If something breaks the stasis, then things can no longer be the way they were, they must change, even if only slightly. The essence of dramatic progression is that every scene should break the stasis of the world of the story in some way. This breaking of the stasis is called an event. Every great scene has at least one major event.

Major Events

In *Shakespeare in Love*, Philip Henslowe, a "businessman with a cash flow problem," is caught by his financier Mr. Fennyman and his henchmen and confronted with the reality of not having paid his bills. A thug lowers Mr. Henslowe's feet onto hot coals, and Henslowe screams for his feet, among other things. The stasis at the top of the scene is that Henslowe has not paid his debts and has failed to convince his financier that he will be able to do so. The stasis is broken with a little torture and Henslowe, with his feet burning, wants to find equilibrium and bring comfort and safety back to his body. Henslowe escapes his torturers by announcing that he can repay his entire debt because he has the rights to Will Shakespeare's new comedy. "It's a crowd-tickler—mistaken identities, a shipwreck, a pirate king, a bit with a dog, and love triumphant," he assures the collector. This bit of information intrudes upon Fennyman's actions (torturing and interrogating), stalling them at first, but then stopping them altogether. Equilibrium has returned to the scene once Henslowe has convinced Fennyman that his money will be returned. The major event of the scene is Henslowe narrowly escaping mutilation by convincing his financier he has a business plan credible enough to pay back his debts. The stasis is broken as the relationship between Henslowe and his financier becomes more amicable. Henslowe has found a way to restructure his debts and must now make sure this restructuring will work. He did not have this burden at the top of the scene. An indication of whether or not a major event has occurred in a scene is if the character, who is the emotional center of the scene, has a different need or objective at the end of the scene than he or she did at the beginning.

10. Stakes: Is There a Great Deal to Lose and No Easy Way Out?

The way to find out if there are real stakes in a scene is to ask for each character if there is a lot to lose and no easy way out. If characters do not have a lot to lose if they fail to get what they want, then there are no stakes in the scene. If a character can walk away from a scene without the risk of suffering a dreadful loss—emotionally, spiritually, or otherwise—then there is nothing at stake.

The stakes are high for Michael Corleone *(The Godfather)* in the scene where he must save his father in the hospital—life and death. If Michael does not get what he wants, to protect his father from the oncoming assassins, his father will die. Is that a lot to lose? Need we ask? Is there an easy way out for Michael? Can he walk away and let his father die? Would that be easy for a character like Michael, who prides himself on "doing the right thing," and has proven his strength to stand up to the family and everyone else in life up until this point? Obviously the very nature of his personality, the soul of his character, would never permit him to walk away easily. The stakes are real, they are enormous, and they operate from a basic human emotion.

In *Jules and Jim,* if Jim breaks off with Catherine for the last time, what will he lose? Perhaps the last chance he will ever have at true love. Is that a lot to lose? Of course it is. Is there an easy way out of this situation for Jim? Let me answer that with another question: have you ever found it easy to walk away from true, passionate love?

Does Henslowe have a lot to lose when he is being tortured in *Shakespeare in Love?* Only his feet, the tip of his nose, and his ear. Is there an easy way out? Not when you are tied to a chair and have a three-hundred-pound thug at your side (as you can see, the stakes have to be even higher for comedy to work). If we dig deeper, it becomes more complex. Henslowe has given his life to the theater. If he is cut off from financing and not able to produce another show, his whole life will come to a halt and his identify will be shattered.

At the beginning of *Secrets and Lies,* Maurice, a middle-class photographer, comes home to find his wife, Monica, distant and cold. He goes to kiss her and she pushes him off with "Mind, out of the way!" He kindly offers her a drink and she nastily retorts "What? If I want a drink, I'll get it myself, thank you!" He is trying his best to defuse her anger, but she clearly wants to start a fight. Maurice's objective in the scene is to keep his connection with his wife, it would seem, at almost any cost. Monica is clearly provoking him; she wants him to get angry at her because she is angry at him—she wants a fight. Both characters work hard to achieve their objectives, and in the end Maurice wins. But it is a lonely victory. He has avoided a destructive confrontation with his wife, but their distance has grown. Are there stakes to this tiny scene? Yes. Maurice, alone, in bed with Monica at night, explains them very clearly:

> MAURICE
> I'm frightened.
>
> MONICA
> Why?
>
> MAURICE
> You don't love me anymore. Not like you used to.

It appears that her love has died. But Maurice loves Monica dearly and he has a lot to lose. It would be very untrue for him to jump ship when he suspects his wife has lost her love for him. This loyalty is built into his character. To walk away from his marriage of many years and the home he has worked so hard to build would be the worst of failures. There is absolutely no easy way out of this situation; he must fight to get her back.

You need to rethink your stakes if your character will only have a bad night's sleep if he does not get what he wants, or he really doesn't have to get what he wants today because there will be other opportunities down the road. Low stakes are one of the most common problems with my students' scenes. Finally, the stakes have to be clear, simple-stupid, and spring from a basic human emotion.

11. What Are the Previous Circumstances?

Beginning writers often neglect to ask the basic question of what happened to the characters just before they entered the scene? By asking this question you will not only uncover new layers in the scene, but you may also crack it open and find a flow for one that has stalled.

Let's suppose Bob is going to ask Susan to marry him today, but right before he enters the scene he learned his mother has died. These previous circumstances give the scene a specific and unique spin. Suppose you wrote the same scene imagining Susan has just come from the doctor's office with a confirmation that she is pregnant and the father is not Bob. How would the scene go then? Or suppose that Susan just saw Bob walking in the park, holding hands with another woman. Or it could be something completely simple and unrelated: suppose Bob has just spilled hot coffee on his pants and is not sure if he has burned his leg? Or suppose Susan just ran a five-mile race in record time? Or Bob ran over a puppy while driving on the highway? Anyone of these choices could make the scene come alive in an utterly unique fashion. Previous circumstances add texture, distinction, and nuance to a scene.

IMPROVISATION ON THE PAGE: PLAYING WITH THE ESSENTIAL COMPONENTS OF A SCENE

EXERCISE

Objective: To isolate feelings, action, objective, and previous circumstances, in order to understand and become aware of how they impact and layer a scene.

FEELINGS	ACTIONS	OBJECTIVE	PREVIOUS CIRCUMSTANCES
anxious	seduce	to win trust	lost your job
in love	heal	prove importance	fell in love
longing	convince	be loved	someone died
abandoned	humiliate	gain approval	discovered a falsehood
grieving	manipulate	expose the truth	had great sex
hopeful	charm	revenge a wrong	won the Academy Award
angry	assure	sacrifice for an ideal	birth of your child
content	threaten	recover something lost	witnessed an execution
envious	control	gain freedom	been dumped
powerful	persuade	connect deeply	had a religious experience
sad	pledge	to get help for others	
confident	deceive	create an adventure	
confused	inspire	do your job well	

Taking two characters you have created, write a short scene choosing one description for each character from each column in the previous chart. The feeling you choose is the emotional life of the character—how they feel as the scene begins. Obviously, as things change in the scene, so will the characters' feelings. The same is true for the chosen action, it is merely the action the character will take to begin the scene. If this action does not help the character achieve an objective (and if there is true conflict in the scene, it will not), the action should be dropped, and the character will employ a new action. The new action should be discovered by the writer while writing the scene. Do not resist these changes. The objective and previous circumstances must remain the same throughout the scene. The length of the scene should be as long as it takes for the writer to arrive at an organic and truthful major event.

Once you have created a scene, revise it using the same characters, time, and place, but this time change the feelings and action used to begin the scene for each character. Keep the same objective and previous circumstance as used before. Write a new scene until you arrive at a major event.

After writing the scene examine what happened when you changed the feeling and action for your characters at the top of the scene? Which set of choices produced the most interesting scene and why?

Revise the scene again choosing different objectives and previous circumstances for each character in the scene, keeping the beginning feelings and actions for each character the same as the last time. Reflect on the effect of these changes on the outcome of the revised scene. When you changed the objective and previous circumstances, how did it change your characters and why? Did it affect the scene in subtle or not so subtle ways? Which choices were most effective?

12. Is the Scene in the Present Tense?

Something is most dramatic if we witness it in the present tense. If a story is about a man proposing to a woman and we do not see the moment when he actually asks her—then we will not get the thrill of being there in the moment.

If you write a scene in which the characters talk about a marriage proposal as something that has happened we get bored. Have you ever sat around listening to people talk about a shared experienced that you have not shared with them? How long does that discussion hold your attention? Not long. It's like watching someone else's home movies. As a screenwriter it is important to keep all matters in the present tense—to show us, not tell us. Make it happen before our very eyes. Don't have a character come into a scene and talk about his or her thoughts and feelings about just getting married. Let us see them get married and learn with them, not after the fact.

13. Have I Fully Considered the Physical Life of the Scene?

The physical life of a scene is what the characters are doing besides pursuing their objectives. They could be washing dishes, removing a splinter from a finger, opening oysters, or shuffling a deck of cards. It is important to give consideration to the physical aspect of a scene, either before you execute the first draft (it is always best to prepare this way) or at least when you are revising.

For example, if Robert were to ask Jane to marry him while repairing a broken doll for his niece, the scene would have greater specificity. The physical object, the broken doll, may also open flow that could reveal something about Robert that we didn't already know. Suppose, in the middle of the scene, Robert reveals that as a child he had a doll that he loved, but because he was afraid of being ridiculed, he hid it from everyone. Suddenly the scene becomes unique, and at the same time, the audience organically learn more about Robert.

In *The Godfather,* Don Corleone, falls and has a fatal heart attack while entertaining his grandson. The physical life of the scene is superb: Brando slices an orange and places the peel against his teeth, pretending to be a monster. It not only adds an interesting texture but also breaks the stasis of the scene when the child bursts into tears and forces Corleone to comfort him. This physical life created a flow and opened the door for a very specific and interesting character reveal. It is also a very original way to write a death scene by juxtaposing play with death. Look for ways to add an interesting physical life to your scene before you execute it. Besides providing rich texture it may provide powerful reveals or break open possibilities for more story. Since the most moving thing about a moving picture is often something moving, a strong physical life will often kick a scene up a notch.

14. Have I Shown Too Much?

One dictum holds true time and time again: start a scene in the middle and get out before the finish. Writers often make the mistake of giving too much information. The audience does not need to know how someone walked into a building, climbed forty stories, picked the lock on the roof door, opened the roof door, tripped on the chair on the roof, and jumped over the chain link fence to get to the edge. Showing that in real time would take twenty to thirty minutes and bore the audience to death. Often all you need to do is show the character entering the building, his first leap onto the chain-link fence, and then cut quickly to him standing on the ledge looking down. The enlarged photo of a movie tells the audience very quickly what is happening and you must stay one step ahead of them at all times. When you are done with your scene, always go back over it to pare it down to the bare essentials, making your point only once and trusting it.

15. Does the Scene Have Rising Conflict?

Earlier we asked if the characters in the scene are in conflict. The scene as a whole must also be examined to see that it has conflict and exactly what type. Lajos Egri, in *The Art of Dramatic Writing*, delineates four types of conflicts: rising, static, jumping, and foreshadowing. The screenwriter should be aware of these four types of conflict and use them as diagnostic tools.

Rising Conflict

When a scene progresses without gaps or transitional problems it has rising conflict. The conflict rises, smoothly, in terms of tempo and rhythm, from beat to beat. A beat marks a change in action in a scene. The transitions from action to action, its beats, must be smooth and steadily increase the tension of the scene until it reaches a climax. A string of minor events should truthfully and fluidly build to a major event. This type of conflict is the result of creating complex, specific characters who pursue clear lines of action. In order for rising conflict to exist within a scene, the characters must be, as Egri notes, "three-dimensional" with clear objectives. A scene that has rising action is one that is well orchestrated with no sense of contrivance when it reaches its climax. The scene's highest point is "the final culmination of everything that was said and done in the scene," as Edward Wright notes in *Understanding Today's Theater*, and is the logical outcome of the forces that were unleashed at the start of the scene.

Let's examine a scene with clear rising action. In *The Apostle*, written and directed by Robert Duvall, Sonny, a preacher with marital problems, enters a trailer home to meet with his wife, Jessie. Before he enters, there is a brief scene where he tells a buddy, "Just sit here in the car and wait, in case I start chokin' this woman to death. If I do, you'll know it!" The audience is set up to understand that Sonny is physically abusive to his wife and cannot control himself:

> A rather quiet but tense scene between Sonny and his wife. She watches his hands during the whole scene.
>
>   SONNY
> For some time.
>
> Jessie nods in the affirmative.
>
>   SONNY
> (Continuing) For a lot longer than this dumb, blind son of a bitch could ever thought about, right?
>
> Jessie looks off.
>
>   SONNY
> (Looking directly at her) What?

                    JESSIE
          For some time, yes.

                    SONNY
          Well, what are we going to do about all this?

                    JESSIE
          What do you mean?

                    SONNY
          Just what I said.

          There is silence for a moment. Jessie shrugs.

                    SONNY
          What? What's that?

                    JESSIE
          I want out of all of this. I just want to be out.
          That's all.

                    SONNY
          Out of what? This marriage?

                    JESSIE
          (Almost inaudible) Yes.

                    SONNY
          I'll have to think about this.

                    JESSIE
          Sonny, there's not a whole lot for you to think
          about. I want to get on with it. And keep your hands
          right where they are.

                    SONNY
          What? What do you want to get on with?

                    JESSIE
          My life!

                    SONNY
          (To himself) That's it.

          He looks at her as we CUT TO her holding his gaze.

                    SONNY
          (Continuing) Now I'm gonna tell you something.
          (Smiling) I may make a little noise about all of
          this, you know that, don't you?

                    JESSIE
          I'm sure you will, Sonny. I'm sure you will.

                    SONNY
          Nobody better mess with my children, especially any
          puny-assed youth minister, you hear me?

> **JESSIE**
>
> Nobody will, Sonny. I can assure you of that
> (pause). I wouldn't make over this too much if I
> were you. I certainly know as much about what you do
> and have done as you think I do, and you know that!

> **SONNY**
>
> Yeah, I guess I do.

> **JESSIE**
>
> Now, as I said, I want to get on with my life.

> **SONNY**
>
> Before I leave this room, would you do me just one
> favor?

> **JESSIE**
>
> What?

> **SONNY**
>
> Would you get on your knees one more time with me;
> just this last time. (He gets on his knees and pulls
> on her wrist)

> **JESSIE**
>
> Why, Sonny?

> **SONNY**
>
> Come on!

> **JESSIE**
>
> Why, Sonny?

> **SONNY**
>
> I want the Lord to hear us together in prayer, a
> prayer of loving understanding, for possible future
> reconciliation for us and for our son and daughter.

> **JESSIE**
>
> No, Sonny, this isn't the time.

> **SONNY**
>
> Jessie!

> **JESSIE**
>
> No, please, Sonny, I don't want to pray with you
> today!

> **SONNY**
>
> Tomorrow or maybe next week.

> **JESSIE**
>
> No, Sonny.

> **SONNY**
>
> I see. There hasn't been a problem we haven't been
> able to solve when we get down to it and you know
> that.

                    JESSIE
He's already given me my answers.

                    SONNY
Our Lord has.

                    JESSIE
Yes.

                    SONNY
Are you sure it was the Lord talking?

                    JESSIE
We've prayed since before we were newlyweds and my
knees are worn out over us. I just don't want it
this way anymore.

                    SONNY
Because of my wandering eye and wicked, wicked ways!

                    JESSIE
Not just that, it goes beyond just that.

                    SONNY
I love my family, I always have. I have a wandering
bug in me, that's why I love to evangelize, but I
love my family, I love my wife and my babies. Do you
know I love you, Jessie?

Jessie just looks at him.

This scene provides an excellent example of rising conflict; it progresses smoothly from beat to beat. Sonny enters the scene and wants to reconcile with his wife. His wife asserts herself: she wants a divorce. The beat changes and Sonny threatens his wife with reprisals if she goes forward with her action. Jessie reassures Sonny that no one will interfere with their children, but asserts her objective of separation. The beat changes again and Sonny requests his wife to pray with him. She will not allow Sonny to take control of her life anymore and reaffirms her position once again. Sonny persists. Jessie takes another tack, and declares that the Lord has spoken to her, has given her permission to break up this marriage. Sonny changes his tack and questions Jessie's statement, putting a doubt in her mind, and challenging her. She will not be swayed; she will take control of her own life. Finally, before he leaves the scene, Sonny declares his love for Jessie, hoping, that in time, they will reconcile.

The rising conflict in this scene grew out of complex characters with internal, external, and interpersonal conflicts operating simultaneously; each character had very clear objectives that grew out of a basic human emotion. The characters changed tack and took different mental actions to achieve their objectives and hence the scene has variety. The moment-to-moment aspects of the scene are superb: one character reacts to the other character truthfully. There are several lesser events that rise nicely to a culminating event—Jessie's declaration that "it goes beyond just that," implying very clearly that she does not love her husband anymore. It is not about his behavior, it is about him, and therefore cannot be worked through.

The scene has clear previous circumstances: Sonny is given moral support by a friend who drives him to his wife's house. Jessie's previous circumstances are not as clearly spelled out, but they could be felt in the scene. By not revealing Jessie's previous circumstances, because they do not come up organically in the scene, the author remained truthful to the moment. The actions and objectives of the scene are played out honestly, simply, and do not break from the truth of the characters.

There is a solid emotional life for both characters at the beginning of the scene— each has a strong feeling and is compelled to do something about it. Everything happens before our very eyes, in the present tense. Positive choices are made for each character and we witness truthful human rationalization. The author does not judge these characters, but allows them their humanity by putting himself in their shoes and seeing and feeling the world as they would.

Sonny traps his emotion in the action: when he threatens Jessie, he takes his rage and traps it in his effort to communicate sincerely with Jessie. Trapping this destructive feeling into a positive action gives Sonny's character more complexity. There are destructive and constructive desires and impulses within Sonny, that are competing for expression and make his character richly and truthfully ambiguous. The stage directions in parentheses note that Sonny is "smiling" while he is threatening Jessie. Sonny wants to reconcile with his wife, and this is an active, positive choice. He is not trying to control, to terrorize, to bully, which would be negative choices. If a writer made such a choice for Sonny even though Sonny does terrorize and bully his wife somewhat because of his suppressed rage, all would disintegrate into the cliché. Sonny would become one note, less human, and less complex. The writer has found a positive way for Sonny to try to get what he wants, which gives the scene more tension, edge, and complexity. Sonny's smile is a superb counterpoint to the rage he evidently possesses. With this strategy, the author has triggered a push/pull response in the viewer, a more complex response. The audience is pulled towards Sonny because they identify with a man who wants to reconcile and who will fight hard to control his rage to prove that he can be trustworthy. The push part of this response is that the audience has been informed that Sonny is very abusive, that he has beaten his wife. This information repels the viewer and creates an underlying tension to the scene.

The scene begins in the middle and gets out before the end. The characters are operating out of their desires and in the case of Jessie, her desire and need are one and the same. The physical life of the scene—kneeling down to pray—grows organically out of the character's desire and the central conflict.

Finally, there are life and death stakes. This scene is about the breakup of a marriage, and even in Jessie's case there is a lot to lose, even though she has a new lover. She will have to face her failure and lose her old identity as a "good Christian woman," which is a tremendous loss. For both characters there is no easy way out of this scene. Because of their orthodox religious beliefs that are absolute and integrated into their lives, they cannot walk away very easily once the matter of divorce has been thrown on the table. To break the contract of the sacred institution is a matter of great shame and sin.

You will notice that this scene successfully answers all of the questions posed in this chapter. The characters have clear wants and conflicts that are internal, external, and interpersonal. There is a clear line of action and the characters' objectives are positive. The previous circumstances are evident, and today is clearly like no other. Finally, the entire scene rises smoothly, from beat to beat, until it reaches a culminating event.

Static Conflict

A scene has static conflict when it goes around and around, back and forth, without ever progressing. It happens when the author does not know what the characters want—here, now, today. If the Sonny and Jessie scene had static conflict, it would be very different, and would probably go something like this:

> **SONNY**
> So how are you today, Jessie?
>
> **JESSIE**
> Good. You know.
>
> **SONNY**
> Ah. Good. (He laughs.) Yeah, beautiful day. Got my friend Joe waiting for me out there in the car.
>
> **JESSIE**
> Oh. That's nice.
>
> **SONNY**
> Yeah. He's a good friend.
>
> **JESSIE**
> We all need friends.
>
> **SONNY**
> Yes, indeed.
>
> **JESSIE**
> Right.
>
> **SONNY**
> So you called me. What's up?
>
> **JESSIE**
> Oh, yeah. Well, you know, I've not been happy.
>
> **SONNY**
> Really, why?
>
> **JESSIE**
> Well, there's this person...

                    SONNY
Yeah?

                    JESSIE
A man...

                    SONNY
Yeah?

                    JESSIE
Well he's a good friend...

                    SONNY
A good friend?

                    JESSIE
Yeah. Maybe more than that...

                    SONNY
More than that?

                    JESSIE
Maybe.

                    SONNY
I see.

                    JESSIE
So. You know.

                    SONNY
You like this man?

                    JESSIE
Oh, yeah. I do.

                    SONNY
You're not in love with this other man, are you?

                    JESSIE
What? Oh, no. I don't think. Most days.

                    SONNY
Most days.

                    JESSIE
Well, yeah, I guess I could say that.

                    SONNY
Oh.

                    JESSIE
So what would you think about a divorce?

                    SONNY
A divorce.

>   JESSIE
> Yeah.
>
>   SONNY
> Are you kidding?
>
>   JESSIE
> No.
>
>   SONNY
> Divorce.
>
>   JESSIE
> Yeah. What would you think about it?
>
>   SONNY
> I think divorce is a sin.
>
>   JESSIE
> Oh, I do, too.
>
>   SONNY
> That's good.
>
>   JESSIE
> Yeah.
>
>   SONNY
> 'Cause I was worried there.
>
>   JESSIE
> 'Bout what?
>
>   SONNY
> That you might want one.
>
>   JESSIE
> Oh, yeah. I don't think divorce is good.
>
>   SONNY
> Yeah, neither do I.
>
>   JESSIE
> Would you like to pray?

This scene never gets to the point. It is flat, dull, and uninteresting because the author (me) has not given the characters clear objectives, three-dimensionality, and a clear conflict. They simply don't know what they want from each other and so they drift and float and bore us to death. If a writer creates a scene with static conflict it is because he or she has not properly prepared.

Rising conflict is obviously preferable to static conflict. A writer may want to use static conflict occasionally to make a point—to add irony to a relationship, to deeply cover subtext, or to communicate the state of boredom. But in general, static conflict is deadly. Writers should be aware of its presence in a scene and try to avoid it.

Jumping Conflict

Jumping conflict occurs in a scene when it literally "jumps" from one action to another, without smooth transitions between actions. Jumping conflict indicates that the author has not fully developed the characters. If we take the same Sonny and Jessie scene and give it jumping conflict, it would go something like this:

> SONNY
> (Calmly, sweetly) Hi, Jessie.
>
> JESSIE
> (Smiling) Hi.
>
> SONNY
> (Enraged, showing his teeth) I know! I know what's happening and I'm gonna kill you!
>
> JESSIE
> (Spitting at him) I want my life back!
>
> SONNY
> (Bursting into tears, falling to his knees) Oh, sweetie I am so sorry. Pray with me.
>
> JESSIE
> (Throwing a vase across the room) I love another man!
>
> SONNY
> (Stroking her hair gently) Pray with me, baby...
>
> JESSIE
> (Bursting out with laughter) I spoke to God! He gave me my answer!
>
> SONNY
> (He slugs her and she flies across the room) You have, have you! I'm gonna kill you if you dare leave me! YOU HEAR!
>
> JESSIE
> (Crying) Oh God, oh God, I'm sorry. I am such a sinner.

Jumping conflict indicates that the author has not done sufficient preparation. In the scene above, the author has focused on the plot points, inventing new twists and turns to kick the scene up a notch, rather than allowing the characters to behave truthfully and organically. There are also transition problems. While there is clearly a lot of action, it does not rise along a smooth line; and it is not organic to the characters. There is no truth in the moment-to-moment play of the scene, it just leaps from one beat to another. If a writer notices that a scene has jumping conflict, I recommend going back to free-writes and spending more time developing the characters. Then, once they have a deeper and truer understanding of their character, I would advise rewriting, being careful not to force the progression of the scene and letting the characters live and breathe. The characters should not be burdened with carrying out the writer's agenda. Characters must be allowed to go wherever their impulses take them.

Foreshadowing

Foreshadowing, the last type of conflict, is tension; it is as powerful as rising conflict, but it does not progress to a payoff. When a scene is driven by foreshadowing, everything is hidden and below the surface. Characters never reveal their subtext; they sit on it while it churns underneath, and the audience can feel this churning in the scene. Foreshadowing is frequently used in many of the so-called art house films such as Jim Jarmusch's *Dead Man* or Hal Hartley's *Henry Fool*. In these films, characters enter a scene with clear objectives, yet a great deal of information remains undisclosed. There is tension in many of the scenes—an implicit promise of conflict up ahead in the story. The characters do not reveal what is driving them underneath, but the audience is fulfilled by payoff later on in the story. When used in the right proportion, foreshadowing has a hypnotic effect, but when overused the effect is soporific.

If a disheveled, obviously agitated man, carrying a butcher knife, walks into a rooming house and rudely asks the clerk if Bob Smith is in his room, there is an automatic tension. If the clerk replies politely, "Who may I say is calling?" and the character snaps back, "Never mind, is he in?" then we have an expectation that there may be conflict up ahead between this man and Bob Smith or anyone in this man's way. If you took any uncompromising character, such as Miss Piggy, and placed her in the same room with another uncompromising character, Oscar the Grouch, you would immediately foreshadow conflict. Miss Piggy would be appalled at Oscar's ways and Oscar would think she is a stuck-up pig. This is precisely what Neil Simon did in the *Odd Couple*: he forced two uncompromising characters to live together and we watched the fur fly.

Foreshadowing works best only if there is payoff. If you endlessly foreshadow and never get to the point, the audience will soon become frustrated. Egri uses the analogy of two boxers who enter the ring and strut their stuff, but never engage in a match. The audience will be disappointed and rightfully so, since the conflict suggested by the foreshadowing has not been fulfilled and completed.

Be careful: foreshadowing can camouflage the fact that the writer really doesn't know what a scene is about or who the characters are. I have noticed beginning authors writing in the perpetual state of static conflict or foreshadowing because they fear they will lose subtlety if they advance their scenes to some payoff. Remember that storytelling is about how much information you should give. Giving too little is just as deadly as giving too much. An audience needs a context in which to view the action of the story, they need to be let into the story. The overuse of foreshadowing can push the audience out of the story because they simply do not know enough about what is going on in the thoughts and feelings of the characters in order to interpret or follow the action correctly. If an audience is left out of the story for too long, they will, figuratively or literally, go home.

In *Secrets and Lies,* Mike Leigh demonstrates an effective use of foreshadowing because it is followed by some payoff. Maurice, a selfless man who is spending much of his energy being the dutiful husband, brother, and head of the family, owns a photo studio. He is proud of his studio, which has provided a good living for his family. One day, out of the blue, Stuart, the former owner of his shop, shows up for a visit. Stuart is drunk, emotionally isolated, a raw nerve, and when he appears at the studio, it puts everyone in the shop on edge. There is obvious tension. Stuart has been to Australia to start a new life, but has failed, he feels like a loser, and he can't stop losing ground:

                    MAURICE
        So, Stuart, are you thinkin' about settin' up again?

                    STUART
        No, forget it. Too much of a pain. You know what
        it's like, Maurice! You sweat your balls off for
        years, you try to make people happy...and what d'you
        get back? Nothing! (Jane gives out mugs of tea.)

                    MONICA
        Thanks. (Stuart ignores Jane; he is flicking through
        Maurice's desk diary.)

                    MAURICE
        By the way, Stuart, this is Jane, my assistant. This
        is Mr. Christian, the gentleman I bought the busi-
        ness from.

                    JANE
        Hello.

                    STUART
        Hiya, Jane! I hope he's treatin' you well.

                    JANE
        He's all right.

                    STUART
        You can work for me any time.

                    JANE
        I'm all right where I am, thank you. (Stuart has
        taken out a hip flask; he pours a drop of spirit
        into his tea. Monica and Maurice exchange looks.)

                    MONICA
        Your wife must've been sorry to have come back.

                    STUART
        Which wife? Oh, that bitch! She never came out there
        in the first place.

                    MONICA
        Oh?

                    MAURICE
So where are you living at the moment, Stuart?

                    STUART
Down at Grays.

                    MAURICE
Essex?

                    STUART
Yeah...me mother's place.

                    MAURICE
Must be nice for her.

                    MONICA
Havin' her boy to fuss over!

                    STUART
She's dead. She died when I was still in Bangkok.

                    JANE
(Sentimental) Aah! (Maurice is quietly amused by
this, in spite of himself.)

                    MAURICE
Sorry to hear that.

                    MONICA
It's a shame.

                    STUART
Didn't see much of'er, anyway. It's my dad I miss.
You win some, you lose some. (He is overcome. He
sips some tea. His hand is shaking, and the mug rat-
tles against his teeth. Pause.)

                    MONICA
(Brightly) You must have had some lovely weather in
Australia!

                    STUART
Too hot. It's too hot over there; it's too cold over
here. (He takes a final swig of tea, puts down his
cup, gets up, and leaves the room abruptly. Maurice
shrugs at Monica, and follows him. Monica and Jane
move to a better vantage point for watching what
happens next.)

This scene is teeming with foreshadowing. Stuart is clearly out of control, on edge,
about to leap at any moment. We can just feel the tension in the scene. Stuart does not
respect boundaries. He is filled with bitterness and hate about his past; failures have
turned him into a crushed man. Cocked and loaded, Stuart is ready to climb a tower
with a semi-automatic rifle and pick off a few pedestrians. He galvanizes the entire
scene because his behavior strongly suggests that at a moment's notice there will be an

explosion, a breaking of the stasis. And Mike Leigh gives us what we anticipate will happen—payoff—in the very next scene, fulfilling the conflict suggested by Stuart's out-of-control intensity.

Stuart picks a fight with the mild-mannered Maurice and his provocation succeeds in bringing about rising conflict. "You've done very well out of my business, 'aven't yer?" asks Stuart. Maruice gives it back to Stuart, at last, "No, Stuart, no. It used to be your business—I bought it from you, it's my business." "I gave you my goodwill. I gave you my clientele. I gave you my fucking reputation!" persists Stuart. "You gave me nothing, Stuart. With all due respect, your client list was shit. I followed it up. I wrote to them, I rang 'em. I didn't get one bite."

At last, the foreshadowing of the previous scene erupts and the surface is broken; the writer digs deeper and we learn about the thoughts, resentments, and perceptions of both characters, Stuart and Maurice.

In skilled hands any one of these types of conflicts—rising, static, jumping, and foreshadowing—can be used to create something dramatic, but it is only with rising conflict that a writer will be able to portray a major event truthfully. Foreshadowing is often used in conjunction with rising conflict. It can set mood, evoke and create atmosphere, tease an audience along, but an intelligent balance must be struck between foreshadowing and rising conflict. This balance can only be determined by the writer, screenplay by screenplay, purpose by purpose.

Dialogue

A great scene has great dialogue. Writing great dialogue is the result of creating real characters; the two are completely intertwined.

It is axiomatic that one of the chief purposes of dialogue is to give the audience exactly the right amount of information at the exact right time. In *Welcome to the Doll House* by Todd Solondz, Dawn Wiener, a pre-adolescent eleven year old, struggles through the rites of passage that most of us found difficult. Solondz uses just the right level of dialogue to give the proper amount of information to keep us interested in the action. In this scene, Dawn is in love with Steve and finally gets her chance to be with him alone when he visits her house one day:

```
INT. WIENER HOUSE - DAY
DAWN is practicing piano exercises when she hears the
doorbell ring. She opens the front door: it is STEVE.

                STEVE
     Hey. Is Mark around?

                DAWN
     No. My mom took him shopping.

                STEVE
     Shit.
```

> DAWN
> He'll be back real soon, though, I'm pretty sure. If
> you want you can come inside and wait.

> STEVE
> (Thinks about it a moment) Okay. You have anything
> to eat?

> DAWN
> Yeah, follow me.

Dawn leads Steve into the kitchen. She starts opening
all the food cabinets.

> DAWN
> You like Yodels?

> STEVE
> Yeah, sure. What else you got?

> DAWN
> Ring Dings, Pop Tarts, Hawaiian Punch...whatever you
> want. And we've got some leftovers, too, in the
> fridge.

> STEVE
> Yeah, like what?

> DAWN
> We've got some fish sticks.

Steve is neither particularly impressed nor interested
by what Dawn has to say. He rifles though the Wieners'
mail, pockets some loose change.

> STEVE
> All right.

> DAWN
> And I know how to make Jell-O.

> STEVE
> Whatever.

Steve walks out of the kitchen and over to the living
room couch. He looks out for Mark's arrival.

> DAWN (O.S.)
> You know, I really like your music. (No response).
> I'm pouring you some Hawaiian Punch. Is that all
> right?

> STEVE
> Whatever.

Now finished preparing a tray of goodies for Steve,
Dawn enters the living room.

>   DAWN
>   Here I come!

She settles the tray on the coffee table and then sits
demurely beside Steve, watching him devour the meal.
Finally, after wolfing down a half-dozen fish sticks,
he licks his fingers.

>   STEVE
>   You not hungry?

>   DAWN
>   No.

He returns to the fish sticks.

>   DAWN
>   You know, I play the piano.

>   STEVE
>   Oh, yeah?

Dawn gives Steve a moment to ask her to play, but when
he doesn't, she takes matters into her own hands, walks
over to the piano, and begins to play.

She fumbles valiantly through a Chopin waltz, the same
one heard over the title sequence.

STEVE is still chewing fish sticks when she finishes.

>   STEVE
>   Hey, that's pretty good.

>   DAWN
>   I could have kept going, but I sprained my finger
>   yesterday.

>   STEVE
>   Yeah, well, you're still better than Barry any day,
>   that's for sure.

>   DAWN
>   You think so?

>   STEVE
>   Oh, yeah. He oughta be taking lessons from you.

>   DAWN
>   Yeah, well, I don't think I have time to give
>   lessons to Barry, but....You wanna see my fingers?

>   STEVE
>   Yeah, I see 'em. (A beat.) Oh, shit, I gotta get
>   going.

Steve rises, starts to leave.

> **DAWN**
> Please wait. Can I play for you one more time? This time with no mistakes? Please?

The front door opens, and MISSY, MRS. WIENER, and MARK appear.

> **MISSY**
> We're home!

The dialogue in this scene gives us just the right amount of information to keep things moving forward without losing the audience. It clearly and simply makes the point that Dawn does not have the slightest chance of winning Steve's heart, given who she is and her stage in life, and then moves on to provide more dramatic information which pushes the audience to the next change of action in the scene. The dialogue supports the author's purpose—to examine the trials of this young girl—and maintains the tone of the screenplay, which Solondz called "the right level of bleakness." The dialogue shapes the black comedy by leaving certain things out and keeping others in, and playing the right card at the right time.

The three most common problems that prevent screenwriters from providing the right level of information that Solondz found in this scene are unmotivated exposition, stating the subtext, and self-conscious or literary dialogue. Let's examine each one.

Unmotivated Exposition

Exposition is information. Generally, in a screenplay, information is given by a character through dialogue. But the information cannot just be spoken willy-nilly in a scene by any character; it must be exposed organically. Information should be woven into the actions and objectives taken by the character in the scene. If the information revealed in a scene is not organically part of the mental actions and objectives of a character, then this exposition is called unmotivated because it is not directly woven into the motives of the character. To illustrate the concept, I have rewritten the above scene with exaggerated unmotivated exposition:

> **STEVE**
> Hey. Is Mark around?

> **DAWN**
> No. My mom took him shopping. She likes to shop at this time of the day, around four o'clock after we kids get home from school. She's been doing this for years. Least as far as I can remember.

> **STEVE**
> Shit. Mark and I are supposed to practice today. I need to get my practice over soon because I have the hots for this other young girl down the block. I want to catch her after she comes home from basketball practice. She's real tall. I like tall chicks.

                    DAWN
        Oh. Well. I'm tall. Tallest one in my eighth-grade
        class. I like standing at the end of the line when
        we all line up to go to assembly. But don't worry.
        Mark will be back soon. You never can tell with
        Mark. He's very irresponsible. But I guess that
        comes with his age. Boys. Who can figure. So. Would
        you like to come in?

As you can see when the characters speak at length about things that are not tied to their objectives in the scene, everything begins to lose focus. The scene is no longer believable because the characters would never expose themselves so easily. This exposure violates their motives and diminishes their objectives in the scene. Characters say only what they need to say to get what they want; if they say something that goes against their objective, it breaks the reality of the characters and the world of the story. Unmotivated exposition also clutters the line of action of the scene and makes it difficult for the audience to discern what the scene is about.

Dawn has a big crush on Steve. She would most likely find it very hard to communicate with Steve because she is so nervous and tongue-tied. Her chattiness would also diminish her objective in the scene, which is to seduce Steve. Dawn is looking for a way to play her cards to give Steve a sign. She wants to find an opening where she can risk showing her true feelings for him without humiliating herself. If she does not choose her words carefully she might push Steve away and never get another chance with him.

If you look at the scene again, with the unmotivated exposition in parentheses, a line of action is clearly discernable.

                    STEVE
        Hey. Is Mark around?

                    DAWN
        No. My mom took him shopping. *(She likes to shop at
        this time of the day, around four o'clock. After we
        kids get home from school. She's been doing this for
        years. Least as far as I can remember.)*

                    STEVE
        Shit. *(Mark and I are supposed to practice today. I
        need to get my practice over soon because I have the
        hots for this other young girl down the block. I
        want to catch her after she comes home from basket-
        ball practice. She's real tall. I like tall chicks.)*

                    DAWN
        Oh. Well. *(I'm tall. Tallest one in my eight grade
        class. I like standing at the end of the line when
        we all line up to go to assembly. But)* don't worry.
        Mark will be back soon. *(I think. You never can tell
        with Mark. He's very irresponsible. But I guess that
        comes with his age. Boys. Who can figure. So. Would
        you like to come in?)*

Sometimes, especially in first drafts, when an author has not completely found his or her characters or has not clearly found a line of action, there will be lots of unmotivated exposition. It is necessary, in terms of process, to over write and then pare down. Often by simply pruning the first draft the real scene can be excavated from underneath.

Stating the Subtext

Unmotivated exposition usually comes about because the writer wants the audience to know all the backstory and history of a character. Another problem, stating the subtext, is the result of the screenwriter being unsure about the specific objectives of the characters in the scene. Unlike unmotivated exposition, stating the subtext is the result of the writer not allowing the characters to be more successful in accomplishing their objectives or not allowing characters to truthfully pursue their objectives.

Subtext is all the hidden thoughts and feelings we dare not say to someone because they are either too personal, private, or inappropriate for the moment. Perhaps these thoughts or feelings will present a side of us that we would rather keep to ourselves. Opening up about what is going on deep inside of us can diminish our chances of reaching our goals—to seduce, charm, threaten, control, and so on. If a salesman wants to sell a tie to a fat man and remarks to this man, "Gee, how many chins have you got there?" then he would certainly work against his objective: to make a sale. The salesman may think this thought about the customer, but it is improbable that he would share his thought with the man when holding a tie up his neck. Every great scene has subtext, especially if you have given your characters three levels of conflict. This time I have revised the Steve and Dawn scene so that too much subtext is stated. We pick up right after Dawn has risked playing the piano for Steve:

> STEVE
> Hey, that's pretty good. I didn't think a nerd like you could have that much talent.

> DAWN
> I could have kept going. I would do that for you, Steve. You know. I don't know....I...get all confused inside, just balled up and...well...I sprained my finger yesterday.

> STEVE
> So. You sprained your finger? So. What are you getting at? You're so weird. Well. Look. I want to change the subject fast because I ain't no dope, I know where you're headed. Look. Let's just talk about Barry and keep it nice and polite. Okay. Here we go. I've gotta admit. Let's see. What can I say? Oh, I know: you're still better than Barry any day. That's for sure.

> **DAWN**
> You think so? My God, that is more than I ever
> expected you to say. If you're saying that, well,
> then, you probably like me. Right?
>
> **STEVE**
> Hey. What are you jumping to conclusions for? Don't get
> all revved up here. Seriously, what I was saying is
> what I meant. Barry oughta be taking lessons from you.
>
> **DAWN**
> (Giggling wildly. Looking into his eyes, seductive-
> ly.) Yeah, well, I don't think I have time to give
> lessons to Barry! But...I have an idea....oh, God, I
> feel so...I don't know what to call it...I ah...you
> wanna see my fingers?
>
> **STEVE**
> Oh, Jesus! You've gotta be kidding me. Now I get it!
> You've gotta be kidding me! What? This is unbelievable!
> Listen. Relax. I see your fingers. Yeah. They're great.
> Keep away from me, would you. I've got my pride.

As you can see stating the subtext takes away the bleak tone that Solodnz was striving to achieve. It also breaks with the reality of scene; these characters would never say these thoughts and feelings because they are not equipped to do so in terms of maturity, self-knowledge, and experience in life. Also, if they were to state the subtext so baldly, the characters would diminish their objectives in the scene. Dawn wants to be loved by Steve and wants to seduce him. She would fail miserably at this goal if she put too much pressure on him by blurting everything out. Pruning the dialogue will restore the scene to something that is both acceptable and true.

Some writers go in the opposite direction and do not write enough of what is really happening underneath a scene, exposing far too little subtext. The subtext is so buried that the audience becomes confused and they have no idea what the scene is all about. The writer who does not reveal enough subtext often thinks that this subtlety will grab the audience's attention. However, the results are the same as the writer giving too much information: the viewer loses concentration and drops out of the scene. The way to find the right amount of subtext is for the writer to inhabit the shoes of the characters and to truthfully allow them to pursue their objectives.

In *Annie Hall,* the screenwriters (Woody Allen and Marshall Brickman) revealed too much and too little subtext simultaneously to create a great scene. Woody Allen has a glass of wine with Diane Keaton and both characters stumble to keep the conversation going. They both want to find out if the other person is attracted to them. On the surface, the dialogue is rather mundane, cocktail party chatter. However, through voice over, we hear the inner thoughts and feelings that they are hiding from each other, which they would naturally do in order to pursue their objectives. This strategy, of simultaneously giving too much and too little information has a comic and sophisticated resonance, and gives just the right amount of exposition.

Self-Conscious or Literary Dialogue

Dialogue is meant to be spoken out loud, interpreted by an actor, not read. A character's dialogue should have a specific tempo and rhythm, which will give clues about the background and immediate needs of a character in a story. The cliché example would be an aggressive New Yorker who speaks with a fast tempo and intense rhythm, or a Mississippi sharecropper who speaks in a slow tempo with a light rhythm. The writer should always be searching for a specific and compelling tempo and rhythm—a musicality—for the language of the characters. The manner and style in which one speaks reveals volumes.

Good dialogue grows organically from character. If all the characters sound alike, with no discernable difference in their emphases, tempos, and rhythms, then the writer has not created specific characters. Like good poetry, good dialogue is chosen as much as for its sound as its sense. Dialogue has the same effect on the audience as a poem. While listening to a poem read out loud, the listener will unconsciously mimic the breathing pattern suggested by the poem and the performance. This mimicry effectively gives the poem, through the performance of the actor, control over the audience member's breathing. Good dialogue also controls the breath of the audience. Since the rate and pattern of our breathing can strongly affect our emotions, good dialogue can elicit strong emotions.

Literary dialogue—dialogue that is really prose—does not work for dramatic writing because, when read out loud, it lacks a musical quality. Not that prose can't have its own musicality, but it is written for the eye to process, not the ear. Good dialogue needs to have an aural presence.

Dialogue that is idiomatic and colloquial rings truer because it sounds like "how people really speak." As Neil Postman notes about court procedure in the United States, the spoken word has the ring of truth. "Testimony is expected to be given orally, on the assumption that the spoken, not the written, word is a truer reflection of the state of mind of a witness. Jurors are expected to hear the truth, or its opposite, not to read it."

To learn how to write good idiomatic dialogue one must study it by simply listening very carefully and training the ear to recognize how people speak. John Millington Synge, a leading playwright of the Irish Renaissance, was known to visit pubs to listen to and record the speech of rural people. About his masterpiece, *The Playboy of the Western World,* Synge remarked "as in my other plays, I have used one or two words only, that I have not heard among the country people of Ireland, or spoken in my own nursery before I could read the newspapers." David Mamet, playwright, screenwriter, and director, spent many years writing down things he overheard people say on the street, in an elevator, or at the local diner. In *Full Metal Jacket,* former U.S. Marines Drill Instructor R. Lee Ermey, was hired as a consultant. He videotaped a demonstration of Marine training in which he flung obscene insults and abuse, non-stop for fifteen minutes, despite being continuously pelted with tennis balls and oranges. Stanley Kubrick was so impressed with Ermey that he cast him as Sergeant Hartman and used Ermey's insults exclusively in the final script.

Great dialogue finally is the result of developed characters. Dialogue is most effective when the author allows the characters to truthfully and believably pursue their objectives.

EXERCISE   RECORDING AN OVERHEARD CONVERSATION

Record several overheard conversations and study the transcripts. Note how real people talk to each other. How often do they cut each other off? How often do they not finish their thoughts? How is what they talk about linked to what they need from the other person they are talking to? What can you infer from the overheard dialogue about the objectives of the people talking?

Make a list of the ten lines of dialogue you found most compelling in an overheard conversation. Examine and reflect on these lines. What kind of scene do they suggest? Make a list of five possible scenes that these lines evoke. From that list, write a scene without using any of the overheard lines. Once completed, revise the scene weaving in the ten lines of overheard conversation. Read both scenes to someone and ask that person which scene feels the strongest and why.

How to Expand and Grow as a Screenwriter

There are virtually endless combinations and possibilities for a screenplay and no hard and fast rules, only choices that may add or subtract from your purpose and the intensity of the experience for the audience. If we discover that a choice is not effective, compelling, or original and therefore is not a positive addition to the screenplay, we discard it and make another choice until we arrive at something better. We eventually make the choice to stop the journey when we believe we have reached a point that completes and fulfills the entire story, having exhausted our intuition and imagination. A screenplay is a set of parentheses around characters and a situation that has both a background story and an afterlife—a narrative that continues after the audience goes home.

A Final Checklist

How will you know the final placement of the parentheses? How will you know when the screenplay is finished? Here is a checklist to help you make that decision. First give your final draft a cooling down period of at least two weeks, when you do not look at or talk about your screenplay. Then read it again, and ask yourself the following questions, being utterly honest with your answers:

- Is there clarity to your story? Are your characters' objectives and the major events of the story clear, layered, and compelling? A screenplay is not complete until each and every page has clarity.
- Does the screenplay move from scene to scene with grace and precision? Is there too much repetition? Have you found the right balance in every scene between how much information to give and how much to withhold?
- Have all the major characters been fully developed? A character-driven screenplay is only as strong as its weakest character.
- Are there real stakes to what the characters want? Have you gotten past the obvious choices and found actions and objectives for your characters that are unique and specific?
- Is there payoff to the story? Have you delivered an intensified experience that rises to a culminating event, which fully addresses the major questions you set up in the beginning of your screenplay?
- Finally, at three in the morning, when you are wide awake and don't know why, ask yourself if your screenplay will make a good movie. If you can honestly answer yes, then trust yourself and follow your heart.

After you have answered yes to each of these questions, give your script to three trustworthy people who have a good understanding about what makes a great movie. After your readers are finished you need to take control of the critiquing session. The first thing I always ask is what were the scenes, moments, and characters that they liked the most and why? What did they find compelling and why? What grabbed their attention and pulled them in? It is very important to understand the strengths of your screenplay before you can understand your weaknesses. If you know your strengths, you always have something to build on. Also, if you do not know the strengths of your work, you may become overwhelmed, depressed, or beaten down by the criticism of your weaknesses. By using this critique format of the good news first, you protect yourself.

When you do hear negative feedback do not act upon it right away. Give yourself another week before you seriously consider a rewrite. Often, during a cooling down period, you will be able to discard the negative criticism that comes from a reader's own biases—everyone has their blind spots and preferences. Try to look for similarities in the comments of all three people who read your screenplay. When you hear the same criticism two or three times, heed it. If you hear more than once that a character is not believable, then you will most likely need to go back over your screenplay and further develop that character. If several of the elements of the screenplay—the structure, pacing, characterization, or story—are not clear to more than one reader, again, you probably have a problem that needs to be fixed.

When you are finally finished with your screenplay, by all means celebrate. You deserve the fun; you have worked hard and accomplished something quite wonderful. After celebrating you have two choices. The first is to take your screenplay and try to make a movie of it yourself. Which is the step I truly recommend. Or you can send your screenplay to producers to see if they will make a movie of it. There are positives and negatives to each route you take.

The first route I believe is the scariest and at the same time the most rewarding. It is a route that requires the screenwriter to, at the very least, become a producer. How a screenwriter does that is the subject for another book, but essentially, it requires that the screenwriter, as producer, put the major elements together so that a screenplay can be made into a movie, including raising the capital for filming and marketing and selecting and hiring a director and line producer. Many writers do not want to take this route because they feel it is beyond their skills and resources in terms of time and effort. Many writers just want to write and if that is the case, you need to take the second route.

In order to get a producer to read your script, you will need either an agent or a professional introduction to that producer. I know of no effective and legitimate producer today that will read an unsolicited script. There are just too many scripts out there and producers need a screening process. Most producers hire readers or development executives to screen scripts from agents or they require professional recommendations before they will read the script.

The best way to find an agent is to first find a resource that lists agents. The book that I like the best, which is on the market today, is K. Callan's *The Script Is Finished,*

Now What Do I Do? The Scriptwriter's Resource Book and Agent Guide. Callan lists not only agencies and their agents, but also gives a good idea of what each agency and agent is looking for in terms of types and genres of scripts. Never send your entire script to an agent. First query them with a letter and resume. The letter should be brief and give the agent a solid idea of what your screenplay is about. The letter should also catch the agent's attention—in an intelligent way. Remember, this letter is the first impression the agent has of you. If you try to attract attention by being sophomoric or overly coy, you will most likely lose the agent's respect. Be direct, confident, and proud of your work when describing it to an agent in a query. Your resume should give the agent an idea of who you are, what you have done, and why you will be a good screenwriter.

If an agent is interested in your query, he or she will respond. I do not suggest following up a query with a phone call. Remember agents are very busy. The good ones have an effective system in place to respond to your query. They will get back to you one way or another. You may lose a good agent by being a pest.

Another way to get an agent is through a professional recommendation. This requires you to use all your contacts. Try to recall the people you have met in the last year or so—filmmakers, teachers, screenwriters, development executives, directors, producers, and so on. Call and ask for their advice and help. Ask for names and recommendations and then call those people and ask the same. Eventually you will have several good contacts to secure a professional recommendation to help you get an agent or a reading by a producer.

Taking this last route means that you will have to wait and endure a lot of rejection and give up a lot of control over your project, since a producer and director will be involved and they will often have a strong influence on a film. If this risk does not bother you, then going through an agent may be right for you.

Remember there is a lot of rejection factored into the whole process of getting an agent or producer and selling a script. Do not take it personally. There are just so many factors that are beyond your control that influence an agent or producer. Many times an agent simply has too many clients or too many projects on his or her plate and no time for a new writer. Or many times your screenplay has a subject matter or type of story that a producer has acquired with another script and simply does not need another of its genre.

It is important to keep at it. It may take a long time, but with perseverance, you will get an agent or producer. Remember, it only takes one person to say yes.

Creating Your Own Support

Recently, while moderating a round table discussion on screenwriting at a local film festival, a young screenwriter remarked to me that he believed today's films had a pervasive problem: they lack craft and content. He spoke of the American films of the 1930s and 1940s and how they were so well crafted. He concluded that the studio system of that age created, perhaps inadvertently, a support system in which writers and other artists could grow and improve simply because they always had work. This constant practice helped them to improve their craft. Director, screenwriter, and actor, Paul Mazursky (director of *An Unmarried Woman* and *Bob & Carol & Ted & Alice*) who was also part of the round table, argued that the young filmmaker was romanticizing the studio days. Mazursky had worked under contract at a studio and felt it was stultifying and soul-crushing. However, I do understand what this young filmmaker was lamenting. He had a hunger for a way to consistently grow and expand as an artist, and in today's world of filmmaking it is difficult to find help to feed this healthy appetite for growth.

I reminded the young filmmaker that many of the writers in the studio system of the 1940s were playwrights, novelists, and tabloid journalists who had learned their craft through many years of practice, before they arrived at the studio gate. I asked him where he thought new writers learn their craft today. Despairingly, he replied, "nowhere." As a graduate of one of our most prominent film schools, he felt that film school was a waste of time and money because no one can teach you how to write. And the problem of working as an independent writer/director is finding the financing for every new project, which is a time-consuming reality. He realistically estimated he would only be able to make a film every five years. His conclusion is that there is no way to become proficient at craft because all of these factors conspire to create very little opportunity for continuous practice.

I disagree with him about both issues. You can learn to write when guided by a good teacher and there is a way to continue to grow as an artist and craftsperson. I have taught beginning writers and they have improved because they have learned craft. I do not think you can teach someone talent, insight, a sense of humor, or prowess, but I do think you can teach that a scene must have conflict and a central idea, and that unmotivated exposition stalls dramatic progression. Knowing these things and integrating them into your writing does make a difference—the writing improves and something has been learned. The support a writer needs to improve slowly and steadily through years of practice, may or may not come from someone else. If it does not, then you can give it to yourself.

Don't Neglect the Realities of Life

To create the climate you need to grow as a writer you must first attend to the matters of real life, making sure the basics are in place. Get yourself a steady job that will pay the bills, but not drain you creatively. Take care of the little things in life, otherwise you will not be psychologically free to focus on the bigger challenges of writing. You cannot create when you are anxious about not being able to pay your bills.

Do not let someone support you, and do not borrow money. This will erode your self-esteem and you will become less creative and imaginative, and perhaps develop a block. If you have a trust fund, do not live on it. Save that money for when you can make a living as a writer, otherwise it will cripple you. You will have too much time on your hands and become counter-productive because you will lose your discipline.

Simplify your life and attend to your everyday responsibilities. Structure your life as much as possible and make it predictable. Save living on the edge for your work. Integrate your goal to finish a screenplay into your everyday existence.

When I first began writing, I use to get up at five in the morning and write for three hours before I went to my temp job at an office in Manhattan. I always told my boss at any temp job that I was a writer and I was temping because I expected to eventually make my living as a writer. I even asked them if would it be possible to use their computers to revise work if I finished all my work and I had free time. Most agreed, and if they didn't, I would ask the temp agency to reassign me. If you have a clear goal and integrate it honestly in your life, the right support will come your way. I found a Fortune 500 company that totally supported my goals; the word spread quickly within the company who I was and what I was about and I was assigned to people who wanted "a guy like me."

Acquire Experience and Build Self-Knowledge

Mature work will only come once you have matured as a person. You get this maturity only by growing as a person through new experiences and knowledge. You don't get this experience of the world, which will ripen and strengthen your work, by watching movies and reading books like this one. You get it by living, experiencing, and having adventures—immersing yourself in the real world. Acquaint yourself with many different types of people and learn about their relationships. Learn your likes and dislikes, your prejudices, and truthfully embrace all sides of yourself. If you cannot face the positive and destructive sides of yourself, then you will never be able to portray them in your fictional characters.

There is a long tradition of writers wandering about and absorbing the world to build a reserve of real experience in order to give grounding, depth, and truth to their work. Think of Hemingway and the Spanish Civil War and James Michener in the South Pacific. If possible, you should travel to places that are unfamiliar and make yourself an outsider. Being an outsider forces you to clarify your likes and dislikes, discover your true point of view, and develop a fresh perspective. This very important apprenticeship is often overlooked or just no longer considered part of the growth process for most young writers today. My greatest work has grown out of my personal experiences: my failed marriage; being a single parent; clinical depression; love affairs; being forced to live in several cities in the world; early experiences as a cabdriver, waiter, cook, and teacher in the South Bronx; and so on.

The recent genre of films about the zany insanity of making a film concerns me. It indicates that many of our writers have limited experience with the demands of the real world—the one outside a specialized subculture of filmmaking. Work that grows out of limited experience with the real world can often be too self-referential, solipsistic, insular, and shallow.

Director Fritz Lang's life provides a perfect example of wandering and observing. After escaping Nazi Germany and arriving in America, Lang wanted to build up a reservoir to draw on for working in a new culture. He "spoke with every cabdriver and every gas station attendant" he met and went to Arizona to live with the Navajos where he learned about sand painting. He also watched American films and read the cartoon strips in the newspapers to get a sense of what it is to be an American. He spent most of his time just soaking up experiences. His first film made in the United States, *Fury*, shows the results of this process; it joins the ranks of his other great works, *M* and *Metropolis*.

When you do sit down to write, having done your preparation in terms of life experience and for a specific script, always keep your expectations realistic. Just play, for the fun of it, and when you do, you will receive brilliant flow. If your expectations are unrealistically high—to be original and insightful, to create the next great American screenplay, or make a killing with your screenplay—you will be dull and blocked, your flow will not flow. Originality never grows out of someone trying to be original. It grows out of someone who, with patience, follows a vision and struggles to express it with clarity. Do no try to manipulate or seek the approval of the audience, just express what you need to express. The audience should be treated with respect and as equals because they are needed to fill out the experience.

Peer Groups

In the end, the screenwriter must build poundage—both in terms of life experience and in number of good and bad scripts—in order to improve. But, given the conditions of our culture, how do you do that? Isolated, day after day, tapping at the keyboard, going backwards and forwards in the chaotic process of writing, it is difficult to avoid despair. It can be, at times, utter drudgery.

Books outlining the modalities of creation (like this one) and the chaos of the market, and pronouncements from the high priests of the seminar circuit do have their benefits. But where do you find support when you are in the midst of the most mundane task of actually creating a screenplay? The answer is to create your own support system. You need immediate and regular feedback in order to continue to create good work consistently. You need to discuss your work with somebody who gets it. How can you hang out with others and talk about your craft? A writer's workshop is the best way to help you get the feedback you need.

A writer's workshop is part salon, part support group. Suppose you need to practice pitching a screenplay before you have to do the real thing. Or you have a germ of an idea for your next project and need to talk it through with your peers. Perhaps you want to do a reading of your new screenplay with actors in front of other writers, because writers give the best criticism. A workshop can provide all of the above. It alleviates the writer's feelings of isolation and generates inspiration by being challenged by our peers. It costs little or no money to do and is one of the best ways to keep yourself growing as a screenwriter.

To find a group, ask your screenwriter friends or check with your local filmmaking association. I have organized or helped to organize several workshops in the theater and for screenwriters over the last decade. What works well for playwrights will work well for screenwriters. Here are the things I have learned: first, to lend you credibility and support, contact an umbrella organization or institution such as a film school, respected journal or periodical, local nonprofit theater, or a YMCA. A screenwriter's workshop will appeal to an institution for many reasons.

For example, I once started a workshop with a small theater company that needed to expand their roster of writers in order to fulfill specific requirements from several of their funders. On another occasion, I began a workshop in a local church because, very simply, the church needed the rent money—as miniscule as it was—and I had a group of friends and colleagues who needed a place to meet once a week. As a group, we collected a small membership fee each month. On another occasion, I went to a local non-profit filmmaker's organization in my community, New York City, and told them that I would organize a workshop and help to lead and manage it for one year. After the success of the first year, the organization then received a grant to hire a staff member to handle the management of our group. It was a win-win situation. A group of screenwriters were able to have a weekly meeting and the organization gained several new supporters and expanded their outreach to the filmmaking community. Make sure the umbrella organization that you choose has a staff in place that can give you some of its time and resources in supporting the workshop, i.e., mailing notices, scheduling, etc.

The workshop must be a safe haven. If its members have agendas other than sharing their work or giving and receiving support, it will not work. Writers need a place just for writers and their concerns. They need a place to bring their work when it is still raw and fragile. If someone enters the group to make contacts or hustle a deal, the workshop will lose its integrity and violate its organizing principle. Keep the size to something manageable. Fifteen writers is more than enough to begin. Organize writers based on talent and experience. If you get people with different sensibilities and interests, the group will be healthy and create an environment where everyone can grow.

Someone is going to have to make the first move and give the time and energy to get things started. Someone is going to have to be the head of the group for no pay—or at the very least, the facilitator. It is just a fact that somebody has to lock up and shut off the lights. It is best if this position rotates within the group. It prevents the consolidation of power, gives everyone the task of being responsible, and strengthens the group. Meet every other week on Monday night. Meeting every week puts a strain on most people's schedules. Monday night is a very lonely night and ripe for the picking. The meeting should last, at the most, three hours. People can listen only so long. Those that have time, should go out for a drink and dinner after the meeting. This social time is important. Just do it. It explains itself.

Tailor your group to meet the needs that arise. Let it evolve and become what it needs to be. It is a participatory democracy. Each group has its own life span. People come and go, drift apart, and the energy dissipates. Don't fight it. Let it disband when it must; if you get three years out of a group then you are doing very well. Organize again. That's what it's all about.

Expanding and growing as a screenwriter also means continuing to train by taking seminars and classes at local universities, film festivals, and professional organizations. It is important to keep in touch with other screenwriters and filmmakers and slowly and steadily build contacts. You can find listings for these types of events in *Filmmaker: The Magazine of the Independent Film* and *The Independent Film and Video Monthly*, both available at newsstands. A very good online resource is the Internet Movie Database (www.IMDB.com) for up-to-date information on just about everything related to filmmaking—reviews, video availability, daily briefings, as well as links to other sites for festivals, professional training, and script exchanges.

On a final note, I would, of course, be delighted if everyone who reads this book makes more money than they know what do with. But a writer should focus on one thing at all times—writing and having fun doing it. If your focus is not on trying to express what haunts and impassions you, you will block flow—the very thing that could help you make a killing. To grow as a writer, you will have to sweat blood at times, but it still should be fun. As the Greeks said, the reward is in the struggle.

Selected Bibliography

Allen, Woody, and Marshall Brickman. *Annie Hall*. MGM/UA Studios, 1977, videocassette.

Anderson, Robert. "Writers and Their Work: Robert Anderson," *Dramatists Guild Quarterly*, Spring 1998.

Baker, George Pierce. *Dramatic Technique*. New York: Da Capo Press, 1996.

Ball, David. *Backwards and Forwards: A Technical Manual for Reading Plays*. Carbondale, Illinois: Southern Illinois University Press, 1983.

Barrett, Shirley. *Love Serenade*. Miramax, 1996, videocassette.

Bentley, Eric. *Thinking about the Playwright: Comments from Four Decades*. Evanston, Illinois: Northwestern University Press, 1987.

Berlin, Isaiah. *The Proper Study of Mankind*. New York: Farrar, Straus and Giroux, 1998.

Berlin, Isaiah. *The Sense of Reality*. New York: Farrar, Straus and Giroux, 1996.

Bogdanovich, Peter. *Who the Devil Made It*. New York: Alfred A. Knopf, 1997.

Brown, Christy, and Shane Connaughton. *My Left Foot*. Miramax, 1989, videocassette.

Callan, K. *The Script Is Finished, Now What Do I Do? The Scriptwriter's Resource*. Hollywood: Sweden Press, 1997.

Cervantes, Miguel de Saavedra. *Don Quixote*. New York: Penguin Books, 1950.

Chatman, Seymour. *Story and Discourse: Narrative Structure in Fiction and Film*. Ithaca, New York: Cornell University Press, 1978.

Chekhov, Anton Pavlovich. *Chekhov: The Major Plays*. New York: Signet Classics, 1964.

Coppola, Francis. *The Godfather*. Paramount Pictures, 1972, videocassette.

Corliss, Richard. "At Cannes, A John Travolta Film Triumphs," *Time*, Vol. 143, No. 23 (June 6, 1994).

Csikszentmihalyi, Mihaly. *Finding Flow, The Psychology of Engagement with Everyday Life*. New York: Basic Books, 1997.

Dancyger, Dan, and Jeff Rush. *Alternative Scriptwriting*, 2nd Edition. Newton, Massachusetts: Butterworth-Heinemann, 1995.

Duvall, Robert. *The Apostle*. October/Boulevard Books, 1997.

Egri, Lajos. *The Art of Dramatic Writing*. New York: Simon & Schuster, 1960.

Gruault, Jean, and Francois Truffaut. *Jules and Jim*. Les Films du Carrose, 1961, videocassette.

Gussow, Mel, "Mario Puzo, Author of 'The Godfather,' Is Dead at 78," *New York Times*, 2 July 1999.

Gustav, Hasford, and Michael Herr. *Full Metal Jacket*. Warner Bros., 1987, videocassette.

Huggins, Roy, and David N. Twohy. *The Fugitive*. Warner Bros., 1993, videocassette.

Kiely, David M. *John Millington Synge, A Biography*. New York: St. Martin's Press, 1994.

Kieslowski, Krzysztof. *Kieslowski on Kieslowski*. Edited by Danusia Stok. London: Faber and Faber, 1993.

Kieslowski, Krzysztof, and Krzysztof Piesiewicz. *A Short Film about Love*. Walter Read, 1988, videocassette.

Kundera, Milan. *The Art of the Novel*. New York: HarperCollins, 1989.

Leigh, Mike. *Secrets and Lies*. London: Faber and Faber, 1997.

Lipton, James. *Bravo's at the Actors Studio: Interview with Sean Penn*. Bravo Television, 1999, videocassette.

Lumet, Sidney. *Making Movies*. New York: Vintage Books, 1996.

Mankiewicz, Herman J., and Orson Welles. *Citizen Kane*. RKO Pictures Inc., 1941, videocassette.

Norman, Marc, and Tom Stoppard. *Shakespeare in Love*. Miramax, 1998, videocassette.

Postman, Neil. *Amusing Ourselves to Death, Public Discourse in the Age of Show Business*. New York: Penguin Books, 1985.

Richardson, John H. "Dumb and Dumber Part I: The Case against Hollywood," *Harper's* (April 10, 1995).

Ryan, James. "Screenwriters, Unite!" *The Independent Film & Video Monthly*, Vol. 18, No. 2, (March 1995).

Schiffer, Irvine. *Charisma*. Toronto: University of Toronto Press, 1973.

Scorsese, Martin. *Mean Streets*. Warner Bros., 1973, videocassette.

Seger, Linda. *Making a Good Script Great*, 2nd Edition. Hollywood: Samuel French, 1994.

Solondz, Todd. *Welcome to the Dollhouse*. London: Faber and Faber, 1996.

Sontag, Susan. *On Photography: The Heroism of Vision*. New York: Farrar, Straus and Giroux, 1997.

Sragow, Michael. "Movies: Realized Ambitions," *Atlantic Monthly*, Vol. 276, No. 6. (December 1995).

Sturges, Preston. *The Palm Beach Story*. Universal Studios, 1942, videocassette.

Truffaut, Francois. *Jules et Jim*. London: Faber and Faber, 1989.

Varda, Agnes. *Vagabond*. Kino, 1992, videocassette.

Weinraub, Bernard. "Independent Films Dominate Oscar Nominations," *New York Times*, 12 February 1997.

White, Jason. *Austin Film Festival Heart of Film Screenwriters Conference*, Vol. 1, Issue 1 (Summer 1997).

Wilber, Ken. *The Marriage of Sense and Soul*. New York: Random House, 1998.

Wright, Edward A. *Understanding Today's Theater*, 2nd Edition. Englewood Cliffs, New Jersey: Prentice-Hall, 1972.

Recommended Viewing

The following is a list of character-driven movies that are recommended viewing. Most are referred to in the book. I suggest them because they offer examples of well-developed characters and fresh perspectives. Collectively, they represent a wide range of styles and types, and are good examples of the many screenwriting strategies discussed in this book.

400 Blows, The (1959)

8 1/2 (1963)

A Clockwork Orange (1971)

Apostle, The (1997)

Badlands (1973)

Before the Rain (1995)

Casablanca (1942)

Chinatown (1974)

Citizen Kane (1941)

Contempt (1963)

Crimes and Misdemeanors (1989)

Crying Game (1992)

Dr. Strangelove (1964)

Full Metal Jacket (1987)

Husbands and Wives (1992)

It's a Wonderful Life (1946)

Jules and Jim (1961)

Lady Eve, The (1941)

Love Serenade (1996)

M (1931)

Mean Streets (1973)

Moonstruck (1987)

Network (1976)

Producers, The (1968)

Pulp Fiction (1994)

Rio Bravo (1959)

Searchers, The (1956)

Secrets and Lies (1996)

Shakespeare in Love (1998)

She's Gotta Have It (1986)

Silence of the Lambs (1991)

Sling Blade (1996)

Some Like It Hot (1959)

Steel Helmet (1951)

The Godfather (1972)

Twelve Angry Men (1957)

Underground (1995)

Unforgiven (1992)

Vagabond (1985)

Who's Afraid of Virginia Woolf (1966)

Index